Change Your AURA
Change Your LIFE

Change Your AURA
Change Your LIFE

A Step-by-Step Guide
to Unfolding Your
SPIRITUAL POWER

Barbara Y. Martin
with Dimitri Moraitis

Wisdom Light Books

Spiritual Arts Institute

Published by: Spiritual Arts Institute
P.O. Box 4315, Sunland, CA 91041–4315
818–353–1716, Fax: 818–353–2269
www.SpiritualArts.org

Change Your Aura, Change Your Life reflects the views and personal experiences of the authors. This book is intended to complement, not replace, professional medical advice, diagnosis and treatment. If you have or suspect you have a medical problem, immediately see your doctor or a professional health-care provider. No medical claims are made as to effects or outcomes of the exercises described in this book.

Editorial: Jo-Ann Langseth
Interior Illustrations: Jeffrey K. Bedrick
Cover Editorial: Melissa Stein
Interior Design: Desktop Miracles, Inc.

Publisher's Cataloging-in-Publication

Martin, Barbara Y.
     Change your aura, change your life : a step-by-step guide to unfolding your spiritual power / by Barbara Y. Martin with Dimitri Moraitis — 1st ed.
          p.   cm.
     Includes index.
     LCCN 2002105830
     ISBN 0–9702118–1–3
     1. Aura.   2. Spiritual life.   I. Moraitis, Dimitri.   II. Title.
BF1389.A8M37   2002
133.8'92

                                                            QBI02–200515

First Printing, 2003
Second Printing, 2004
Third Printing, 2005
Printed in the United States

This book is lovingly dedicated to all students of metaphysics searching for the truth.

TABLE OF CONTENTS

S ECTION   T HREE

Unfolding Your Spiritual Power

FIGURES

FOREWORD

It has been an honor to contribute to the writing of *Change Your Aura, Change Your Life.* I have known Barbara for many years and the changes that have come over me as a result of working with the aura and spiritual energy have been miraculous. In my case, it was not so much a matter of my overcoming a trauma or personal tragedy. As a matter of fact, I came from a well-adjusted home life. I grew up with loving parents and a brother who's my best friend. What I did have was an inexhaustible desire to tap into the spiritual side of my life. That desire has been realized to a greater degree than I had ever imagined possible through my association with Barbara and this work.

At the time we started working together, Barbara had very little organized information covering these marvelous teachings. She had been teaching for many years, but most of the instructions were given orally. For those who have been with or studied great souls, this mystery becomes understandable. It often becomes the duty of the people around such an inspired teacher to organize and distribute the teachings presented. It remains the teacher's job to maintain the spiritual connection necessary to be effective and accurate. So in addition to my becoming her student, we became writing partners, which eventually led to our collaborating on *Change Your Aura, Change Your Life.*

In all the time I've known Barbara, her teachings have remained entirely consistent and reliable. I've never once had reason to question the integrity of these instructions. I've been a witness to many healings and transformations received by others, demonstrating all the more the validity and usefulness of spiritual energy.

No book can replace the direct experience of working with the aura and Divine Light. Yet I hope with all my heart that *Change Your Aura, Change Your Life* makes that magnificent journey to enlightenment a little brighter and more understandable for you, as it has for me.

DIMITRI MORAITIS, *collaborator*

INTRODUCTION

A miraculous spiritual force operates in the midst of us. Although invisible to physical sensing, it is vividly alive and active. It is a part of us and we are a part of it. This force is known as the human energy field—the aura.

In the following pages, we'll explore what the auric field is and how to improve it by working with spiritual energy. This book is designed to be a hands-on training manual in how you may work with the aura to improve the quality of your life. It introduces a powerful meditation tool for accessing an unlimited source of spiritual power that is simple and easy to follow.

The depth of activity that goes on within each of us, unseen by the physical eyes, is truly amazing. For anyone who has studied this subject, one fact becomes crystal-clear: There is far more to the unseen part of life than there is to the seen. If nothing else, it is my hope that this book will give you a greater knowledge of yourself, who you really are, and your unlimited potential as a spiritual being.

Every spiritual process described here has been shown to me through my own direct clairvoyant observations. I was born with the gift of spiritual sight; clairvoyance is a natural part of life for me. From early childhood, I could see auras, and had countless other spiritual visions as well. These experiences have always seemed very normal. As a matter of fact, when I was very young, I assumed that everyone saw what I did. It was a rude awakening when I found out that they didn't.

Clairvoyance (French, for "clear seeing") is the ability to observe the normally invisible spiritual processes of life. I was about three years old when my spiritual sight opened to the beautiful world of auras. I began by seeing them around people and things. Though I had little comprehension of what I was seeing, I remember watching the auras around my parents and siblings and noticing how the colors would change according to their moods and actions. I remember taking trips into the country and seeing the auras around trees and flowers and thinking how beautiful life is. And how God must be everywhere.

I had an experience when I was about four that taught me an important lesson about my abilities. My father was a Greek Orthodox priest who had wonderful engineering skills as well. The archdiocese would send him to various towns to build a church and then build up a congregation. He did this in many places around the country, always with great success. As a result, our family constantly moved, which wasn't always easy on us. I had three brothers and two sisters. Living on a priest's salary was quite a feat, especially considering that we moved so often. How my mother was able to keep us happy and well cared for could be a book in itself—she did a wonderful job.

One day, we all went to the dedication of a new church. It was a major event, and, of course, our family was a big part of it. The archbishop had come from the Archdiocese of New York. There were thousands of people. The archbishop stood very regal, resplendent in his tiara and cross before the altar. Beside him, to his right and left, were two bishops who were officiating with him. I studied the aura of the archbishop and found his energy field to be very menacing. Instead of brilliant, uplifting colors, he had dark, grotesque colors emanating from him. However, the bishop to his right, who was lower in rank, had a very beautiful aura with striking pearl luster colors.

In the Greek Orthodox faith, it is customary to kiss the hand of the officiating archbishop, priest, or bishop. When it was our turn to go down the aisle and kiss the hand of the archbishop, I refused. My mother insisted. In front of the whole congregation, I screamed, "No, he's a monster! He eats children!" Needless to say, my mother took me out and gave me a good spanking.

So, I learned that this gift could be a curse as well as a blessing. Who wants to see ugly energies around someone—especially a family member or loved one? I learned to keep quiet about what I saw and to shut off these gifts when I needed to, so I wouldn't be overwhelmed.

In my teens, I began to realize that it was possible not only to observe the aura, but to change and improve it. I also became aware that I was not alone in this process, that I was being helped by beings from the spirit world. From childhood, I could see them, but as I grew older, they were making their presence much more known to me.

In my twenties, I embarked on a training program with these spiritual beings, who instructed me in many facets of the spiritual world. This training eventually led to my becoming a teacher of metaphysics and to most of the principles imparted in this book. I also had a few spiritual teachers in the material world, who taught me and helped prepare me for the rigors of teaching.

When it came time for me to begin my professional work, I hesitated. I was working at an insurance company at the time, a single mother supporting two children, and this spiritual work seemed like a risky venture, even though I knew its value. I also knew how much responsibility was involved in being a spiritual teacher and wasn't sure I was up to the task. However, I was prompted—in the most unusual of ways—by many who saw that I had something to offer. By the time I was in my early thirties, I had given up my job and begun teaching metaphysics full-time. I've been teaching ever since.

I wish to emphasize that the exercises in this book are by no means a replacement for trained professional guidance. Sometimes your own spiritual efforts will not be enough to remedy a condition, and you will need experienced outside help. Certainly, if you are experiencing serious physical or psychological disorders, you should consult a doctor, counselor, or experienced spiritual healer to complement any spiritual work of your own.

A note about the illustrations: While I have made every effort to show the aura as accurately as possible, a certain amount of interpretation is inevitable. In addition, it's almost impossible to see the whole aura, *in toto*, at the same time. When I'm reading a person's aura, I focus on one part before going on to the next. In these auric illustrations, I have tried to show specific qualities of the aura as well as the human aura as a whole. Most of these renderings are cross sections of the auras described. In actuality, the aura is very much three-dimensional and has movement.

I wish to thank the many friends, family members, colleagues, and students who have been so patiently supportive during the writing of this book. It has been many years in the making. I would like to acknowledge my collaborator, Dimitri Moraitis, for his tireless work. Dimitri has been a dedicated student and friend for many years and has developed a thorough understanding of the knowledge presented here. I drew on a great deal of past knowledge as well as fresh inspiration for the material in this book. It became Dimitri's job to distill the information in an organized, literary form. The shape this book has taken is largely due to his creative contribution.

I hope this book will inspire you to new spiritual heights. I have been teaching for many years, and it has been fulfilling to see how working with the light has helped people to grow and express more of their true potential. Someone once said that it's wonderful to build bridges or magnificent buildings, but that the greatest feat of all is to be builders of men. I couldn't agree more.

BARBARA Y. MARTIN

How the Aura Reflects Your Life

Chapter 1

Your Spiritual
Bank Account

Imagine a bank account in your name, with unlimited cash reserves awaiting your use. First you'd say it was impossible, but if you saw the account and were actually able to make a cash advance, things would change, wouldn't they?

Right now, you have the ability to tap an unlimited, spiritual reservoir of energy that can help you in every aspect of your life. Think of it as your spiritual bank account. Need more love in your life? Bring in the energy that is the embodiment of love. Looking for new inspiration? Call on the energy that inspires new ideas. How about more prosperity? Draw in the very power that manifests wealth. This spiritual account of Living Light is far more valuable than any cash account could ever be, and nothing is asked of you other than to use it.

This gift from God is one of the essential keys to developing a better life. By tapping into this spiritual account, you can greatly quicken your personal and spiritual progress. You can produce what you want faster, solve personal problems more effectively, and be able to help others to a greater degree.

This divine power can be perceived as a brilliant, iridescent light, with colors far more splendid than anything found in the physical spectrum. Spiritual light has its own source and purpose, which is very different from the light we see with our physical eyes. I have seen this spiritual light mend relationships, pull people out of suicidal depressions, heal physical, mental and sexual abuse, create harmonious marriages, help overcome addictions and perversions, get people out of financial disasters and take them to spiritual heights they never dreamed possible. The more these people dedicated themselves, the more the light could work for them. Some of these transformations were instantaneous, others took time, but all were realized.

Throughout the centuries, spiritual light has been depicted in scriptural writings, literature and art. In Genesis, one of the first acts of God was to bring forth light. In the New Testament, the dove of peace blesses humanity by beaming rays of light from its mouth. The Light of Christ temporarily blinded Saul while he was on the road to Damascus. Countless pictures show angels and archangels beaming light to suffering souls to heal and restore them; most benedictions show the recipient anointed with light. People who have reported near-death experiences almost always acknowledge the presence of a magnificent light. Divine Light is the backdrop to almost every heavenly scenario, and the centerpiece of every religion.

If you've studied metaphysics, you're familiar with the white light. People use it in specific situations, such as for protection, or to illuminate a condition. The image is very strong: light dispelling darkness. The white light is definitely part of your spiritual reservoir. In addition, there is a vast array of other spiritual energies at your disposal for personal and spiritual development. Just as physical light can be divided into its spectral colors, spiritual light reaches you in rays of various colors—with each ray serving a different spiritual purpose.

How does your aura fit into all this? First, your aura is energy. Everything you feel, think and do radiates a spiritual energy that comes through in definite colors and intensities. This essence is the aura. It is through the miracle of the aura that the Divine Light expresses itself in you. Your aura, then, is an individual expression of the Divine Light in action. Just as the spiritual reservoir is your divine bank account, your aura is a spiritual bank statement that registers and keeps record of how you're using that spiritual energy. When you draw in spiritual energy, you first draw that energy into your auric field before putting it to use in your life. So, by making a change in your aura, there will automatically be a corresponding change in your life. Change your aura, you change your life. That's one of the spiritual laws.

Spiritual energy may be defined as the Divine Light that propels the life force of God to all creation. In other words, there has to be a power that sends the love of God, the peace of God, the wisdom of God, and all the attributes of God to each of us. Spiritual light is the power by which this goal is accomplished. Without this energetic conduit, we would have no means of receiving anything from God.

Spiritual light is part of the divine radiations that emanate from the very heart and mind of God. It is this energy that sustains all life and is the power behind all activities, physical and spiritual. From its purest state, light flows from the highest spheres and planes of creation down into various gradations, to fulfill many applications. If you need more love, the light will bring to you a flow of Divine Love. If you need prosperity, the light will take on a different quality and bring you the consciousness of wealth.

As the light flows from this celestial source into your aura, it generates the spiritual power necessary to create whatever it is you are focusing your attention on. To give you a personal example, when my eldest brother Philip was young, he wished to become an opera singer. He had an incredible voice, and everyone felt he was destined for greatness. When he started out, he had little training or money. His voice teacher gave him complimentary lessons because he saw his potential. In my brother's aura, I could see the spiritual power connected to creative talent—a bright electric-blue light. I also saw a deeper royal-blue energy, which showed his determination to succeed at his art. These colors were the beginnings of what would become the fulfillment of his spiritual purpose. As I watched his aura through the years of training and struggle, his auric colors gradually brightened as his talent and skill increased. At one point, I began seeing a sparkling turquoise in the energy coming into his aura, indicative of prosperity. This energy was showing itself, even though it had not yet materialized in his life. It was then that I knew good things were around the corner for him. His aura had all the earmarks of success, and sure enough, he soon became very successful in his field.

We all have the ability to change and improve ourselves. It doesn't matter where we are or what we've done with our lives; we are all here for a purpose and have been given the spiritual tools to succeed at that purpose. By working on ourselves we attract the spiritual energies that improve our lives. We go through the experiences of learning and growing, while behind this developmental activity we're also gaining in spiritual power, which is the key to manifesting the fruits of our efforts.

Your Spiritual Booster Shot

The most important act you can perform is to earn light. It's the key to all activities in life. You earn light by your every constructive thought, word, deed and feeling. Every positive thing you do, however small, recognized or unrecognized, adds to you. The more light you earn, the brighter your aura becomes and the higher in consciousness you climb. That's why it's so important to conduct yourself in a spiritual manner and treat your fellow man kindly.

You may ask, "Why not just be a good person?" Why not simply do the best you can and let God do the rest? Why go through this very focused process of working with the aura and divine energy? Of course, doing and being good is an essential part of spiritual growth. It's the hallmark of an evolving soul. But just being good in itself doesn't complete the whole spiritual picture. You need to combine a loving nature with effective spiritual tools to be successful in your personal and spiritual growth. There will be many times when you will get stuck somewhere in life's pursuits and could benefit greatly by tapping into your spiritual reservoir. How many times have you been aware of a problem or a fault and are motivated to correct that fault, but no matter what you do, it just doesn't seem to happen? How can that change come about if the power to make it happen isn't there?

Let me give you a few examples of how working with spiritual energy helps accelerate change. I had a student who asked me if I could help her sister. Her sister was a clothes designer, and I went to see her at a small studio she had in Hollywood. When I walked in, I saw an attractive, kind-looking woman, but one who also appeared to be bedraggled and confused. Her hair was disheveled and she had circles under her eyes from lack of sleep. Despite being such a brilliant designer, she was wearing a shabby coat and clothes that looked like they came from a thrift store. Clearly something very dramatic had happened, and she needed help desperately. She told me she had hardly eaten in days, so the first thing we did was go to a restaurant to get some food in her.

She quickly told me her story. It turned out that her husband, who was also her business partner, had just up and left her, taking all the money they had. They owned a small design studio that was doing well, yet somehow he'd decided to abscond with all the funds, which left her penniless. She was trying to stay in business, but without funds of her own, she'd lost all the accounts and her business quickly collapsed. She even lost her home. When I met her, she was sleeping in her studio and using the pattern table as a makeshift bed! She was confused, angry, bewildered and frustrated. She couldn't understand how her husband, who helped pay her way through design school and start the business, would take advantage of her in such a callous and cruel way.

When I first met her, I could see that this was a very talented person. She had the electric blue and powder blue in her aura, indicative of talent and inspiration. That she was spiritually astute showed in some gold and white light above her head. But she had allowed the experience to muddy many aspects of her aura, and it was very disoriented. There was a lot of gray, showing fear and worry. There was also a scratchy tan-colored energy, showing lethargy: the traumatic experience had put her in a mental fog. Although she was trying, she had no idea how to get out of her predicament. There was anger toward her husband, which came through in vitiated red. There were also dark brown, dark green, and little black energies around the emotional aspects of her aura. These colors were reflecting her dark feelings and desires for revenge.

I told her I could help if she was willing to work at it. Happily, she was *very* willing, and took to the light right away. She worked with spiritual energy daily, and diligently used many energies to get the job done. To her amazement, she started feeling the effects of the light right away, and almost immediately began to regain the hope and optimism she needed to get her life going again. She used the purifying rays to cut loose the dark thoughts and emotions that were building inside her. She used the dynamic energies to rekindle her self-confidence, as the whole experience had left her self-esteem very low. She worked with the balancing energies to bring her life back into harmony and spiritual rhythm once again. There was a great deal of forgiveness work done with the love ray, as well as working with the reenergizing energies to build up her vitality and spiritual power.

Within three months, her diligence had paid off. Her aura had dramatically improved. It was much brighter and more luminous. The grays and muddy disoriented colors were gone. Her vengeful feelings toward her husband were gone too, and she forgave him. The muddled energies that had been clouding her thinking vanished, and now her mental body was sharp and clear, with lemon yellow and silver. Emerald green was also strong in her aura, showing that her life was much more balanced, her thinking much clearer. Perhaps best of all, she was expressing her loving nature once again, which showed up as a deep rose-pink light. Her whole demeanor changed, and she was a better person than ever before.

This change in her aura was reflected markedly in her life. She found a place to live with a studio where she could do her designing. Although the business she had started was gone, she enrolled in school again to expand her expertise and soon found a job in a manufacturing company as a designer. She had landed on her feet and was thriving! And she's been doing well ever since. She's now a high-powered executive working in New York. Another wonderful blessing is that the two of us became great friends. This is the power of spiritual energy.

In another situation, I counseled a compulsive spender. He was married, with four children, and making good money as an accountant. Yet, he was in deep financial waters because of his overspending. He would buy himself cars, yachts, or whatever popped into his head, until all his funds were depleted. Then he hadn't even enough money to care for his family, and was always strapped for cash. His wife was so stressed by his behavior that she eventually left him. His kids were just as angry. He knew he was causing great pain, but in the grip of a raging compulsion, he felt powerless to resist.

He went to several psychiatrists, seeking help. In therapy, he discovered that his problems stemmed from childhood experiences with his parents. Pathologically frugal, they would deny him toys and other things that he wanted. Whenever he desired something, they would usually refuse him. As a result, he'd always felt deprived and emotionally insecure. Now an adult, and making good money, he felt an intense urge to overcompensate by buying all the things he wanted—buy them outright, buy them *now*. Yet, not even his newfound insight could stop him from compulsively spending.

When I first met him, he was very up-front about his problems. He was a good man, and really wanted to fix things and save his marriage. To his great advantage, he was open to working with the light. His aura showed that the negative energy he was creating hadn't had time to really settle in, but that he obviously had several areas to work on. He had lemon-yellow and silver energies radiating from the mental part of his aura, proof positive of a good mind. It was, however, clouded by some gray energies mixed with mustard yellow, showing depression and disorientation. There was also a gray cloud of worry above his head, born of preoccupation with his condition.

Despite some worry vibrations around him, the bright orange in his aura showed him to be an optimistic person. Dazzling blue energy in the emotional part of his aura declared his passion for life. He was always out there, trying to make the big score.

His obsessive desire for material things showed up in his aura as a bright red energy. The fact that this energy was bright revealed that there was nothing inherently wrong with his wanting these things. His problem centered on the way he was going about getting the things he wanted. However, he also had cocoa-brown, signifying that he could be petty—which accounted for his lack of attention in family matters.

In the upper part of his aura, just beyond the shell, he had some blob-like thought forms. A dark green-and-black thought form on his right side showed envy, as well as hatred of others who had more money or things than he did. A thought form on the left was a vitiated red energy. This showed his aggressive approach to being one step ahead of the next guy, no matter what.

Fortunately, he'd become disciplined from his accounting training and was able to dedicate himself to his transformational work. First, he worked on cutting loose the anger he had toward his parents. Using the white light, he transmuted old memories and the frustrations he felt from never getting the things he wanted as a boy. He worked with blue-white fire to build up new life force, and deep rose-pink to forgive his parents for what they had done. He gradually began to see that it was his parents' right and free choice to give or not to give him things. They had their own reasons, and he couldn't blame them for that. He also worked with the orange-red flame to cut loose the thought forms of compulsive spending that he had created as a result of his anger. He brought in a lot of gold and silver light to illuminate the immaturity of his actions and to build logic and discipline in his spending habits. Finally, he worked with the emerald green ray to help regulate and stabilize his thinking habits.

Once he started to get a handle on himself, he began to use the deep rose-pink light on his family, so they would forgive him. He prayed for his wife to come back to him. Once she saw that he really *had* changed his ways, she forgave him and went back, as she was still very much in love with him. The whole process took about a year, but he saved his marriage.

His aura had greatly brightened. He still had the silver and lemon yellow in his mental center, but gone were the lethargic and depressing energies, as well as the destructive thought forms that were encroaching on his aura. He had a lot of rose-pink light, showing the high degree of love he had developed. He was also expressing a beautiful royal-blue energy, demonstrating the deep loyalty he now had for his family. No longer would he put his own desires and ambitions ahead of his family's needs. A brilliant emerald-green light expressed the balance and harmony he was now feeling. He stopped spending on himself and used his money for his family's needs instead. With his spending habits now under control and his accounting skills to help him, he was able to get out of debt.

Could these people have worked things out on their own, without tapping their spiritual bank account? Of course they could, but it would have been a slow, grueling process, with the likelihood of many setbacks before they could get on their feet again. The point is: Why go through any unnecessary struggle or setbacks when God gives you the ability to access spiritual energy that will definitely facilitate growth?

Life gives you all the time you need to achieve the great goal of improving yourself. Yet, once you're awakened to the greater possibilities of life, you're much more motivated to pursue your spiritual unfoldment. By drawing from your spiritual bank account, you can make changes in your life faster and more effectively, your chances of sustained success far greater than if you went at it on your own.

How to Use This Book

In the following pages are many examples of how to work with the light in very practical situations. Yet, to gain the greatest benefit from using this book, I want you to think of your light work not only as an opportunity for help in the everyday challenges of life, but as an opportunity to come closer to God. That is the ultimate purpose of the light work. By using the light to help you in the challenges of life, you are actually drawing closer to God in all His infinite variety, closer to His love, His peace, His joy, His wisdom, etc.

It goes without saying that you draw on this spiritual light *only for constructive purposes.* The light is not a genie or magic wand designed to service your every whim, but a divine tool in your spiritual arsenal. It's an opportunity to invite God to come closer into your life. If you use the light beneficently, for the good of all, access to your spiritual reservoir is naturally strengthened and increased. If you misuse the light persistently or maliciously, you won't be able to draw on the reservoir as before until you're back on the right track.

The spiritual light facilitates change by giving you the power to step into a greater spiritual awareness of life. That is the secret of spiritual light. As you draw more power into your aura, you're expanding your spiritual awareness. Light and consciousness walk hand in hand. The more light you have, the higher in consciousness you can climb. And as your consciousness heightens, change is inevitable.

For example, a nurse who attended one of my classes was skeptical of the light. She was dedicated to helping people, but thought some of these metaphysical ideas were a little far-fetched. One night, as she waited in a bar with her friends for dinner, two men nearby began arguing at the top of their lungs. The argument soon turned into a fight. She had learned about healing relationships with the love ray in class that week, so she decided to test its power. As the men argued, she silently asked that they receive the deep rose-pink ray of spiritual love. To her great surprise, the fighting stopped within minutes. The men looked at each other, wondering why they were fighting at all. It turned out they were good friends who had gotten a little drunk and were arguing over nothing. They ended up hugging and buying each other drinks.

The woman was dumbfounded. She came to class the next week and related her extraordinary experience. Her skeptical mind could easily have dismissed the whole thing as coincidence, but she knew better. She said she'd never doubt the power of the light again.

How did the light stop these men from fighting? It didn't. The light helped these men receive a spiritual quickening of love, so they could see for themselves what they were doing. Once quickened, they chose for themselves to stop fighting. The fact that they were already good friends made it easier to receive the light. And although the nurse was not a firm believer, the fact that she was willing to give the light a fair chance made her an effective emissary.

So, drawing in light brings more divine awareness of whatever we're working on. If we're calling on the light to increase prosperity, we're actually drawing in more divine consciousness of prosperity to create conditions of abundance and supply. Or if we're calling on the light to receive peace, we're expanding our awareness of divine peace which will create a more peaceful condition around us, and so on. Under the umbrella of the spiritual light, all our earthly interactions and situations are opportunities by which we may grow and develop. Daily life becomes a sacred experience. And as we grow, we begin to see the light of life all around us: in the face of a friend or family member; in a moment of adversity or in the ecstasy of inspiration; in the homeless person we greet on our way to work every day; in all our fortunes and misfortunes.

Seeing the Light

One of the biggest questions I am asked is, "Does the light work for me if I can't see it?" Of course it does! The light works for you always. Actually, you're drawing in the light already but probably don't realize it. Without this spiritual energy, you couldn't exist. You depend on its steady flow of nourishment to keep yourself spiritually and physically alive. This power is drawn unconsciously, much as your subconscious mind controls and regulates 98% of your bodily functions.

When you first begin your light work, you may not see the energy in activity. That's very normal and to be expected. You don't need to see the light any more than you need to see your heart to know it's beating. Most people start by feeling the light as a rush of energy, a physical vibration, or heat. Regardless of how you perceive it, the light is going to start working for you immediately. As you grow with it, you'll become more attuned, and the light will become your greatest ally. The majority of people I work with do not see energies, but they see the effects of spiritual energy in their lives, and that's the key. So, the sooner you start working with the light, the sooner you'll see the results.

The Metaphysical Tradition

The study of the aura and spiritual energy may appear new, but it is actually part of a heritage thousands of years old. This ancient study is called metaphysics.

Metaphysics is the study of the spiritual root of physical life. It comes from the ancient Greek, meaning "that which comes after the physical." In this way, metaphysics shares similar goals with other noble studies such as philosophy, general spirituality, theology, mysticism, theosophy and ontology. Traditionally, there are two branches of metaphysics—theoretical and practical. Theoretical metaphysics is mainly an intellectual study practiced mostly by scholars and philosophers and is not the subject of this book. Practical metaphysics bases its knowledge and understanding on direct spiritual observations and experience. In its purest form, higher metaphysics is a sacred art, practiced by trained mystics who can see beyond the physical veil of life. The study of spiritual energy and the aura falls into the realm of practical metaphysics. All metaphysical references in this book refer to this practical, higher application.

Definition of Terms

Throughout this book, we will be referring to certain words and making particular comparisons. I would like to clarify a few of these basic terms.

The Enlightened & Unenlightened Consciousness

The enlightened consciousness is one that is filled with the awareness of its Divine Self. The unenlightened consciousness does not have this spiritual awareness.

Positive & Negative Energy

Positive and negative energy have nothing to do with polarity, as in electricity. In metaphysical terms, positive energy is spiritual energy charged with divine essence. It operates at a very high frequency. All references to light, spiritual energy, power rays, and so forth, refer to this positive energy. Negative energy is positive energy corrupted through misuse of its original design. In this form, negative energy is void of any divine essence. As a result, its frequency has been greatly reduced and has a draining and destructive effect on the aura. When we refer to this type of energy, it will be clearly spelled out as such.

Spiritual Evolution & Devolution

Evolution in metaphysics means the building up and unfolding of our soul qualities. Devolution means the tearing down and stagnation of the soul life. The evolution of the soul is generally not a vertical line upwards. There are highs and lows, upward and downward motion, as the soul evolves and devolves in its growing process until it becomes strongly dedicated to the spiritual life.

Divine—Spiritual

The word divine pertains directly to the world of God, our original source. The light we speak of in this book is an abbreviated term for Divine Light, and refers to the spiritual emanations as they flow from the God source.

The word spiritual has its root in the Latin word *spiritus* (breath, air, breath of life), but in metaphysical terminology is actually a more generic term. It refers to all realms that are nonphysical. In other words, negative energy is technically still spiritual energy because it is not of physical origin, yet because it is corrupted, it's definitely not divine energy. But unless stated otherwise, we'll use the word 'spiritual' interchangeably with the word 'divine' to mean the higher, pure world of God.

Anatomy of the Aura

One afternoon when I was very small, I was playing with a favorite red ball in our family living room. I was bouncing the ball around in all directions when it knocked against a piece of furniture and rolled into the kitchen. I ran after it. My mother was at the sink washing dishes. She was alone and happily singing to herself. I grabbed the ball and looked up to see if she had caught me. She hadn't seen me at all. Suddenly, as I looked at my mother, I could see a glow of light all around her. In this glow were all kinds of bubbly pink and lavender colors moving around. I was startled, yet fascinated. What was this? For a moment, I thought I was dreaming. I remembered having seen bits of color around people before, but this was so unmistakable, so real. There was no question about it—I was seeing the aura. At the time, I didn't even know what it was called, but the aura has been a part of my life ever since.

In this chapter, I would like to explore the fascinating world of the aura. For all the years that I have been working with the energy field, I still find it captivating. It teaches so much about ourselves and how we are all part of an incredible spiritual process. The auric field gives us tremendous insight into who we are as spiritual beings. As we have seen, the aura is crucial to our spiritual growth because it is where we make changes in our lives first. To create any condition, to see it manifest physically, we must first have the spiritual energy present. The aura is where we generate that spiritual power. By understanding how our aura works, we gain a much better grasp of how to make effective and lasting improvements.

As the anatomy of the aura is explained in this chapter, try to get a sense of what your own aura looks like. Again, you do not have to see it to gain an understanding of it. By learning about its various components and how they operate, you can ascertain where you are in your energy field even without seeing it. This evaluation of your auric strengths and weaknesses will give you a much better idea of where in your aura to focus the light.

The aura may be defined as an invisible (to the physical eye) vibratory essence that surrounds all living things. Humans, animals, plants and all objects in nature give forth a vapor or cloud, indicative of their real constitution. Inanimate objects also have an aura or auric emanations. A person's state of mind, physical health, emotional nature, and spiritual makeup all radiate energy, which together comprise the aura. The ancient philosopher Ponchidius wrote, "The human aura may be described as a fine, ethereal radiation or emanation, surrounding every human being." He should have gone further to include animals, plants, and so on.

The aura is, in essence, a blueprint of our active soul qualities. It's not the actual soul but the expression of the soul. As we attract spiritual energy through our various thoughts and activities, those energies register in the auric field. Our talents, strengths and weaknesses are all laid out in our auras. There's no guesswork. In physical life, we can hide our true character from others if we choose to. In the aura, there can be no concealment or deception: our true character is clearly visible. If we have done evil deeds, those deeds register in our aura. If we have done wonderful things, those wonderful energies will also appear. All the variations in-between show up, too. As a result, the aura is completely consistent and reliable in displaying our qualities and spiritual makeup.

Does everyone have an aura? The answer is emphatically *yes*. Every single person on this Earth has an auric field, regardless of who he or she is. The aura is common to everyone. Even if a person is deathly ill, there is still an aura. The only time an aura diminishes in power is when a person is ready to make their transition from this Earth life. In this case, the aura does not dissipate; rather, along with the soul, it withdraws its power from the physical plane of existence and returns to its spiritual origin. Other than this, the aura is always active and visible.

We don't have to actually see the aura to know its operation and power. Most of us can feel the aura, because the aura vibrates. People say, "Oh, I don't like that person's vibes." Why? Although we may not see an aura, we intuitively react to its energy field. As a result, a person with a rarefied aura will automatically feel uncomfortable around someone with a dark aura, and much happier around a person who has a similarly bright aura. Likewise, a person with a very dark energy field will feel more at home with someone of like vibration than with someone whose aura is very bright. The old adage "Like attracts like" holds very true with the aura.

Most striking about the aura are its dynamic colors. Our thoughts and feelings all radiate colors indicating the quality of thought or feeling being expressed. These colors, to the untrained clairvoyant eye, first appear to be random, but they're not. Each color is there for a specific reason and as a result of a particular way we have attracted and used the Divine Light.

As we change our mental and emotional states as well as our actions, our aura changes accordingly. This change can sometimes be dramatic. Parts of the aura can be tranquil as water one moment, then impulsive as flames the next moment. Other parts change much more gradually over a long period of time as our character changes. This dynamic quality is our saving grace. We're never stuck with an aura the way it is.

Shape of the Aura

Let us begin our study of the aura by looking at its shape. The aura is not something amorphous or vague: it has definite form. For the most part, the shape remains constant throughout our lives. Other emanations within the aura can fluctuate, giving the appearance of contraction and expansion, but the basic shape remains the same. This "shell" is the basic framework in which the other aspects of the aura reside.

Within the basic shape are bands or zones of various colors. They look like compartments filling the shape. There are nine of these zones. The physical body appears contained within this shell and its compartments. These zones are stationary and their colors change very slowly. It can take a lifetime to bring these colors into their fully illuminated state. Generally, the upper compartments will have brighter colors, showing the enlightened energies the person has developed, while the lower compartments will be darker, indicating that the person is trying to work out of those lower vibrations.

The Rounded Shape (Figure 2–1A)

This is not a perfect round. There is a slight oval at the top and bottom, but it's mostly round. The top is approximately six inches above the head and extends a little beyond arm's length. The outer rim is usually silver or gold but can change according to the needs of the individual. The rounded aura shows a soul in the process of gradual spiritual growth.

The Square Shape (Figure 2–1B)

The square-shaped aura is actually slightly larger than the rounded aura and literally looks like the person is stuck in a cube. The physical body is slightly off-center within the shell, with more room at the bottom than at the top. The square shape shows a devolving state of consciousness. We are not born with an auric shape like this. Over time and with repeated misuse, our auras can change from the rounded shape into this square shape.

The Pointed Oval Shape (Figure 2–1C)

The pointed oval-shaped aura is pointed at both top and bottom. It's about as wide as the rounded aura but reaches up about twenty-four inches above the head and below the feet. The pointed oval shape is the mark of a master. The circumference is usually gold for protection. A person with this shaped aura is either very near to, or ready to blossom into, his or her Divine Self.

Divisions of the Aura

Within the auric frame are what we call divisions. Many people think of the aura as splashes of colors and symbols when, in fact, the aura is a vast, intricate manifestation, just as man is. Nowhere can this intricacy be more clearly seen than in the auric divisions. The divisions may be seen in and around the auric shell. They cover a broad spectrum of our nature, and together comprise the sum total of our character traits. By improving the qualities of these divisions, we can vastly improve the corresponding quality of our lives.

Health Division (Figure 2–2A)

The health division takes in the entire physical makeup, including all organs, glands, tissues, and one's general condition.

A – The Rounded Shape

C – The Pointed Oval Shape

B – The Square Shape

Figure 2–1: **The Three Auric Shapes**

This division has health lines, or striations, that move out from the physical body to the perimeter of the auric shell on both the right and left side. When a person is in excellent health, these striations come through in very strong silvery-white energies that shimmer. They are exceptionally beautiful to see in this condition and immediately demonstrate that one is in radiant health. When a person falls ill, the health lines start to lose some of their luster and change to a dull metal gray. If someone is very ill, the lines become dull and droop closer to the body, depending on the severity of the illness. And when a person is approaching death, the health lines will droop very close to the body and continue to deteriorate to a dark metal-gray energy. In this condition, the person is ready to depart from the physical body.

In addition to health lines, the physical body itself radiates an aura of about two inches along its contours. You will see reds and oranges when the body is robust and strong. These radiations look similar to the auric emanations seen in Kirlian photography. There are also auras around each organ. Healthy organs usually have a rosy hue, while sick organs will have a dull gray aura around them.

Mental Division (Figure 2–2B)

This division, which also goes by the term mental body, deals with our thinking. Thoughts are among the easiest of areas to disturb in the aura, and therefore one of the most important areas to keep alert and clear. The mental division is one of the primary areas of the aura on which to begin work.

The energies of the mental division may be seen moving in and around the head. A gold band, giving power and strength to the mental body, is visible above the head. There is also a glow of lemon yellow light, crowning the very top of the head, that indicates the intellectual capacity of the individual. In the average person, this energy will radiate a few inches from the head, but with a mental giant or a genius it can extend quite a bit farther.

In the center of the forehead is the mental chakra (center). This center is part of the mental division and will be radiating an energy corresponding to the quality of the person's thoughts. Most of us move back and forth from enlightened to unenlightened thoughts, with the two sometimes bumping into each other. Many times, we don't even know when we're in the unenlightened state. We sense the confusion or disorientation but don't identify it as unenlightened thinking. We generally know when we are in the enlightened state because there is such bliss involved.

Emotional Division (Figure 2–2C)

This division is located in and around the solar plexus and extends to the outermost part of the aura. The emotional division is the total makeup of our emotional natures—good, bad, or indifferent. If we are angry, dark red energies will shoot out like firecrackers and can extend quite far if the outburst is very intense. If we are in love, beautiful fuchsias and pinks will radiate.

The feeling nature is an intense, powerful place within the aura. We more often act out of our feeling nature, without allowing our mind levels to direct our lives. We all know how feelings can color the mind. The emotional division acts somewhat as a center or anchor for the aura, balancing the whole auric field. Someone who is a master of his or her emotions will have very bright, radiant oranges, pinks, greens, or blues in this division. These energies will move out quite a bit farther than the mental radiations. The emotional center is in the middle of this division.

With someone who's very destructive emotionally, there can be dark browns and greens and even black, showing intense hatred. The energies in a volatile emotional condition move contrary to their natural flow. Notice the expressions, "sick to my stomach" and "gut-wrenching." The emotional "gauge" lies within the solar plexus.

For most people the emotional division is a mixed bag, including both positive and negative emotions. Someone may have the love flow, which brings in the pinks, but may be very jealous, which would move in dirty, avocado green energy. Like the mental division, it's critical to keep this division as clean and clear as possible, so we don't dissipate our spiritual powers.

Magnetic Division (Figure 2–2D)

This division is very interesting because it shows the creative talents and abilities of an individual. Its center of energy may be seen on the left side of the chest, a little above the heart. It is round in shape, similar to the energy centers. It's about two inches in diameter and peacock blue in color. From this blue point, rays of light shoot out when the division is active.

The magnetic division reveals to what degree a person has developed talents and abilities. If bright electric blues and oranges are radiating from this point, it means the person is actively using their abilities. For example, if a person is an excellent pianist and actively playing, the energy coming out of the magnetic division will be bright and radiant. On the other hand, if that person has neglected the piano, the energies will become dull. The talent is there, but inactive. One must use his or her particular gifts—otherwise, the energy will fade.

Geniuses have a very pronounced magnetic division because they are using their gifts to a high degree. The talent and abilities expressed can be in any area, including music, literature, art, medicine, engineering, physics, computer science—you name it.

Color Division (Figure 2–2E)

Interpenetrating the other divisions, the color division amounts to the total character of the individual. Habits, attitudes and motives all play a part in this area. About eight inches thick, it forms an oval shape that extends from about eighteen inches to two feet all the way around the person. The colors in this division move in small pinpoints of light that resemble heat rising from a sidewalk on a hot day. These points of light are so thick you can barely see through this division when really focusing on it. In the color division of an enlightened aura, these points of light sparkle in a rainbow of pearl luster colors, making the whole aura iridescent and creating a euphoric effect. To elevate this division, we must first elevate the character of the other divisions, and the changes will automatically appear here.

Spiritual Division (Figure 2–2F)

The spiritual division reveals the spiritual advancement of an individual. This division is seen about two feet above the head in arching bands of light. There are seven of these bands. They are about a half-inch thick, fanning out upward in various pearl luster colors and creating the effect of a rainbow. We all have these spiritual bands to varying degrees of intensity. They are the accumulation of spiritual light we have earned in our evolution. The brighter these bands of light, the more we have advanced spiritually. The colors can move into pale pinks, lemon yellows, and light greens. In a very advanced individual, there can be seen a pronounced indigo in one of these bands. It's a beautiful sight to behold and one of my favorite aspects of the aura to watch.

Understanding the Energy Centers

Now we come to one of the most important aspects of the aura, especially as it relates to working with spiritual energy. These are the energy centers, or chakras.

In the aura, there is a linking up of spiritual power through energy centers. Many people use the East Indian word "chakras," which is another term for energy centers. The word chakra is Sanskrit for "wheel of light" or "wheel of force." Actually, the centers are *spheres* of light, sparking out rays of various colors. The centers look like miniature suns, varying in size from about two and a half to three inches in diameter, with a pearl nucleus of light in the center. Their color is basically gold, but each one has its own dominant color particular to its individual purpose and character. They can also appear to be multicolored because of the energies that move in and out of them.

These energy centers are extremely vital in our processes of spiritual transformation because they are where we will be making changes in our aura first. When we draw light into our aura from our spiritual bank account, the first place the light makes contact are these energy centers. So in working with the Divine Light, we become intimately acquainted with the operation of these points.

Each center is responsible for a different aspect of our being and activity. They are given to us when we are born and stay throughout our lives. The reason we have these points is to receive and transmit energy, and we're constantly doing one or the other. These centers, then, are focal points of the tremendous power moving in and out of us.

When these centers are in alignment and the consciousness is flowing, there is complete harmony of mind, body and soul. When the energy field is in this beautiful state and the energy is being received and sent accurately, these centers will spin in a *clockwise* motion (see Figure 4–2). If one or more of the centers is spinning in a counterclockwise direction, then there is disharmony, which throws off the balance of the other centers and diminishes the power and accuracy of the energy being received and transmitted.

In attempting to understand the character of each center, there are two basic ways to interpret them—in the contemplative mode and the dynamic mode. The Tibetan and Indian schools of metaphysics, which have long directed great attention to the centers, emphasize the contemplative mode in their writings. Their purpose is to help the spiritual aspirant understand the inner life of his or her being. By placing attention on these centers, students can discover aspects of their inner nature that would be otherwise inaccessible to them. Such contemplative states may lead to moments of heightened awareness. There are stories of yogis entering blissful states by contemplating the beauty of the opened Crown Chakra, for example.

The dynamic interpretation of the centers focuses on the active expression of these points in daily life. Our focus will be on the dynamic expression of the spiritual centers because it is this flow we are most concerned about in the light work. Inasmuch as the centers have a direct impact on our day-to-day existence, working with them can have an immediate effect on our lives. Improving the flow of light through these centers is what will facilitate swift improvements in our outer world.

The number, basic appearance, and location of these centers are the same for everyone. Some of the earliest illustrations of these centers, which again came from the East, focused on seven main centers lined up in a straight line from the base of the spine to the top of the head; all had either a flower- or disk-like appearance. This was a symbolic representation of the spiritual centers and not intended to be taken literally. It was the way early spiritual writers chose to teach the principles of the chakras to the uninitiated. I have tried to illustrate these centers exactly the way I see them, without symbolic embellishment (see Figure 2–3).

The Crown Chakra (White)

Most books on chakras will point to the top of the head as the location of this center, but that is incorrect. This point is actually about six inches *above* the head. The Crown Chakra reveals how awakened a soul is in its spirit self. For most people, the Crown Chakra is closed. The majority of us haven't yet reached that state of consciousness of being spiritually aware. When this center is closed, it is oval-shaped, like the bud of a flower that hasn't opened, and is pure white. It does not rotate or radiate any energy. There's nothing wrong with the center being in this state. The person can be fully active in life. It just means that he or she hasn't started developing that side of his or her nature.

As a soul begins to open spiritually, the Crown Chakra, or the thousand-petaled lotus as it is also called, begins to light up. As the spiritual vibration starts to move in, each petal begins to unfold, and the center becomes glorious to behold. Its petals shoot out about eighteen to twenty inches upward and outward, very much like a lotus blossom. The predominant colors are white and gold. In this condition, it resembles a crown sitting on the upper part of the aura, and makes an unmistakable statement as to where we are in our spiritual development.

It takes time and effort to open this center: no matter how we may meditate or pray, this point cannot open until we have *earned* that power and vibration. By improving ourselves and working with the light, the Crown Chakra will unfold gradually. We don't have to concern ourselves directly with this center in working with the light. One interesting note: when we pass on from this world, the soul leaves through the Crown Chakra.

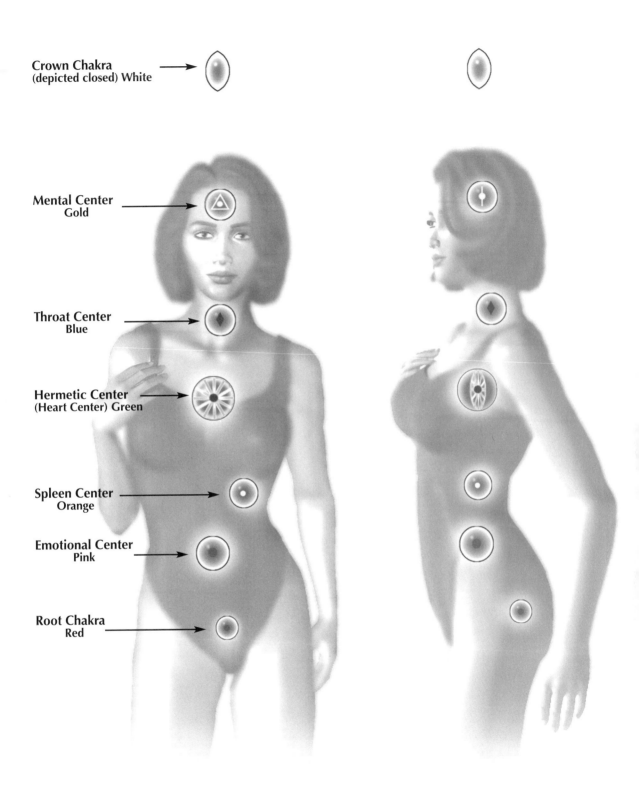

Crown Chakra
(depicted closed) White

Mental Center
Gold

Throat Center
Blue

Hermetic Center
(Heart Center) Green

Spleen Center
Orange

Emotional Center
Pink

Root Chakra
Red

Figure 2–3: **The Energy Centers**

The Mental Center (Gold)

The mental center is the nucleus of the conscious thinking levels. This energy point, located in the center of the forehead, is esoterically called the Trinity Chalice. This center is gold in color and about three inches in diameter. Within this center is a triangle of a lighter, golden hue with a beautiful diamond point of white light in the center. The center spins quickly because of all the activity going on, but the triangle remains stationary.

The mental center is a hub of intense activity. It's constantly receiving and transmitting thoughts, and these thoughts are extremely potent. This energy point sends power to the rest of the energy centers, especially the emotional center. When thoughts are in the enlightened flows, the connection between emotion and thinking and the subconscious levels will be working successfully. When the thinking level is very high, silvery sparkles move out of the mental center. This is indicative of a quick, intelligent and aware mind. There is usually a pronounced amount of lemon yellow as well.

The mental center keeps all levels of consciousness in harmony and balance. It is the highest point of light within the body and therefore the gateway to higher or lower levels of consciousness. The mental center is the director of our conscious life. This means we can either shut off the higher flow and be ego-centered, allowing little of the higher energies to influence us, or we can receive direction from the Divine, and use that inspiration to guide our conscious lives.

The Throat Center (Blue)

Esoterically known as the Eternal Ego, the throat center is the voice or the sound vibration part of us. It is located, appropriately, in the middle of the throat. It, too, is a golden sphere about three inches in diameter, slightly smaller than the mental center, with a magnificent royal-blue diamond nucleus.

Through this center, we project the power of our word. Our words radiate tremendous spiritual power. We may think we're just making sounds, but behind those sounds is potent spiritual power. This is why we must be very careful about the words we speak and to choose our words thoughtfully.

The spiritual energy that radiates out of this center moves in one of two ways: spiritual tone, or harsh sound. In beautiful, spiritual tones, there is a blue range of color emanating from the nucleus. These energies can stream out about a foot and a half in all directions. Great singers like Caruso, or inspired orators such as Emerson, will have this blue moving out from their throat center. The average person will radiate a ray of light that extends about a foot from either side of the center.

The spiritual energy behind destructive words moves on the harsh sound level and will come through on broken and jagged rays. The colors will vary according to the exact words, emotions, and intentions behind the words. I've actually seen snakelike energies streaming from the mouth of someone who was being very deceptive. It is important to bring more purity, love, and idealism to the spoken word. We have to watch very carefully not only the words we speak but also the motives behind those words. We must speak truly and kindly, for every word has an impact, for better or for worse, on those who are listening.

The Hermetic Center (Green)

This center is in the middle of the chest and is more commonly known as the heart center. I use the esoteric name, Hermetic Center, following the traditions of mystical teachings. This center is gold with a brilliant emerald green point in the middle. It's the largest center in the body.

The Hermetic Center deals with our world affairs—everything that is part of the outer world. This includes persons, places, things and situations. That's quite a bit! From the spiritual point of view, there are twelve avenues to our human earthly affairs and within the Hermetic Center there are twelve related power rays. These rays resemble spokes on a wheel. Seven of these avenues pertain to our day-to-day affairs and are called the seven solar rays. They are represented by the colors green, blue, turquoise, yellow, white, pink and red. Then there are five unnamed spiritual colors that appear white and pertain purely to our spiritual development.

It is critical to protect this center from undue pressures of the outside world. It can feel burdened when we take everything to heart and try to carry all the world's woes. We must strive to be "in the world, but not of the world." We can look at the world and be keenly aware of what is happening, but refuse to claim its troubles as our own.

The Hermetic Center is also known as the seat of the soul. The soul cannot be seen in a direct way. Yet behind the emerald green point within the center is a golden glow of light, which is the indicator of the soul connection. This connection has several names. It has been called the Ark of the Covenant and the Holy of Holies. This is our secret door to the inner realm. Since this center is the seat of the soul, it keenly responds to how the soul feels. Joy, exhilaration, love, sadness, weariness, anxiety, frustration, disappointment, depression—these feelings all come through and affect the

Hermetic Center. As a result of this connection, intense experiences regis-ter more deeply in the heart center than perhaps anywhere else.

The Emotional Center (Pink)

Located just above the navel, this center is esoterically known as the Spiritual Heart. It is the second-largest center in the body next to the Hermetic Center and is gold, with a beautiful deep rose-pink nucleus. It rotates at moderate speed.

This center deals with our emotions. As we know, emotions are very powerful. They are the engines that give strength and motion to our thoughts, and a thought with emotion behind it is very potent indeed. If someone brings in destructive emotions and then sends them forth, the neg-ative energy harms not only all in its path, but is certain to eventually boomerang back, with even greater force, to its sender. This is why it's so important to refine the emotions to the point where feeling and thinking blend well together in high positive flows. If we are in a good place emo-tionally, there will be beautiful streams of pinks, orange and reds emanating from the pink nucleus.

The Spleen Center (Orange)

This point is not a center as the others are, but rather a very important focal point of energy. The Spleen Center is about two and a half inches in diameter and is located on the left side of the body, close to the spleen. It is orange in color with a golden nucleus of light, and spins in a clockwise direction at a slower speed than the Hermetic Center.

The Spleen Center is a distributor of energy. One of its big jobs is to receive and distribute the sun's energy throughout the physical body, espe-cially the bloodstream. It's also a storage place for solar rays, so that when we need energy, it can be called upon. This point is responsible for helping to keep the physical body vital and full of stamina. It also brings in harmony and joy. When it's in a healthy state, red, orange and gold light will shoot out from the nucleus of this center. Lots of sunshine will benefit the Spleen Center.

The Root Chakra (Red)

The Root Chakra is located at the base of the spine toward the tailbone, and is actually easier to see from the side or the back. It's gold in color with a carnation red nucleus of light. This point does not rotate but remains stationary. It has an entirely different type of flow than the other centers.

One of the Root Chakra's jobs is to deal with experiences of the past. These are memories that are still being carried in the consciousness and need to be worked out. The Root Chakra holds the excrement, or the refuse, of our unenlightened thoughts and deeds. This is where the spiritual expression "going down into lower Egypt" or "coming up out of lower Egypt" comes from. Once cleared, the Root Chakra is a powerful ally.

In addition, the Root Chakra strongly connects with the creative and sexual part of us (see Figure 8–4). When we are in a healthy state sexually, the energy will be moving upward toward the emotional center in a beautiful flow of carnation red. For the person who is redirecting the sexual energy for other creative endeavors, this energy can move up even higher, sometimes to the mental center or higher still, if we're talking about a spiritual master. However, if we wantonly misuse sexual energy, the flow can move downward and the color will turn a dark maroon red.

This center works with another very important energy called kundalini. When active, kundalini is a spiraling, serpent-like energy, rising upward along the spine. Kundalini is a spiritual power already within us, but lies dormant until we begin to spiritually awaken. The purpose of this energy is to help strengthen and energize the spiritual centers. When someone is evolving at a good pace, the kundalini naturally opens without any conscious effort. The soul is slowly earning the vital power of the kundalini. This way, the person is able to handle the kundalini energy, and its unfolding becomes a beautiful, sublime experience.

Some schools of yoga teach opening the kundalini by conscious effort. However, I have found emphasizing the kundalini in our natural, spiritual progression to be unnecessary. It opens in its own time and rhythm, without conscious intervention as we work with the light. A word of warning: kundalini energies are nothing to fool with. I have counseled several people who were severely traumatized because they opened the kundalini too early. They were seeking instant spiritual illumination but found out, the hard way, that that's not the way it works.

Energy Center Radiations

Flowing out of our energy centers are various types of emanations. These radiations show the variety of activities within each center. In developing the aura, our main purpose is to elevate and enlighten the quality of these radiations. There are four distinctive types of energy center radiations.

Active Emanations

Active emanations represent the current flow of energy at any given moment. These are often the most expressive indicators of a person's immediate thoughts and feelings. Active emanations fluctuate with our every thought, word, feeling, and action. Generally, they are seen as straight rays of light, but they can take a great variety of forms, as you will see in many of the illustrations throughout this book. The colors can run the gamut, from the highest white to the blackest black, and everything in-between. These emanations are the ones that receive help from spiritual light most quickly.

Fanning Rays (Figure 2–4B)

Fanning rays are among the aura's most beautiful emanations. They shoot out from the nucleus to either side in a solid color of light. The extent of their radiation depends on the development of the person and begins to appear in the aura after a person has reached seven years of age.

Fanning rays show the *tendency* of energy in a particular center (note that there is no fanning ray in the throat center). Whereas active emanations can change with every word, thought, act and deed, fanning rays will stay the same color unless the whole direction of energy changes. For example, say a person has a pink fanning ray radiating from the emotional center, which demonstrates a loving nature. This person can still have days here and there when they feel irritable and out of sorts. This doesn't necessarily mean that the emotional fanning ray will change color, because the thrust of the person is still to be loving. But if that person were to become irritable on a regular basis or stop caring about people, then the fanning ray would definitely change color.

Spiral Rays (Figure 2–4C)

Spiral rays spin with the movement of the center and reflect the spiritual progress of the individual. At birth, these radiations are white and gold in color. After seven years of age, they begin to develop. They turn into colors similar to those shown here and continue to develop throughout life.

Stabilizers (Figure 2–4A)

Stabilizers help keep the flow of energy moving steadily. They move out in three to four straight rays and are gold in color. They stay the same color regardless of what's happening to the individual.

The Mixed, Devolved & Enlightened Auras

Let us now put together all aspects of the aura that we've been exploring, and look at the energy field as a whole. Of course, there are as many variations in auras as there are people, but in my experience, auras fall under three broad categories.

The Mixed Aura (Figure 2–5)

The vast majority of humans have mixed auras. Even souls that are high on the spiritual ladder will have the mixed aura until they near the spiritual pinnacle. The mixed aura has a rounded shape and has both positive and negative energies active at the same time.

A soul with this type of aura is in the process of evolving and is going through the human condition in all its vicissitudes. The soul with a mixed aura might be that of a fine artist who has a drinking problem, or someone who is very smart and inventive but also selfish and mean. A person who is fundamentally good, yet weak-willed and gullible, would also show a mixed aura. Variations are endless. Over time, it becomes the job of the soul with the mixed aura to use enlightened parts of that aura to transform the unenlightened parts until all are in Divine Light.

In the illustration here, the soul is on an upward swing but still has plenty to work out of. The darker compartment of green across the emotional division reveals a jealous nature that must be overcome. The dark green cloud formation to her right shows that this person is actively expressing that jealousy in some way. The gray compartment in the lower part of her aura shows she's overcoming a lot of fear. The brown compartment harbors pettiness, suggesting that she can be mean at times.

This person has many redeeming qualities as well. The light green band of light to her left shows she's growing spiritually despite her weaknesses. I see this band of green often around people who have awakened to the spiritual life and are learning spiritual truths. The gold pyramid above her head shows she is searching for truth. The pink bubbles of light to the right show she is in love with someone, but the other person is not returning her affections, which might account for some of the jealousy vibrations.

This soul also has creative energies. The winged forms above her head show inspired enlightened thoughts; the light blue formation to the left shows creative vibrations. However, its position indicates that she has not yet expressed this creative power. Vitality is apparent in the red energy coming from her hands, and good health is shown by the bright health lines moving out from either side of her body. Emanations of blue coming from her throat center tell us that she speaks positively; purple waves of light at her feet show she has overcome some tragedy or adversity. Her color division is clear with bright colors, and her spiritual division is fairly bright—she has developed spiritual powers somewhere in her evolution.

From this stage of spiritual development, we eventually realize the enlightened state; however, if we refuse to express our higher nature, we can fall into the next auric expression—the devolved aura.

The Devolved Aura (Figure 2–6)

This square-shaped aura reflects a soul that has consistently misused its spiritual powers. As a result, many of the energies have been corrupted. Such an aura has become square-shaped because, by its persistent refusal to connect with its higher nature, it has restricted the spiritual flow to the point where very little Divine Light can get through. During the sixties, the expression "He's a square" was often used. Ironically, someone really *can* be a square! This soul has a long climb back into the light, not only because of all the work needed to redeem it, but also because living in the dark propels it on to ever darker thoughts and deeds. Such a soul could be a tyrant or mass murderer, but doesn't have to be. I have seen this aura around what you would call "normal" people who hold no conspicuous positions in life.

The devolved aura seen in Figure 2–6 is very muddled; the lower half is especially disorganized. The black compartment holds sustained hatred which he has tried to control. It may also indicate that he has been involved in murder.

The dark green and brown compartments on the lower left indicate a conniving, cheating nature, compounded by cruelty. His emotions are all mixed up. There's a lot of anger, shown by the blotchy energy to his left at the emotional division. The health lines are turning gray and beginning to droop at the bottom, which means that his misdeeds are leading to physical illness. The head area has a brownish yellow energy, showing pettiness and a lethargic quality to his thinking. The dark green shooting from his forehead shows he is planning some sort of deception. The black thought forms around his aura show hatred toward someone that has recently been expressed. The dark, dirtied blue compartment across his head area shows he's constantly moody and brooding over his life. The sparkles of his color division are much smaller than the color division of the mixed aura, and many of the points of light are dulled and dirtied. Notice too that the energies radiating from his centers are filled with darker colors and do not reach as far as with the mixed aura. This shows he's in an active state of depression. His spiritual division remains unaffected, but he has no access to those powers until he turns his life around.

Despite his condition, there are some bright colors in this aura. A lemon yellow energy compartment above his head shows intelligence and a strong mind when it isn't clouded by wrongdoings. Red and orange compartments across his torso show he is energetic and motivated. This energy and motivation are often the most redeeming qualities in the devolved aura. The purple compartment on the lower left side of his aura shows he can be calm when necessary. Bright green and gold rays shoot out from the center of his chest, indicating he is active in world affairs, and probably successful. And isn't that often the case? Very destructive people can be quite successful in the work world and financial arena even though they are far from living life correctly. This often confuses people around them into believing that their actions are meritorious.

Fortunately, a soul in such a devolved state is something of a rarity. I have seen maybe a hundred devolved auras in my life, but that's a hundred too many. A soul like this is certainly not past redemption, but has a lot of work ahead to turn things around.

The Enlightened Aura (Figure 2–7)

In sharp contrast to the devolved aura is the enlightened aura. The enlightened aura is the ideal we all aspire to. In building our images of the things we most want in life, this is the auric image we need to implant in our hearts and minds.

The evolved aura has the beautiful pointed oval shape. There is also an outer gold aura that can radiate an additional two feet, creating a feeling of great expansion. All components of this aura are in full operation and well developed. Its colors are in the high pearl luster ranges and are moving in beautiful flows and striations. The compartments of the auric shell are clear, definite, and well organized. Notice the gold in the upper compartment, showing the high spiritual state of this soul. In addition to the pointed shape, a striking feature of the enlightened aura is a lack of dark colors. Occasionally, a ripple here or there may show up, but there are no defiled energies within the enlightened aura. The illustration here can only hint at the beauty of such an auric field.

A halo of lemon yellow light filled with diamond points shows the keen intelligence this person has. There are triangles inside each main spiritual center, signifying that the centers are working at optimal power. Notice the expanse of radiations coming from these centers: they reach almost to the edge of the auric shell. These beautiful flows show he has control over his mental and emotional nature and is living his life in ways that only add more light to his aura. The Crown Chakra, above his head, is fully opened, displaying a beautiful white lotus flower shape. This soul is fully awakened in its spiritual nature and is fully aware of its purpose on Earth.

Enlightened created forms are all around this aura. The white stars to his left show purity of thought. This person's mind is completely focused on God. This man has spent untold time refining and developing his divine attributes. The beautiful formation to his right shows he is in pursuit of a spiritual mission, or higher purpose. This soul, if not already a master of life, is very close to that level. The purple at his feet expresses the tremendous peace and spiritual stability this soul has attained. The color division is similar to that of the rounded aura, but the colors are now primarily gold and purple. The bands of light above his head are very bright and vibrant. This soul is a blessing to be around and creates only good wherever it goes. From here, the aura can expand even further, for perfection is never static: we grow from "grace to grace."

I have seen such an aura maybe a handful of times in my life, yet it is the destiny of all of us to have such an aura.

The Colors You Are

As I started seeing auras, one of my first reactions was to wonder what a particular color meant. Why was that color around this person and not around that person? I knew certain auras repelled or attracted me, but beyond that, I couldn't understand why one person would have certain colors around him, while someone else would have very different colors. I tried early on to find some information or material about what I was seeing, but there were no teachers I could turn to for help. And since no one else was seeing colors, I had no way of putting my experiences into perspective. All that changed when I was eleven and enrolled in a private drama school run by a woman named Dorothy LaMoss.

Dorothy headed one of the best stock companies in the Midwest. She had also gained a reputation on Broadway and in Hollywood. She was an eccentric woman. On the outside, she had an appearance of austerity, but once you got to know her, she had a good sense of humor and could be quite charming. We got along well together. She knew her craft and was a demanding teacher who produced results.

One day after I had been with her for about six months, she asked me to come on a Saturday to see her. I arrived that Saturday, wondering what she wanted from me. At the time, we were rehearsing a play, and I thought she was going to drop me. When I got there, she started asking me questions that had nothing to do with the play. She asked *how* I perceived things. I told her I saw things just like anyone else. Then she asked if I could see colors around people. *That* got my attention.

"Why do you ask me that?" I asked.

"Because you can see the aura," she said.

When she said the word 'aura,' I jumped.

"Is that what it's called?" It was the first time I had heard the term.

"Yes," she said. "And I would like to pass on to you what my grandmother and mother have taught me. I am a hermetic scientist. My mother and my grandmother, who were very advanced in metaphysics, were also hermetic scientists. I would like to teach what I know and give you a better understanding of your gifts."

Thus began my first encounter with real knowledge of the aura. Every Saturday, I would study with Mrs. LaMoss in private. She had several ancient books on hermetic science covering many aspects of metaphysical work. The books were hundreds of years old and were, in turn, based on writings that were thousands of years old. I spent many hours at her home, copying reams of information from the hermetic teachings. Dorothy also had diagrams and drawings that showed the various types of auras. Charts included auric colors, in all their shades and degrees. These were broken down very clearly, and the meanings of those colors were given in detail. It was an illuminating time I shall always remember. Even today, with interest in the aura and metaphysics blossoming, I have yet to see the same depth of information I was given by Dorothy and those sacred texts. It became the basis of my spiritual teaching years later and is one of the reasons I am writing this book: it's time to share some of that knowledge with a wider audience.

Spiritual colors in the aura range from the beautiful, high, pearl luster colors of the advanced soul to the inky blacks, dull metal grays, and dirty maroons of the undeveloped individual. As we have seen, most people fall into the middle range, with both higher and lower colors moving in their aura. When the soul is ready to progress to the next level of development, the shade becomes lighter and is frequently mistaken for white.

The auric emanations seen around a highly developed person are far more real and vivid than colors perceived in the physical world. Blues and greens, as beautiful as the colors of sky or leaves, are even more vivid and powerful in spiritual energy. The opposite is also true. The colors seen around a devolved aura can be grotesque and hideous. In addition to the unappealing color, there's a feeling and vibration accompanying the color that does not exist in the physical realm. Luminous colors are uplifting and scintillating, while colors of the lower vibrations actually take on depressing and often chilling qualities.

As you review these color definitions, reflect on how they pertain to you. Again, you needn't see the colors to recognize their operation in you. By knowing their meaning, you can pretty accurately determine what colors you have in your aura. For example, if you're a loving person, you can bet there's deep rose-pink light, which is elevating and enhancing your aura. If you find you're getting angry a great deal, chances are you're expressing vitiated red in your aura that you'll need to work out of.

Enlightened Colors (Figure 3-1)

Enlightened colors are spiritual energies that we have attracted and earned as a result of our positive thoughts, actions, and deeds. They express the spiritually attuned part of our nature. These energies have retained their divine essence and purpose, and are actively working to realize our spiritual potential. It's also with these positive energies that we are helped to transmute the darker parts of our aura.

White

Along with gold, white in an aura is considered one of the highest colors. It means purity. It symbolizes the Light of God bringing wisdom to humanity. Many spiritual attributes are connected with the white light. This energy, in any degree in the aura, unquestionably indicates a spiritual, often visionary, soul. Revelation is connected with white. A great deal of gentleness comes with this color as well. Pearl white represents kindness and a forgiving quality. The oyster white, which has almost a very light yellow in it, means the soul is steadfast and trying hard to learn lessons. Crystal white, the purest form of white, shows that the soul has acquired complete mastery; it represents the blending of strength, courage, vitality, determination and perseverance.

Gold

Gold is the color of wisdom, illumination, self-confidence, faith, inner strength and courage. It is also a very strong protective energy. If we have gold in our aura, we have the power, the will, that can master the lower self. We have the confidence of knowing who and what we are. We know what we can accomplish, what we can do. We move and act decisively. Gold brings in strong dynamic powers that can cut us loose from the mesmerism of feeling futile, frustrated, and inadequate.

Silver

Silver is the energy of spiritual intelligence. Silver in the aura shows a person with keen powers of perception and a quick, alert mind. This person will think for himself and not let others do the thinking for him. I often see silver sparkles or diamond points of light moving around a person's head. The brain and flesh cells have silver radiating from them, as well as from the health lines, in a healthy, active individual.

Blue

This color is often seen around a person who is in pursuit of spiritual truth, and this is more or less a royal blue. This individual, as a rule, will overcome all obstacles in the search for truth. Bright blue in the aura shows integrity, sincerity, and natural wisdom. Often, someone with predominant blue is involved in science or the arts. Royal blue also means a very loyal, devoted person. Consider the expression "true blue." It shows honesty, good judgment in material affairs, and can signal a very religious soul. Madonna blue, a light but not quite powder blue, shows obedience, and fulfillment of duties. This person obeys God's will. Primary blue is one of the strongest healing colors and is seen around doctors and healers. Aqua is also a very healing color, high in vibration. Along with violet, it can bring in peace, and help quiet the nervous system. Peacock blue shows talents and abilities. Blue-purple indicates accomplishment with God's power.

Powder Blue

This is a light blue and brings in high, creative inspiration. It is one of the pearl luster colors. In the aura, it shows an artistic person who loves beauty. Light blue shows devotion to noble ideals. Great artists will have powder blue strongly marked in their auras.

Turquoise

Turquoise is the energy of prosperity, and this means in all departments of our lives—an abundance of ideas, friends, and material goods. It's a "good luck" energy. Turquoise holds us in the consciousness of wealth and freedom from limitation and restriction. A person with this energy in his or her aura thinks in unlimited terms and knows that the money or the resources will be there for them when they need it, even when the outside world appears to show the opposite.

Pink

Pink is the color of love. Spiritual love comes in the shade of deep rose-pink. This pink is absolutely devoid of jealousy, selfishness, or any other human negative emotion. It is expressed with great beauty, and lives in the planes of creation. Pink is a universal color expressing joy, comfort, compassion, human love, upliftment and abundance. It comes through in many shades, from the high pearl luster to the fuchsia and rose-red pinks. Crimson shows a natural, unpretentious loving nature. A pearl luster pink, which is a lighter shade than the deep rose-pink, shows a soul's pure love for God.

Green

Green is recognized as the color of growth and renewal. Emerald green expresses balance in an individual, and is a very important color to have. This individual has his or her life in order. Emerald green is also the color of harmony of mind, body, and soul. It's seen in a person who, growing in knowledge, experiences harmony in many facets of life. It reveals one's love of nature and the outdoors. Pale, delicate green is sympathy. Apple green shows new spiritual growth and hope, loving service and cooperation. Green is restful to nerves, good for overcoming fear. Green-blue indicates a trustworthy, helpful nature.

Lemon Yellow

This energy brings in powers of concentration. It deals with the intellect. People who have this color strongly in their auras may devote their entire life to the study of higher truths. They will be able to embrace a subject and stick with it until it is learned and mastered. Lemon yellow in the aura shows mental vigor in artistic, creative, and scientific endeavors. Yellow, for example, will be seen in a schoolroom around children who are learning. Teachers, of course, have a great deal of yellow. Yellow represents a healthy body, mind, and intellect. It is beneficial in dispelling fear, worry, and nervousness. Bright, optimistic people have this lemon yellow in their auras. Yellow and orange together can be very inspiring.

Orange

This is a bright orange, like the fruit. The color orange means that the person has strong motivation, enthusiasm, and good organizational abilities. This energy can also show a burning desire or ambition. A very determined individual, one who almost always overcomes obstacles and meets his goals, will earn this color. Straight orange expresses thoughtfulness, consideration, and soul energy. The person is a dynamic leader, a live wire. Golden orange is wisdom and energy, heightened mental and spiritual abilities, and self-control—a high spiritual vibration not often seen.

Red

This is life energy, especially ruby red. It radiates a lot of vitality. Red is a color that can also mean righteousness. It indicates an enthusiastic individual with high aspirations. It's the passion part of us. People with red in their auras have insights into other people, and they work well with others. They are not defeated easily. Ruby red is usually physical vitality, endurance. Red invigorates the body. Rose red represents an active love; rose red and orange together help to create a glow of well-being, promoting a healthy outlook. These are predominantly strong and uplifting colors, bringing brightness and a feeling of warmth, a desire for living. Clear red is faithful; orange-red is a healing and cleansing color. Coral is indecision, unhappiness in one's surroundings. Scarlet red can indicate egotism. Red-purple represents power of the body, and individual effort.

Violet

The person who has violet possesses an aura that is serene and calm. He or she expresses an inner and outer poise. This person is always willing to be of service to humanity. Violet brings in high spiritual power, true greatness, unselfish efforts. Violet offers mental protection. If the violet moves into lavender, a worshipful character is revealed. Orchid, which is the slightly deeper shade, denotes humility and, as the first cousin to lavender, is holy and spiritual.

Purple

This color in a person's aura means deep peace. Also, a person with purple in his or her aura is deeply religious in a mystical way. Yet, purple also expresses ability to deal with practical and worldly matters. Purple-indigo indicates that one is seeking spiritual power. Waves of purple bands under the feet show a person who has overcome adversity.

Indigo

This color gives inspiration and deep inner strength of a purely spiritual nature. It is an extremely high color and seldom seen in mankind to any marked degree. One who has this color has come a long way, as it means that he or she has awakened in the spirit self. It doesn't take much of this energy to have a powerful effect on the aura. Indigo-violet shows someone who is searching for a spiritual experience.

Unenlightened Colors (Figure 3–1)

Unenlightened energies show some type of defilement or corruption of the Divine Light. They are divine energies that we have somehow misused and are now void of the divine essence they were originally imbued with. For instance, a bright clear mind would have the lemon yellow energy in it, but if the person became lethargic and lazy, then the bright yellow would move into a dirty creamy, mustard energy. The brightness would vanish because the person was not utilizing spiritual energy as it was intended to be used and there is no longer the divine essence in that light as there was before. This person would now have a difficult time making decisions. Mustard yellow could also signal sickness. If it gets very dull, it can even show a savage person. Bright orange is the color of drive, enthusiasm and ambition, but if it turns into a burnt orange, the person has become filled with self-pride. Dark brownish orange shows a lack of ambition stemming from repression. In addition to the dark color, these energies have a repulsive, cold vibration if they are predominantly in the aura. In other words, they're no fun!

If we recognize some of these energies operating in us, it's simply a sign of where we need to work to improve: we needn't worry or hit ourselves over the head about it. Remember that our auras are constantly changing, and there's not one aspect we can't elevate and transmute. If our thinking is lethargic, it can become astute. If we're mean, we can become kind, and so on.

Every one of us, at one point or another, has created dark light. It's part of our human experience to rise above these conditions. The thing to always remember about unenlightened energies is they are not part of God's divine emanations. They're artificial and not part of our true divine nature. Therefore, we do not need to claim these negative energies as our own. We just need to clear them out of our auras and not create any new destructive vibrations. The best part of all is that these negative energies are powerless before the Divine Light. They have no real influence unless we invite them to operate in us. The more good we do, the more of the high colors we attract and accumulate, and the more we displace these lower vibrations.

Gray

Gray is associated with fear, gloom and depression. Gray is the color of illness. When someone tones down to gray, that person is a worrier. Gray appears in the auras of people who can't presently see their way out of whatever dark cloud they've fallen into. However, if there is silver moving in with the gray, it shows someone who has known despair and suffering but is fighting his way out. Charcoal gray indicates despair, and gray-black is heaviness, dullness, grief and loss.

Vitiated Red

This energy comes through in a dark, dirty, maroon red. It shows lustfulness. This person is mainly operating from the lower animal, instinctual levels of consciousness. They can be intoxicated by sex and have an insatiable appetite for more. It can suggest perversion, and a definite misuse of the sexual energy. Vitiated red also shows deterioration of the person. Deep, muddy red shows strong anger, nervousness, a bad, domineering temperament, and strife.

Avocado Green

This is a very dark green, like the outside of an avocado. It reveals deceit in an individual. This is someone who is out to cheat and take advantage of people. A traitor would have avocado green in his aura. It shows a person who is greedy. Avocado green is also present in the aura of a person with a consuming jealousy. It is a very insidious energy I have seen too often in people. Olive green, which is lighter in shading, shows envy.

Dark Brown

Brown, especially cocoa brown, shows someone who is cruel and petty. This energy stimulates selfishness and selfish desires for power. It can show someone who wishes to achieve and grow with intense feelings, but in the wrong directions. Dull brown denotes avarice. Greenish-brown shows petty jealousy. A brownish mass of color can mean miser. Brown can also express guilt and repression.

Black

Black is the lowest vibration of all the colors. It is totally absent from the higher vibrations. It indicates someone who is open to dark influences, even vicious evil. Inky black clouds around a person are indicative of malice and hatred. A soul with this energy may be prone to murder, or has already committed a heinous crime. This person is capable of committing even more terrible crimes without hesitation or conscience. Lighter, smoky black indicates a "dark night of the soul," someone in the depths of despair. It can mean sorrow and suicidal impulses.

The Aura in Action

Let's apply our knowledge of spiritual colors and the aura as we look at some illustrations of what the aura is like in action. Some people have the mistaken impression that their aura is something impersonal or removed from everyday life. Nothing could be farther from the truth. The aura is an intimate, dynamic, and active part of everyone's life.

Like snowflakes, no two auras are exactly alike because no two people are going to use the life force of God in exactly the same way. If we spend our lives planting seeds of hate, we will not display the auric splendor of those who plant seeds of love. If you are a violinist and I am a stockbroker, our auras will not be alike because our jobs require different focus and skills. In addition, the aura clearly shows that all events happen in a person's life for a reason. Whether filled with strife or filled with love, our lives are entirely dependent on the kind of energy we have created for ourselves.

This gallery of auric portraits depicts auras of actual people I have known. I have chosen auras that show a dramatic use of spiritual energy, either for positive or negative purposes. Again, these auric conditions are nor static or permanent. The aura is active and changing constantly, its shades of expression as varied as the people who express them.

Romantic Love (Figure 3–2)

Here we see the aura of a 20-year-old college student who fell in love with a young musician. The musician returned her affections and an intense romance began.

In this aura, a cloud of pink above the girl's head shows that she is strongly thinking of love, and of her beloved in particular. Around the whole aura is a bubbly pink champagne energy moving in a circular motion, joyously expressing the perpetual state of euphoria her love creates. It also reveals that the love is being reciprocated, and that she is experiencing a vibrantly loving relationship. For the energy to be as intense as this, love has to be reciprocated.

Notice the active emanations of emerald green, royal blue, and gold radiating from her Hermetic Center, showing steadfastness, determination, and strength of soul. This girl could not be shaken from her feelings. Hers was an all-consuming love. Active emanations of pink radiating in star-points of light from her emotional center show the actual expression, the feelings of love. The two were constantly expressing their love for each other. Energy such as this will stay in the aura for as long as the bond of love is sustained.

In such a relationship, the lovers will do anything for each other. Feelings go beyond sexual attraction. They're best friends, and neither would dream of hurting the other in any way. They're always looking to please one another and enjoy what the other does for them. This aura is fun-loving, optimistic and supportive. Sometimes there will be possessiveness, which can bring in some lower energies, but in this case, it wasn't there. Her feelings revolved around an intense desire to be with her love. This soul is monogamous, and immune to outside temptation. I know this sounds like a fairy-tale romance, but it does happen. I have seen many auras expressing love, although I've seen it to this degree less often.

Intelligence (Figure 3–3)

This is the aura of an atomic scientist I observed in one of my lectures. Naturally, the energies in his mental division were particularly strong. He had a band of yellow light just below the gold band connected with his mental division. This band had been built up through constant use of his powers of concentration. Another salient feature often accompanying such a brilliant mind is the solid silver triangle within the mental center—a mark of exceptional intelligence, even genius. That he was in the midst of intense mental work is evident in the upper part of his aura, where equation-like thought-forms, some of which were quite long and complicated, were being projected from his subconscious, because he was so focused on his work. Brilliant souls such as this also have a highly developed magnetic division.

The weak links I have found in studying the auras of scientists and intellectuals are in the emotions. One would think that highly intelligent people would also possess well-balanced emotions, but this is often not the case. Emotionally, this man still had things to clear. The imbalance in this case showed up as avocado green rays shooting out from his emotional center. Strong irritability, manifesting in jagged dark red lines, also projected from his emotional center. An absence of pink in his aura suggested that he probably was a little cold in his relations with people.

Hatred (Figure 3–4)

This is an aura of a woman who'd been molested as a girl by her father. Although many years had passed, the result was a basic distrust and hatred of men—not pleasant for the men in her life. This aura shows the misplaced hatred she was directing toward her boyfriend at the time.

When I first met this woman, her aura wasn't so bad. She was actually very artistic—shown here by the active magnetic division—but as problems in her relationship developed, they triggered this kind of auric reaction. It took several months for the energy to build to this degree. A black cloud began to form above her head, showing persistent thoughts of longstanding, festering hatred. The fact that it was *above* her head means that although the thoughts were focused in hate, her mind could nevertheless be clear in its dark thoughts. Occasionally, I will see a cloud of hatred in and around the head area, which is indicative of confusion and poor functioning, but this was not the case here. The woman owned her own business and was doing quite well. Lightning bolts of maroon and black were also in her aura, showing rage born of hatred. Black radiations from the Hermetic and emotional centers testified to the consuming and destructive effects of hatred: she was making life very difficult for herself and the people around her. Such an aura must be closely monitored because a person in this condition is prone to rash acts. This woman talked about how her boyfriend was no good, and how she thought about killing him.

And yet, this is by no means an evil aura. The woman actually had spiritual inclinations and, interestingly, clairvoyant abilities as well, but she was disturbing those energies by creating such dark light.

Anger (Figure 3–5)

Anger is perhaps the most dramatic of the negative emotional states seen in the aura. This illustration represents the energies of a man who constantly lashed out at his wife. She didn't have to give him much of a reason to launch one of his tirades. The situation ended tragically. The wife eventually became ill because of all that happened, and died.

This anger extended beyond the perimeters of the auric shell. Squiggles and thunderbolts of vitiated red shot through the aura, along with streaks of red and blotches of olive green—unmistakable signs of extreme disharmony. The Hermetic Center held clouds of dark brown and other muddled colors, showing the heaviness he was carrying on a constant basis. Broken lines of brown energy moved from his throat center when he was on one of his tirades, yelling cruel words at his wife. His emotional center was one big jumble of jagged vitiated rays of anger and irritation. Black dots showed the hatred this man felt, even though the wife did nothing to warrant it. Of course, it wasn't only his wife he was angry with. He was like a walking time bomb that was ready to explode at the slightest provocation.

Wealth Consciousness (Figure 3–6)

One of the most prosperous energy fields I've ever encountered was that of a prince of royal German lineage. He was a man of immense wealth when he was forced to flee Germany after Hitler came to power. He managed to take a large chunk of that wealth with him to the United Stares. Highly educated and with many skills, he was a diplomat and geologist, as well as an astute businessman. He owned his own oil company. Above all, as evinced in his aura, even though he was displaced from his homeland, he maintained his high level of wealth consciousness. He was in his seventies by the time I met him, but still very alert and active.

Looking at his illustration, you can see pronounced turquoise energy moving around him, which means that this prosperity consciousness was longstanding. There is also a foundation of turquoise at his feet, establishing it as a steady consciousness that did not waver; he would most likely carry his prosperity consciousness into every situation for the rest of his life. The preponderance of turquoise in this aura showcases a man who has continuously attracted and manifested abundance. The turquoise around his Hermetic Center shows the day-to-day activity of the prosperity flow. The orange active radiations express his enthusiasm and motivations—this man really enjoyed what he did and was not operating out of greed or pridefulness. As a rule, this kind of aura is very upbeat and fun to be around.

Poverty Consciousness (Figure 3–7)

This aura represents a negative reaction to a tragic event. The illustration is based on a woman who was widowed and left with three children to care for. She found work as a maid and was good at it, but it was a rough go with three kids to raise. Fortunately, the townspeople helped her as best they could, but it was still hard for her. To compound the problem, she developed a pessimistic, gloom-and-doom attitude. The reason her aura was adversely affected was not so much her trying situation as it was her negative handling of that situation. Depending on him totally, she had put all her trust in her husband, and when he was gone, her world fell apart. Had this woman been able to put her faith in God, or even in herself at this challenging time, she would have fared far better and bounced back more quickly.

Notice the dark energy around her head area. She feels sad, downtrodden, fearful and without hope. Most of us have experienced this feeling to some degree. There's a feeling of failure. One has to work hard to get out of this consciousness. Most people make the mistake of seeing financial woes as permanent, and here's where they make their big mistake: feeling stuck and with no way out, they marshal little motivation to make the necessary effort. But if the condition is seen as temporary, and open to change, there is much more motivation, much more faith and hope that better days are in the making.

Also by this woman's head is a heavy thought-form concentration of avocado green, gloomy blue, and cocoa brown, reflecting the constant darkness of her thoughts. I remember seeing it undulate as her thoughts took on their generally petty, degrading forms—the woman this picture represents was always sad and often belittled herself. The fact that this thought-form obscured part of her head shows that the condition was definitely clouding her thinking. Above this blotchy energy, note the gray cloud of fear. When I knew her, she was constantly fearful of what might happen next.

Around the Hermetic Center was a maroon energy that signified negative conditions in her personal affairs. There were also brighter colors of royal blue—loyalty to her children, despite a bleak outlook on life. Emerald green showed an attempt to keep balance in her life. She was not a bad person by any means, but had succumbed to the hardships that befell her. In her emotional center, pink radiations of love showed her to be a warm person who loved her children very much. Mingling with that love pink were gray radiations, signaling fear of the future.

Fear (Figure 3–8)

This auric illustration is of a man who was afraid of losing his job. Fear and worry energies are very similar in the aura. They can be about a particular thing or situation, a chronic condition, phobia, or an anticipated event. The fear may be justified or not, but when present to this degree, it's all-consuming. This man's worries had been building for months, which was reflected in a charcoal gray cloud above his head. If his fear were to diminish, then the gray would also lighten. Drooping gray lines emanating from the emotional center suggest that this man was withdrawing from the challenge rather than facing up to it. The fact that the radiations were moving downward means that the experience itself was pulling him down, creating a devolving situation. Royal blue still emanated from around the throat, but the energy was broken, showing the lack of confidence and weak will that accompanied his fear. In this case, the man's fears were based on a real threat, but things ended up okay. He kept his job. Yet the energy he expended in his worry sapped him of valuable energy, which took time to rebuild.

The Spiritual Aspirant (Figure 3–9)

The aura of the spiritual aspirant is one of growth, as the soul begins to develop its spiritual powers and potential. This aura belonged to a minister at a metaphysical church, an energetic, enthusiastic and knowledgeable person.

    This soul had begun its conscious pilgrimage to its Eternal Home and was working on bettering itself. Light bands of apple green and light blue may be seen above her head, between the top of the aura and the spiritual division. I see these bands often in spiritual aspirants. The silver sparkles above the head show this person being quickened in divine intelligence to receive new ideas and inspiration, and to have greater spiritual awareness. The lemon yellow present *within* her mental center attests to this person's highly developed powers of concentration. Waves of purple light, strong at the feet, show she had overcome many obstacles. Emerald green emanates from her Hermetic Center, indicating that she was working hard to balance her world affairs. The orange of enthusiasm, also coming from the Hermetic Center, shows the thrill of spiritual discovery. Notice that the Crown Chakra has opened several of its petals, evidence that this soul has begun its awakening to its spiritual awareness.

    Emotionally, however, there was still a mixed bag as this soul was working out of its lower emotional nature. This lower state comes through in the vitiated red of anger and the dark gray of fear, showing the war within this soul as the false self fought to resist transformation. But as long as this woman continues to focus on her spiritual development, she will triumph over her lower nature. This type of aura is not uncommon, especially today, with more and more people waking up to the spiritual realities of life.

Meditating
with Divine Light

Six Steps to Change Your Aura

A unique feature about tapping into your spiritual bank account is that you're drawing energy from a spiritual source *outside* yourself, and from a greater place and dimension. This is the reason the light can be so effective. Because the Divine Light comes from such an exalted place, it has potency far beyond anything connected with physical life. The six-step technique presented in this chapter is a simple yet powerful meditation to draw the light from your spiritual reservoir into your aura. It's a technique that's been a part of the metaphysical tradition throughout the world for centuries. I have taught this technique to thousands of people, with astonishing results. It has no formal name, but I call it the Higher Self meditation.

As you explore the Higher Self meditation and the myriad ways to work with spiritual energy, keep in mind three simple keys. They represent the process you will use to employ light in any situation.

- Decide what you want the light to do for you.
- Draw the light into your aura.
- Apply the light to effect the change you desire.

Decide What You Want the Light to Do for You

Before meditating, it helps to have a clear idea of how you want the light to help. When you meditate with light, you meditate with a purpose. So, the clearer you are about exactly what you want the light to do for you, the more definite your results will be.

There are countless situations in which you may call on the light for spiritual assistance, from meeting daily challenges to working out deeply embedded character flaws and traumas. If you already know where you want to focus the light, then you are ready to begin the meditation. However, since you're taking the time to develop yourself, I recommend that you first step back and take personal inventory of your strengths and weaknesses. This way, you can better see where you are in your consciousness and spiritual progress. It was Socrates who said, "The unexamined life is not worth living." As part of your normal routine, you need to take time out from life's pursuits to reflect on what you're doing in order to gain a fresh perspective. The list you compile from this self-inquiry can become a reference point, not only for what you need to work on but also as a signpost of your progress.

Recognition Is Half the Battle

The first step in any type of self-inquiry is recognition. We have to recognize that there are parts of us that need improvement. Despite the desire of many of us to improve our lives, there is often resistance to the whole process. It's not easy to recognize our faults or weaknesses. Many people go through the greater part of their lives unaware that they may be doing things that are hurting themselves and others. Recognition of a personal strength or weakness is a giant step in the right direction. There is tremendous liberation in the simple realization of why things are the way they are.

In some fortunate instances, recognition alone is enough to break through whatever blocks we may have. More often, though, recognition is the critical first step toward transformation. Also, our recognition doesn't have to be limited to faults. It can be an earnest desire for overall improvement. It can be the recognition of a virtue or strength that we were not fully aware of.

Take Responsibility

The next step in conducting an effective self-inquiry is we have to take responsibility for our actions. We will not get far in our spiritual growth if we constantly assign blame for our troubles to other people or outside circumstances. In my counseling work, people come to me with endless complaints, usually accompanied by self-pity. I say to them, "Do you want to be the master or the victim of your life?" We must stop projecting our own faults onto others and blaming the other guy for what's going on in our lives. *We create our own world.* From our thoughts, desires and emotions, we have created the personal environment we're living in. So, if something's not going the way we want it to, rather than saying, "Why is this happening to me?" we need to say, "What did I do to create this situation?" It's that simple. Take charge of your life and watch how things will change.

Listing Strengths & Weaknesses

To begin your self-inquiry, get a notebook and assign space for six categories. Label them: Thoughts, Emotions, Personal Affairs, Relationships, Career, and Finances.

Then simply make a list off the top of your head of what you feel are your strengths and weaknesses in each category. Take inventory of the traits you're very conscious of. After you write down your observations, check to see how honest you are with yourself. Are you being too easy, too hard, or right on target? Which trait seems to stand out the most? That's probably the one you should focus on first.

If you're having trouble looking at yourself objectively, conduct a weeklong self-survey. Take a week and keep a log of these six qualities in action. Don't steer your observations in any particular direction or judge anything. Don't change any of your daily habits. Take the week just as it comes: boring, average, exciting. Any activity is going to bring out qualities in you. Just *observe,* and keep track in your journal of what you're doing. At the end of the week, review your entire survey. The beauty of this kind of survey is that there's no arguing with yourself. If you got angry a lot that week, you got angry. If you were impatient, you were impatient. Things are clearly seen for what they are. Of course, not everything will come out in these preliminary exercises, but what you need to know *will* be apparent.

Draw the Light into Your Aura

Once you know where you want to focus the light, you're ready to meditate. The beautiful thing about taking inventory is that not only does it give you direction as to which way to go with the light, it also helps to get you in the frame of mind to work with spiritual energy to begin with.

There may be several areas that you want to work on. I recommend focusing on one area at a time until you have achieved the transformation you desire, or made strong progress in that direction, before beginning another. This way, you'll see results faster and build more confidence in the power of the light.

Understanding the Higher Self

Before beginning the Higher Self meditation, I must familiarize you with one more part of your spiritual anatomy—a very sacred part. As we have explored, you can change your aura by first tapping your spiritual bank account. Yet, how do you actually tap into this creative flow? You have this magnificent source of power, and you have the expression of this light in your aura, but what is the mechanism by which this light actually reaches you? There needs to be a link between you and your spiritual reservoir that can guide the whole light process. Fortunately, this link is already a part of you. It's a magnificent aspect of your spiritual design that already has the divine intelligence and awareness to relate to the light directly, as well as relate to the soul part of you. This link—or emissary of light—is your Higher Self.

The Higher Self has been mentioned so many times in spiritual litera-ture that it has become part of the nomenclature of metaphysical study. Many teachers recognize it as a guiding force in man's evolution. Helena Blavatsky, the great metaphysician, co-founder of The Theosophical Society, and author of masterpieces such as *Isis Unveiled* and *The Secret Doctrine,* called the Higher Self "the divine prototype," "the reflection of the universal spirit [divine spirit]." The famous European mystic Rudolf Steiner called the conscious awakening of the Higher Self a "spiritual rebirth." Other teachings call it a "lifeline," or a beacon by which a ship lost at sea can find its way home; the awakened soul is answerable to and looks for guidance from the Higher Self alone.

All the spiritual light you receive from your spiritual bank account has to first pass through the Higher Self. After it receives the light from the realms beyond, it can then transmit that light to you. It does this automat-ically, but when the process is attended to in a conscious and direct way, it can greatly increase the light your Higher Self can give you. If it were not for the Higher Self, you would have no way of connecting with the Divine Light.

The beauty of your Higher Self is that it's already in its divine awareness and therefore in a state of perfection. It's a greater part of you, completely aware of the spiritual realms above it and yet keenly aware of what is happening to you, here and now. You can completely rely on the Higher Self. It has no blemishes, no human traits to disappoint you. It's totally reliable and is a guiding force in steering your soul in its evolution. The Higher Self is always with you and always working for you, whether you are aware of it or not. As you align yourself with its power, its effectiveness greatly multiplies.

The Higher Self is often contrasted with what is commonly termed the "lower self." The lower self refers to the unenlightened human parts of your consciousness. These are the parts of you that have not yet spiritually developed. For many people, the lower self is all they're aware of at this point in their spiritual evolution.

In addition to channeling light, the Higher Self is one of the tools you will use to help transcend your human awareness and reach into your spiritual knowing. This consciousness will help you awaken to the spiritual path and your divine potential. It also helps you to consciously become aware of the light process.

Fortunately, the Higher Self is not simply a metaphysical concept. It is an intimate and sacred part of you. In the aura, the Higher Self appears as a point of light twenty-four inches above the physical head. If you wish, you may call this the eighth spiritual center. Its full name is the Higher Self Point of Spiritual Knowing (see Figure 4-1). It's about three inches in diameter (similar to the other centers) but it does not rotate. It's gold, with a point of lighter gold in the center. From this center, thousands of gold and white thread-like rays shoot out about fourteen inches in all directions. Many depictions of spiritual blessings, such as *The Coronation of the Virgin* by Velázquez, interestingly place the source of the blessing current at the Higher Self Point. The more developed and connected to the Higher Self the individual is, the more radiant and extended these rays will be. As a particular energy is drawn into it, many of the rays will take on the color and quality of the light being called upon.

Since it is above your head and above the mixed elements of your human aura, the Higher Self Point can receive the light clearly and directly. Think of the Higher Self Point as like a satellite in space. An orbiting satellite can receive a signal from deep space much more clearly than a receiving station on Earth because the satellite has no interference from the atmosphere. Without human interference, the Higher Self Point becomes a gateway to the greater realms of light and life. It's an indescribable sight. I was in my early twenties when I began seeing the Higher Self Point, and it was even later that I learned how to work with it.

The Higher Self Meditation

To begin the Higher Self meditation, first find a quiet, relaxing place. It should be a place where you feel good and can concentrate without interruption. You don't want to be around a lot of people when you are doing this meditation. If you don't already have one, I recommend finding a spot in your home that is conducive to meditation. Ideally, it should be an area that others don't spend much time in. It may be a corner of your bedroom where you have your own special chair—anyplace where you can work consistently. This way, the energy will have a chance to build, which will make your light work all the more effective. If you live with other people, let them know what you are doing, and that your meditation time is to be uninterrupted time. You may also work outdoors, which is excellent. Being in nature is certainly an effective way to work with the light. Again, find a place where there aren't many people nearby, such as your backyard or a park. I've even pulled my car off the street, found a quiet neighborhood, and have done a meditation right in the car.

Again, the point of any type of meditation is to become still, and shut the world out, so you can tune into your own divine nature. Meditation is a way to get closer to God. In the activities of daily life, it's hard to feel your divine oneness unless you're able to periodically tune out that activity. I had a student once who said she was meditating every day, but that things weren't happening fast enough for her. So I went to her house, and she showed me how she meditates. To begin with, she had the radio blasting. She also had the phone right next to her and picked it up twice during her "meditation." She had food on the stove and would get up periodically to check it. In other words, she was doing *everything but* getting into her divine oneness. How could the light work be effective this way?

The Higher Self meditation is actually a form of meditation and prayer. Meditation is getting into the stillness to receive, and prayer is petitioning God—whether it be for love, illumination, faith, or to send light and prayers to others. You will be getting into the stillness to receive the light as well as petitioning God for the kind of light you need.

In first working with the light, ten to fifteen minutes are all you need. Light a white candle and place a bowl of water next to the candle. This will help to set the right vibration in the room for your work. You can also place flowers near you if you like. It doesn't matter what time of day you meditate. I like to meditate in the morning because it helps to start my day off right. I even suggest selecting some clothes that you will wear every time you meditate, such as a robe, because with each meditation you're putting light into those clothes. Over time, so much light will be held in your meditation clothes that you'll find yourself in the mood to meditate just by putting them on.

The six steps to the Higher Self meditation are:

1. Relax
2. Establish Protection
3. Check Your Spiritual Centers
4. Connect with Your Higher Self
5. Down-Ray the Light
6. Ground Yourself

Step One—Relax

Take a few moments to simply relax. Let go of the world's clamor and your own preoccupations. It doesn't matter what's going on around you. You're in a sacred place now, where you're making your connection with the Higher Power, and you want to be as clear and lucid as possible. This relaxed, passive state is not a sleepy state, but an awakened calm.

If you're upset or disturbed by something, be sure to first calm down before starting the light work. You don't want to start the work angry or disturbed. Take a break and go for a walk or a drive, and don't think at all about what is bothering you. If you're having trouble relaxing, begin by playing some music to calm you. You can also start with some slow, deep breathing.

Step Two—Establish Protection

When you do any type of meditation, you're putting yourself in a very open, receptive place. Spiritual protection is important at every level of life and doubly important while in the meditative state. There's a lot of activity in the world, a lot of negative energies coming at you from people and places that can affect you—if you permit them to. So, before you start your meditation, make sure to call for protective light around you.

Once you have found your place to meditate and are relaxed, start by placing yourself in a bubble of light. To do this, stand up, hold your arms out, and envision yourself surrounded by a golden bubble of light about arm's length from your body. This bubble of light is all around you—in front of you, behind you, above you, below you, and on either side of you. Envision seven flows of living light surrounding you, and keeping you in perfect safety while you say the following prayer.

Golden Bubble of Protection

"Encircle me now in a golden bubble of protective light. I ask for seven flows of this light to surround me, keeping me perfectly protected."

Once you feel you have established your protection, you can start. Over time, if you are consistent with your meditations, you will build your protection very strongly, and won't need to stand. You will be able to reinforce your protection sitting down.

Step Three—Check Your Spiritual Centers

In working with the Divine Light, you're going to be sending the light from your Higher Self Point to four spiritual centers most frequently. These are:

> The Mental Center
> The Throat Center
> The Hermetic Center
> The Emotional Center

These four centers are going to be focal points for receiving and distributing the light throughout your consciousness. It's not that the other centers don't come into play; they're just not designed to be the kind of receiving and transmitting stations that these centers are.

When the centers are moving in their proper flow and rhythm, they should be spinning in a *clockwise direction* (see Figure 4–2). Imagine a clock, attached to your chest with its face out, its hands rotating in their normal direction. This is clockwise. If your centers are moving counterclockwise, you can be opening up to all sorts of disharmony, and the centers will make

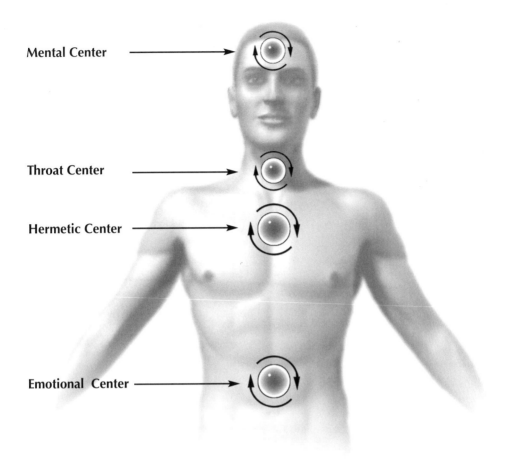

Mental Center

Throat Center

Hermetic Center

Emotional Center

Figure 4–2: **Moving the Centers Clockwise**

a poor point of contact for the Divine Light. Even if only one center is moving counterclockwise, it can throw the others off. Begin by placing your hands, right hand over left, over the center you want to check. Start with the emotional center and work your way up. Become very still and try to get a feeling of how your center is moving. If you sense that the center is moving clockwise, move on to the next center. If the center is off, envision the pure white light going into that center and changing its direction, moving it clockwise. Continue until you have checked all four centers.

Step Four—Connect with Your Higher Self

Now you're ready to make your connection with the light. To begin the Higher Self meditation, sit upright in your chair, uncross your legs and take your shoes off so the energy can flow freely (see Figure 4–3). During the meditation, keep your hands on your emotional center, right hand over left, to help polarize the energy as it flows through you. You will begin your meditation by placing your attention at your Higher Self Point, twenty-four inches above your head. By effectively placing your conscious attention at this point, you are making a strong connection with your Higher Self. It's very possible you will feel elation, or a heightened awareness of the Higher Self, but such an experience is not prerequisite to conducting an effective meditation.

When you're ready, start by saying the following invocation out loud. This invocation is a signal that you are calling for help. It affirms your connection with your Higher Self Point and helps you to get in the divine state you need to work with the light.

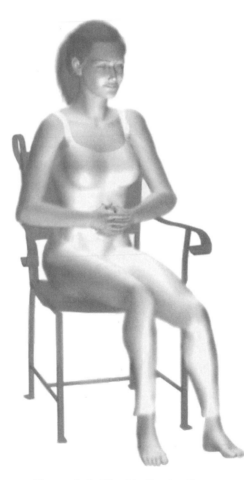

Figure 4–3: **The Meditative Pose**

Invocation

"Heavenly Father, Holy Mother God, I raise my consciousness into Thy consciousness where I become One with Thee. I ask to receive that which I need and that which I need to know now."

As you say these words, place your attention into your Higher Self Point, becoming one with its divine essence. Feel and sense that you are in the clarity of spiritual knowing, a place of peace, serenity and harmony. The centers within your body can be tainted and corrupted, but not this Higher Self. You have placed your consciousness above the human levels of your being; you have moved into a pure divine part of you.

Step Five—Down-ray the Light

Once you have established a connection with your Higher Self, you can petition the light verbally. Verbalization is important because it helps you to focus, while also making you a much more active participant in the light work. You're going to be calling on a particular light ray to do a specific task. If you say it silently, there's a tendency to let your mind wander a little. Verbalizing your prayers is a strong affirmation of the light, and also brings into play spiritual tone through your throat center.

In calling on the light, the key verb you will use is *down-ray*. The Divine Light is going to be down-rayed from the higher realms to your aura. Remember, this is not a spiritual supply that comes from within you; rather, it is energy that you are drawing from a source that is above and beyond you.

As you ask for the energy you need, first see that energy down-rayed to the Higher Self Point. See the color of the energy you are working with touching into and activating this point. From the Higher Self Point, envision a beam of light moving down into the four spiritual centers you are working with (see Figure 4–4), or wherever you're asking the light to go. As the light touches into each center, hold it there for a moment to feel the connection being made, knowing that these centers are being ignited with spiritual power. See the center completely filling with the colored light you're asking for, and out-raying about a foot in all directions. Then ask for the particular divine quality you want the light to bring you.

You will be calling on the light by saying a meditative prayer. These prayers give the directions you want the light to take. There are many examples of meditative prayers in this book, suited to a variety of situations and conditions. I recommend using them verbatim in the beginning. Eventually you will get into the rhythm of the light work and come up with your own prayer for the exact need you have. Don't worry about goofing up the exact wording. Yes, there is a nomenclature to the light work, but as you work with it, it will come to you. Working with the light will become an art as well as a spiritual exercise. If you can memorize the light prayers, that's great. If not, then simply read the prayer.

As the light is being down-rayed to you, you may feel it as a rush of energy or a tingling sensation. You may feel heat, depending on what it's doing and the degree of your sensitivity. I repeat, even if you feel nothing, the light is still working for you. Eventually you will get into the feeling of the light. If you sense resistance, don't push against it. Be gentle, and go at a pace you feel comfortable with. If you're working with more than one energy, give yourself a few minutes between energies to allow each one to settle before calling on the next.

If you're not sure about something, ask Divine Intelligence to guide you. Don't worry about hurting yourself if you choose the "wrong" energy. Sometimes, I have asked for one ray and seen a completely different ray come in. Your Higher Self knows exactly what your needs are. Always ask that you receive the light "to the degree of my need." You can't really overdose on the light because the Higher Self watches that you get only what you can handle, but you do want to be in the rhythm of the light work, and saying this is helpful. In addition, you want to ask the light to touch into "all levels of my consciousness." This way, the light can be directed to other areas of the aura that need work, in addition to the centers.

Step Six—Ground Yourself

After you have received the light, be still for a moment to let it stabilize throughout your consciousness. This way, you are grounded in the light. You don't want to suddenly jump up and get on with your day. When you feel that the light is established in you, ask that it be anchored into each point, sealing in the light. It's a good idea to ask that the golden ray of protection surround the light you have just received. Through your meditation, you have been blessed by the most precious energy of light. You don't want to lose that light or have it usurped. In closing, remember to use the following prayer to thank the Higher Power for all the work done for you, and to acknowledge all that you have received.

Closing Prayer

"I ask that the light I have just received be protected, sealed and anchored into my centers and all aspects of my aura. I thank Thee that this is so, and so shall it ever be. So be it."

Once you feel yourself grounded, get up and go on with your day.

Apply the Light to Effect the Change You Desire

Now that you've completed the six steps of your meditation, finish your light work by applying the light in your life. Occasionally, a meditation alone can make the change you desire, but for the most part, you're going to have to actively apply the light after receiving it. You can't expect the change to come just by doing the light work and not applying the spiritual energy where it's needed. You must become the example of what you want. The whole key with light meditation is to integrate the light received into your active life. If worry is one of your weak points, you must make a concerted effort not only to work with the light, but to refuse to give in to worry, and instead express faith and spiritual trust. With the light work, you will release those worry energies much faster. But if you constantly go back into those muddy waters, the light will have little positive effect. If you're really determined to correct a fault, you have to be steadfast about it. You have to see it all the way through. Likewise, if you're building self-confidence, you'll work with the gold light a great deal, but then as opportunities come up to express that confidence, you must do so. Through repeated application, you build the power in your aura until it becomes a steadfast part of the aura. The spiritual path is not an escape from life's duties, but the fulfillment of them. It's an enhancement of all life's processes. The light gives you a much needed spiritual booster shot, but it is not a shortcut to spiritual unfoldment. Regardless of your knowledge or talent, you still have to go through all the steps of growth. Tapping into your spiritual bank account simply helps you get there faster.

Be receptive after doing a meditation. Sometimes, the light works for you in ways you're not expecting. Yet there is great joy and freedom in the process. Once the light starts working in your life, you may see that some people you thought were friends are not really friends at all. You'll need the courage to forgive and let them go, and allow new, like-minded friends to come into your life. Or, you may discover that you're in the wrong job, and will need to start looking for a new and better one. You want to be adaptable, and trust the light. It will always steer you in the right direction.

Chapter

5

Tapping the Power Rays

Nature is full of God's bounty. Everywhere you look, you can thrill to God's richness and splendor. Nature produces an almost endless variety of physical creations—trees, flowers, insects, animals. Even physical light is not just one color but *many* bands of colors. The same variety holds true of spiritual light. There are myriad spiritual energies, each serving its own purpose. You need this diversity because each power ray draws in a different spiritual attribute, and there are many attributes of the spiritual life you need to draw on. The ten power rays described in this chapter represent ten different qualities of the spiritual life that you can incorporate into your physical life. These spiritual energies have been specially designed to help you in your spiritual pursuits.

As you work with the rays, do your best to visualize the color of the ray working. If you can actually see the power, that's great but not necessary. Your ability to receive the spiritual light will not be diminished if you don't see the energy. Above all, don't worry about it. I have had students questioning whether they really got the energy, and wondering why they couldn't see the light while others could. Doubting is counterproductive, as it can get in the way of receiving. Simply *know* that you are receiving. These power rays are no fantasy. This is not an intellectual exercise or a play of imagination.

They are real. You really are drawing these energies to you, and as you work with them, you will get into a place of knowing.

The duties of these color rays can overlap. Sometimes, the rose-pink love ray will purify negative energies more effectively than the orange-red flame. Other times, the gold will come in for illumination, rather than the pure white light. You'll get into the feeling and sensing of exactly how to use these rays. Best of all, your Higher Self knows just what you need. If you call in one ray but another is more appropriate for you at that moment, you will get what you need.

Bear in mind that these power rays do not operate like physical light in the sense that blue and yellow make green. Each ray is a power that works independently of the others.

A meditative prayer accompanies each ray. These are general prayers that you can use anytime you need these power rays. For example, if you're feeling jittery, you can use the meditation prayer for divine peace to calm yourself down. In the following chapters, we'll go into the various ways to work with the light in particular situations, and the individualized meditative prayers that go with them.

Purification

The power ray to use for spiritual purification is called the orange-red flame. This ray is specifically designed to help release negative buildup in the aura. The dominant energy is orange, which is the purifier, but the red is strong too, which brings in purification quickly, and with great vitality. The orange-red flame purifies by "burning up" negative energy in the aura. This ray breaks up the destructive energy into a fine powdery substance called black and gray atoms. Once cut loose, the unredeemed atoms are taken into the mineral kingdom, where they are reconstituted in the Divine Light. Nothing is lost. Even defiled energy is recycled.

Spiritual purification is essential in developing your aura. In physical life, the body can build up many toxins from a variety of sources. It must release these toxins or it will become increasingly polluted, stressed, and diseased. In spiritual purification, you need to release spiritual toxins for the aura to operate properly. These spiritual toxins are the negative energies you have either created or picked up from others. Such energies linger in the aura, disturbing and draining the entire energy field. Fortunately, the aura has a built-in self-replenishing system that operates on an eight-hour cycle to cleanse the energy field. Yet, sometimes this is not enough.

For example, say my aura is in great shape with no dark radiations to speak of. I get into an argument, and I unleash a huge outburst of anger. The anger will change my aura, and some of those once beautiful energies will now move to the vitiated red. I have dirtied my aura as a result of my emotional outburst. Eventually, the negative radiations will subside, but this will take time. Even with the self-cleansing system working round the clock, an intense outburst of anger will take two weeks to completely leave the aura. During those two weeks, I will be susceptible to additional outbursts and other negative energies if I'm not careful. If I succumb to more emotional outbursts, I only build up more negative energy, thus restricting the natural flow of the aura. If I'm not vigilant, I'll attract other kinds of destructive energies, compounding the problem enormously. The result can only wreak havoc in my life, resulting in tension, accidents, illnesses and other problems.

The orange-red flame is usually the first step in effecting change. So, you're going to be calling on this ray often. Purification is an almost daily requirement; probably right up to the day you leave this world you're going to be purifying yourself. It's almost impossible not to create or pick up some negative energy along the way. There's always something that wants to come at you, and you can absorb these negative energies unintentionally. With the orange-red flame, you don't have to worry. This energy can get you out of any spiritual entanglement. The orange-red flame is also an essential tool for releasing the buildup of destructive energies accumulated from the past. You'll be using this spiritual scrub brush often in releasing bad habits and faults. It's a tremendous power ray. Without this energy, man could never rise out of the negative energy he has created or acquired.

Meditative Prayer for the Orange-Red Flame

"Down-ray the orange-red flame of purification to all levels of my consciousness, releasing me from all black and gray atoms and taking them into the mineral kingdom to be dissolved in the light."

New Life Force

The ray to call on for new life force is the blue-white fire of eternal life. This ray is very powerful and is connected to what is called "the breath of God."

It's one of the highest energies you can use. I've often said that if you only have time to use one energy, use the blue-white fire. It's a powerful, replenishing energy that brings in new life force to your consciousness. It's a spectacular energy to see. The predominant color is a rich sapphire blue, almost like the blue flame of a gas stove, with sparkles of white and silver light shooting out, creating an electrifying effect. Again, it appears more like a ray than an actual fire, but it works in you very much as a spiritual life-giving fire. There are actually seven attributes to this power ray, and many times you can see a kaleidoscope of colors moving with the blue and white, which is why this ray is so beneficial.

The blue-white fire will be used very strongly in conjunction with the orange-red flame. After you complete your spiritual purification, always follow up with the blue-white fire. Having finished using one ray, you are now replenishing with another. The blue-white fire has an amazing capacity to rejuvenate and charge up your aura, making other energies assimilate better. Like pulling up weeds from your garden before planting new flowers, you want to prepare the soil so the new seeds will grow well. Using the blue-white fire is like tilling in new soil.

In addition to this recharging ability, the blue-white fire has many applications. If you're depressed, the blue-white fire can help you move out of depression. The blue-white fire is also one of the greatest healing energies. It helps sustain the physical body. You can see its power coursing through the physical organs and bloodstream. Without the blue-white fire, the physical body would lose its vitality and not be able to function well. In essence, it's part of the cosmic life force, capable of healing and restoring life energy to all areas of your being.

Meditative Prayer for the Blue-White Fire

"Down-ray the blue-white fire of eternal life, charging and recharging all levels of my consciousness in a clockwise motion with new, electrifying life force."

Wisdom

The ray to call on for wisdom and illumination is the golden ray of wisdom light. It appears as a brilliant golden ray and is the spiritual essence of the dynamic power of God. You will use this energy a great deal in conjunction with divine guidance. If there is an important decision you're trying to make, bring in the golden ray of wisdom light, especially to your mental body, and ask for illumination to help you make the right decision. If you find you're wishy-washy in general, the golden ray is the energy that will help you become more decisive.

Wisdom is one of the major attributes of a mature soul. The word wisdom bespeaks spiritual insight and knowledge, strength of character, and strong moral fiber. A wise person makes decisions from a place of inner knowing. Spiritual wisdom is a result of applied knowledge and not repeated, drilled-in information. A student can memorize many spiritual principles, but this doesn't make him spiritually wise. Until that student has assimilated the knowledge into his or her knowing, it's not really wisdom. There's an old spiritual saying, "You know that you know that you know." It takes time to truly build wisdom. This is why an aura with the predominant gold in it is one of the highest auras of all. It shows that the soul has gone through countless experiences, tests and trials, and won the victory of true spiritual knowledge and mastery.

The gold light is the most dynamic of all the rays, and you need to be expressing your dynamic nature. It would be very hard to get anything accomplished in this world, especially anything spiritual, without dynamic energy.

Many people in the spiritual work misunderstand the dynamic nature of life. They often confuse being spiritually dynamic with being humanly aggressive, and so they shy away from expressing their dynamic nature. The dynamic nature of life is the "giving out" aspect—the builder and the initiator of life. Being spiritually dynamic is a *divine* trait that operates under the direction of divine will so that your actions are in harmony with life. In this way, your actions are in no way detrimental to others. It becomes a win/win situation. People who are dynamically active will radiate a beautiful golden light. By contrast, being aggressive is a purely *human* trait that manifests as human will, pushing for what it wants without regard to how that aggression will affect others. More often than not, aggressive or coercive acts have an adverse effect on others. It's usually a win/lose situation. And instead of the golden ray of the dynamic action, people who are overtly aggressive will radiate a dirty maroon red energy.

Because golden light is such a dynamic power, it has many applications in addition to building wisdom and illumination. The golden ray may be called upon to build a dynamic will, confidence, courage, divine power, faith, and inner strength. It's also the best energy for protection, even better than white light.

Meditative Prayer for Wisdom Light

"Down-ray the golden ray of wisdom light to all levels of my being, bringing forth Thy wisdom and illumination and all the divine, dynamic attributes of this power that I need now."

Spiritual Love

The deep rose-pink is the energy to call on for spiritual love. As the golden ray brings in strong wisdom, will, and action, the deep rose-pink draws in love, compassion, and kindness. Its essence is the magnetic nature of God. In the high spiritual realms there are basically two forces operating—Divine Mind and Heart of Spiritual Love. Love is the bond that holds the universe together. More than anything else, Divine Love brings you into oneness with God. Once you are in that unity, you will have love for yourself and compassion for others, because you will be connected to the source of love.

The love ray is one of the easiest energies to sense. When working with it, you can feel its softness and gentleness. There's often a feeling of bliss when using this ray, and people see its energy more often than any other. The deep rose-pink ray may be used to create a more loving environment for yourself and others around you. It can also work as a great healing energy if you have been hurt or are feeling lonely or unloved. It's an essential energy to use in mending relationships, working on forgiveness, increasing your trust and understanding, and becoming less selfish. It's the greatest healer of the soul and can mend the deepest of wounds to the heart.

All human fears, frustrations, loneliness, and worries can be dissolved by the deep rose-pink love ray. This Divine Love helps to inspire a selfless attitude toward life. It is the pure unconditional love that gives without thought of return. This is not the love of selfish wants and vested interests; it's the sacrificial love, the love of service to humanity. This high love leads to the ultimate universal love of God, that loves all of creation equally and unconditionally.

Meditative Prayer for Divine Love

"Down-ray the deep rose-pink ray, quickening my spiritual centers and filling my entire consciousness with this Thy love, bringing me into perfect beauty, rhythm and tone, as one body in Thy body of Divine Love."

Divine Peace

The deep purple is the ray to call on for divine peace. There is also a gentler version, which is violet in hue. The deep purple ray is essential for quieting the mind and emotions. It seems the word most often used in the world today is peace. People are crying out for peace. In this stressful and fast-paced world, in the midst of the whirlwind, you need to quiet the consciousness and commune with your own divine nature and God. The only way to do this is to turn to God for your peace. This ray offers one of the best ways to help you release the stress and strain of the world and to get into that calm state. It releases any sense of burden or heavy-heartedness.

This is the energy to call upon to bring you into the divine stillness, the spiritual silence. When you're at peace with yourself, there is no conflict. There's a relaxation in divine knowing. You can only be truly at spiritual peace when you are in that divine knowing. A person with a lot of purple in their aura is very advanced indeed because that person has truly let go and let God take over.

Many people hold on to their worries and troubles to such a degree that they leave no room for God to enter their lives. They let stresses burden them to the point that they can barely function. When there's a lot of anxiety, the aura is affected. The energy doesn't flow as it should and becomes jagged and irregular. This ray can smooth out these bumps in the aura. It's great for soothing the nerves. If you are grieving, or have experienced something shocking, the purple ray is the energy to use to help you come out of that grief.

Meditative Prayer for Divine Peace

"Down-ray the purple ray of divine peace, touching into all levels of my consciousness and bringing me into the silence of peace and the peace of silence."

Balance & Harmony

The power ray to call on for balance and harmony is the emerald green ray. Without harmony and a centering of the consciousness, nothing will work right in your life. The more spiritually centered you stay, the easier things will go for you. The emerald green ray helps balance and harmonize all the different aspects of your life, so they move smoothly. In music, harmony is defined as the blending of two or more musical sounds in a pleasing manner. In the same way, you want the different departments of your life to be moving well together. You can use this energy to help maintain balance between mind, body and soul.

The emerald green ray is very important in your day-to-day life. This energy helps to keep your spiritual equilibrium, no matter what obstacles you face. If you feel disoriented in your earthly affairs, call on this energy to balance things out. You undoubtedly have many things going on at the same time and need to keep them all moving smoothly. Maybe your home life is fine, but your professional life is chaotic. Your relationship with your friends may be strong, but not with your own family. You may have suffered a trauma that threw your life out of balance. These are all situations that need the emerald green ray. A person whose life is balanced will be able to handle many things with efficiency and ease. There will be fewer extremes in his or her life, and when extreme situations do come up, they will have far fewer devastating effects.

Your Hermetic Center is in particular need of this ray, as there is so much activity in this center connected with the outside world. This energy also helps to reverse counterclockwise movement in the aura.

Meditative Prayer for Balanced Power

"Down-ray the emerald green ray of balanced power to flow directly into my centers and entire being, bringing me into perfect harmony of mind, body and soul."

Divine Intelligence

Like silver light in the aura, the silver ray brings divine intelligence. Intelligence is different from wisdom in that it is based strongly on perception. Many people are intelligent but not wise. Yet, you need intelligence to perceive wisdom. The silver ray works strongly on the mental levels of the aura to quicken your powers of perception. The silver ray facilitates clarity and is great for quickening perception when you're having trouble comprehending a lot of information.

This ray accelerates progress. Say you have a business transaction that seems to be dragging. It's clear what has to be done, but there is endless red tape. Papers are not getting signed, people are not returning phone calls. You can call on the silver ray to quicken the whole process and break through the stagnation. It's the ray of choice when you need guidance in your routine, everyday human affairs. The silver ray works very well with gold, lemon yellow and white light. It helps to enhance the effectiveness of other rays as well, so that you receive them more easily in the aura. You can also call in this ray to help guide you when you're not sure which ray to use in your meditations.

A person who is utilizing his or her divine powers of intelligence will have uncanny understanding and resolve when facing the challenges and problems that arise in life. Have you noticed how certain people seem to handle pressure very well, making clear decisions that seem to turn out right? This kind of person is very close to the divine nature of this power, whether on a conscious or unconscious level.

Meditative Prayer for Divine Intelligence

"Down-ray the silver ray of divine intelligence to my mental body, quickening my brain and flesh cells and all levels of my conscious brain/mind thinking, sharpening my powers of perception."

Concentration

The lemon yellow ray brings in tremendous powers of concentration. If you're studying for a test or trying to master a subject, this is an essential ray to call upon. It gives you the ability to focus on a subject without distraction. As you build this power, you will stimulate your ability to study and increase your enjoyment of learning. If you need to dispel mental lethargy, this is the ray to use. Although it's primarily a mental energy, it may be used throughout the aura to help steady the vibration.

The lemon yellow ray is important in becoming a trained clairvoyant. When I was developing my own clairvoyance, I spent nine months just working on concentration to get me to the level that I needed to develop my sustaining power. It's difficult to hold certain clairvoyant perceptions for any length of time. Without this level of concentration, I would not be able to sustain my spiritual vision throughout a whole lecture—which may include my reading of many auras.

Meditative Prayer for Concentration

"Down-ray the lemon yellow ray into my mental body, quickening my mental, brain/mind thinking, and bringing me powers of concentration."

Prosperity

The turquoise ray is the spiritual energy of prosperity, abundance and supply. Its color is a bluish-green, very much like the bluish shade of the turquoise stone. If you believe you are lacking the spiritual awareness of prosperity, this is the energy to work with. This power ray is especially designed to help you build an awareness and flow of unlimited wealth. In physical life, there is often a tendency to limit oneself. This ray can help you get out of the narrow, boxed-in consciousness of limitation and expand your horizons. With this power ray, you will step into an expanded flow of light. This energy works especially well in the Hermetic Center to multiply and amplify the positive conditions in your life. It can help you to create more money, as well as attract friends, ideas, and assistance in building fresh new circumstances.

As discussed in Chapter 8, prosperity consciousness is one of the natural, inborn attributes of your soul. As a child of God, you have the power to create prosperity. To express these gifts of abundance is a matter of nurturing and developing those inborn qualities. If you're lacking in physical resources, it just means you've disconnected in this area from your spiritual heritage. Somehow, the turquoise energy is not balanced in your aura. To build your prosperity, you have to draw on this energy often. You must also think, speak, and feel prosperous. It's especially important to get into the feeling of this energy; you need *to feel wealthy* to establish it in your consciousness. Your emotional body needs to feel this spiritual richness, whether your pocketbook agrees with you or not.

If you're in a financial crunch, you can use this ray to help generate income. If you're anxious about money in general, you can use this ray to help build a more spiritual consciousness of money. This way, your faith and knowing will carry you through any rough times financially. If you are in the true consciousness of prosperity, it won't matter how much you have, because you are directly connected to supply and know that you will always have what you need.

Meditative Prayer for Prosperity

"Down-ray the turquoise ray of abundance and supply, touching into my Hermetic Center and quickening persons, places, things, conditions and situations, bringing me into perfect prosperity."

The Pure White Light

The pure white light is a wonderful elevating and redeeming energy. It brings in the very essence of God. It has a tremendous ability to transmute negative energies. If you have done something you know is wrong, you'll want to call on this energy to help redeem your soul, lift you out of the dark energy you've created, and repair any harm you may have done to others. It doesn't matter how deep the pit you may have fallen into. White light can pull you out of any quagmire. This ray is strongly connected with your evolutionary climb. The pure white light will bring you into the purity and holiness of the God experience that you normally would not have in the human arena. It works wonderfully with confrontation in relationships, helping to lift you out of that abrasive energy. It's essential to use during sex to keep the energy moving on a high level. It's one of the primary energies to use in developing clairvoyance. The pure white light is also an illuminating and revelatory ray, especially when you're asking for illumination of a purely spiritual kind. It has protective properties as well, and works well with the gold for protection.

Like the orange-red flame, the pure white light can release negative energy, but it particularly focuses on *redeeming* the negative energies. With negative energy you have a choice: you can either cut it loose or transmute it. In redeeming negative energy, you're restoring defiled energy to its divine essence. It's like the cells of the body. Some cells are discarded when they are old and beyond use; others are replenished because they're still useful and can be restored, even if some impurities have contaminated them.

Meditative Prayer for the Pure White Light

"Down-ray the pure white light to equalize, align, center and attune all levels of my consciousness, uplifting and bringing me into the purity of Thy oneness."

Energy in Action

In the beginning, working with these rays may take a little getting used to. You have to become familiar with the whole process, as well as comfortable with the greater flows of energy you will be receiving. Yet, once you get into the rhythm of the light, it will quickly become second nature. What you are actually doing in the Higher Self meditation is following the natural course the light takes in reaching you. By working in conscious cooperation with this natural process, you're simply enhancing the spiritual power you can receive.

A wonderful artistry unfolds as you get into the rhythm of working with the light. In the beginning, speaking the words might feel like a recitation, but eventually those words will feel like your very soul expressing itself. The nomenclature of the light work will become your own sacred language, and you'll find your own form and beauty of expression. Also, give yourself time to get used to the greater vibrations of light you'll be receiving. It will come in small doses in the beginning until you're acclimated to this new level of spiritual activity.

In your transformational process, the light essentially does three-fourths of the work while your own hard work takes care of the other fourth. The three-fourths entails a whole intricate process of sending the light to you, which you need not concern yourself with. Your part consists in doing the spiritual meditations and, above all, keeping yourself as strong and as balanced a channel of light as possible. You can't work with the light by day and debauch yourself by night. I've had students say they decided not to work with the light because it was too much effort! As if all one had to do is wish for something to happen, and it would. As they say, "If wishes were horses, then beggars could ride!" You have to do your best to become the example of what you wish to be.

People have asked me how many meditations it takes to clear something from the aura. This is the million-dollar question, and the answer depends on several factors. First, how deep is the situation? A recent irritation will clear more quickly than a long-term resentment. Another factor is the determination of the individual. A lackluster approach to light work will be far less effective than a single-minded approach. Perhaps the biggest impediment is the element of backsliding. In a perfect world, even the most tangled of energies could be cleared in a relatively short time. Yet in practice, there is almost always a seesaw effect. The light process begins, but then something reenergizes the negative condition, and the light process must begin again. This can go on for some time before the momentum swings in favor of the light.

Think of the light work as pouring clean water into a cup that's filled with dirty water. If you keep pouring clean water, eventually all the dirty water will be displaced, and there will be only clean water. Generally, a single isolated negative energy in the aura that has not gained momentum can be cleared in five to ten effective meditations.

Effect of the Light Process

Most times, the meditation process is a catalyst for change. It generates the initial movement of spiritual energy that begins the transformational process. It's a little like a tiny snowball rolling down a snow-packed hill—it generates momentum and grows bigger and bigger. The light work gets the ball rolling.

The initial destination for the light is the energy centers. The light comes down from the Higher Self to the extent that we need it, and does the job it was designed to do. When it is finished, it then withdraws and returns to its source of emanation. During this process, light is retained in the energy centers where it shows up as active emanations; it is these emanations that can really help to get the ball rolling (see Figure 5–1). This is why it's critical to use the energy you receive right away, or it begins to fade almost immediately.

Over time and with constant effort, the aura takes on a whole new glow and vibration with the Higher Self meditation. One very dramatic example of this process could be seen in a woman I counseled before I began teaching full time. I was working at an insurance company at the time, and she worked in my department. I didn't tell people I could see the aura at that point. Yet, since I could see problems, I would try to help people in an indirect way, or would occasionally teach some of the principles to friends who were really in need and open to such ideas. I had to be careful as I was doing this at a time before metaphysical ideas were as accepted as they are today.

I could see in this woman's aura that she had problems. One day, I asked in a casual way if something was bothering her, and she told me her troubles. It turned out her husband of thirteen years had just upped and left her with six children to care for. They'd married when she was only seventeen, and now she was barely thirty and on her own with six children. Deeply shaken, she had fallen into a serious depression.

Her depression showed clearly in her aura (see Figure 5–2). Her mental center was spinning counterclockwise, and there was a creamy energy around it, showing mental confusion. In addition, there was a gray cloud above her head, denoting intense worry. The fanning rays in all of her centers were gray, the very color of her depressed thoughts and feelings. She also had dark blue active radiations emanating from her Hermetic Center, expressing her gloom-and-doom attitude. Proceeding from her emotional center were avocado green active emanations, showing she was developing some darker emotions of deceit. This expressed in her trying to see what she could get away with on the job and in her personal life.

The orange-red flame and blue-white fire rays were used to cut loose depression and the pessimistic assumption that she would never find another love. Emerald green light gave her balance because desertion had left her shaky and very disoriented. The deep rose-pink was needed to boost her self-esteem. This was probably the hardest part for her. More painful than the anger toward her husband was the feeling that no one would ever want her again. The fact was, she was still a young and attractive woman, and there was no reason she would not fall in love and marry again. I told her there was an excellent chance that she would remarry. She'd always answer, "Who would want me, with six children?"

After about eight months from the start of this whole process, her aura looked great. The dark clouds and muddied areas were completely gone. Her mental body was sharp and clear. Instead of gray clouds, there were now silver diamond points of light, attesting to the development of much keener powers of perception. Lemon yellow fanning energy coming from her mental center showed alert and focused thinking. Her Hermetic Center had emerald green fanning rays, illustrating the balance and harmony she had achieved in her life. There were beautiful bright blue active emanations coming from this center as well, signifying dedication and loyalty to her children. Her emotional division was also in great shape. There was a beautiful rosy pink fanning energy coming from her emotional center, expressing her new love of life. There were also bright blue active emanations in this center, showing the now-steadfast and stable quality of her emotions. Of course, her whole outlook on life was much rosier.

One day as we were having lunch, I saw the image of a man in her auric field. I couldn't see any specific features, but I intuitively felt that this was a man she would meet, someone who was a potential husband. Amusingly, when I told her that she was going to meet someone soon, she was still skeptical! Had she been able to see what good shape her aura was in, she would not have questioned me at all.

Before a month had passed, she received an invitation to her high-school reunion. She went, and whom did she meet? She met an old high-school sweetheart. It turned out he had married, fathered two children, and was also divorced. The attraction was still there. A month later, she married him, with her six children and his two children participating in the wedding cere-mony, the littlest girl being the flower girl! This experience had a profound effect on me as well. Helping her marked the beginning of my teaching career because, from then on, this woman kept telling people who had prob-lems, "Go to Barbara; she knows something!" As a result of her prompting, I began conducting some of my first public metaphysical lectures.

Developing a Spiritual Point of View

One last point I wish to reemphasize is the importance of working with the light from the spiritual point of view. Remember that life works from the inside out. Everything we experience in physical life was first created on the spiritual plane. This is why the aura comes first in any transformation process. What often hinders our spiritual unfoldment and lessens the effectiveness of our connection with the light is that we look at life from a physical point of view. Even when it comes to spiritual matters, most of our knowledge and understanding is perceived and interpreted through the five senses. I have seen the aura described as an electromagnetic field, as if it were only a radiation of the physical body. People have tried to equate spiritual light with physical light. It's natural to do this because we're comfortable and most familiar with our physical surroundings and experiences.

The spiritual light and aura will make little sense if viewed strictly from the physical standpoint, because the Divine Light is not of the physical world. It can greatly affect the physical world but the light is part of the inner, spiritual world. Although the spiritual and physical worlds are part of the whole of life, in practice they operate very differently.

The spiritual world is the creative world, the originating world. It's the world of God. Everything we see physically was conceived and originated in the spiritual world. So the spiritual dimension existed before the physical one. It's from this divine source that we draw the light, and it's in this spiri-tual life that the aura exists and is perceived. Because the spiritual world is the original world, it is not dependent on the physical life for its survival: its life is independent of physical existence.

In addition to being creative, the spiritual world sustains life as well. It sustains all life on Earth, including each one of us. Without this divine power holding the universe together, all of creation would cease to exist in an instant. The spiritual world is, therefore, in a constant state of giving. The Divine voluntarily pours out its life that others may partake, which places us in intimate and constant contact with the source of our being. There is great joy in this process because it is in giving that there is creating. This creative nature of giving is the essence of our spiritual character as well. When we are spiritually minded, we are always creative, original, and in a selfless state of giving.

The physical world, on the other hand, is a created world. It's the result of creative acts that originated in the spiritual realms. It has no power of its own. Without the spiritual world to nourish and sustain it, the physical world could not maintain its form and would return to its source of emanation. Because of this, the physical world is in a constant state of receiving. In receiving life from the spiritual world, the matter of the physical world is organized and sustained. So, the nature of physical life is to take. As spirit wants to give, matter wants to take. The physical world will seek to draw into itself all it can to maintain itself and will resist any idea that compromises that goal. Form is always seeking to hold its own. In this way, it's inherently selfish. It depends on this holding power to survive. The same is true of us. If we are thinking only physically, we will always be narrow-minded, selfish, and with no true understanding of what we're doing to our fellow man.

The secret of understanding our aura lies in the recognition that if life is first spiritual, then it follows that we are, above all, spiritual beings. This means that the same attributes that apply to the spiritual world apply to us. Our spiritual character, then, is the essence of who we are. It's the core of our being, the real us. And all the spiritual qualities we admire are already our true nature.

The only reason we're not automatically aware of our divine nature is that we're in a process of spiritual unfoldment. This unfoldment is part of our design. The divine attributes in us are *potential* powers, waiting to be developed. And as we develop these powers, they become more and more a part of our active life. If our lives do not presently reflect the spiritual essence within us, it's only because we have yet to develop those latent qualities.

The part of our spiritual essence that's unfolding is what we call the soul. The soul is like a seed planted in the ground. A seed starts out as a tiny thing. Yet, all the potential for developing into a beautiful rose or a mighty oak tree is already there. All that is needed are the right elements in which to grow: air, water, sun and earth. The seed, if nourished and undisturbed, cannot help but become that great flower or tree. In the same way, the soul of man is like a seed that God plants in the garden of creation. All the potential for realizing its divine nature is already in the core of the soul. To realize that potential, the soul must embark on a pilgrimage through creation where it grows, eventually making its way back, fully realized, to God. And like the plant that needs water, the soul needs the spiritual nourishment of Divine Light to grow.

So, to effectively change something, we must start from the spiritual foundation, even though it may seem unrelated to our immediate physical problems. By working from a spiritual perspective, we can improve anything. Problems, character flaws, and dilemmas that we face on this Earth are a result of a disconnection from the divine root of life. Fix the connection, and we correct the problem.

Unfolding Your Spiritual Power

How to Change Mental & Emotional States

Thoughts and emotions are the most important areas in which to begin your auric transformation. You will find that the majority of problems in your life stem from some erroneous thought or emotion lurking somewhere in your consciousness. For that matter, most of the problems in the world today can be traced to wrong thinking and feeling. By working on these areas, you will be adding immeasurably to uplifting your aura and relieving yourself of much stress.

A negative mental/emotional condition is never permanent—you can change any condition you find yourself in. It doesn't matter if a thought or emotion appears overwhelming or has been with you for a long time. Because these negative states are not the spiritual reality of who you are, they can be transformed. In the same way, you are in control of your reaction to outside influences. No one can tell you how to think or feel unless you permit that to happen. Yet, this is exactly what many people do. They let others run their lives and wonder why they have problems.

Fortunately, use of the Divine Light is extremely effective in transforming mental and emotional states, and cutting loose those negative energies at the core. If you're careful not to recreate negative conditions, you will be clear of destructive momentum altogether. The light can also help to build new, spiritual power that sustains high, positive energies at the thinking and feeling levels.

The first step in your process of transformation is to recognize that the spiritual part of you is the true guiding force behind your entire thinking and feeling. If you try to divorce thoughts and emotions from their spiritual foundation, you will be creating erroneous thinking and feeling that will take on a life of their own. This can only produce problems somewhere down the line, and you will never receive the answers that you seek. You may see the problem, but its resolution will always elude you because you are not connecting with the source that can really help you.

Thoughts and emotions have enormous power in the auric field. Together, they comprise a vital role in keeping consciousness moving harmoniously. The mental and emotional divisions are also where we see the greatest fluctuations in the aura. This is especially true of the mental division because you're always thinking about something. As you change the tendency of your thoughts, your colors change, and as you emotionally react to your thoughts, your emotional colors change as well. The thoughts of an unenlightened mind are like monkeys in a cage going all over the place. This is exactly the way it looks in the aura—chaotic and disoriented. Of course, the emotions will react accordingly.

In working with thoughts and emotions, keep in mind the following principle; it describes the fundamental operating relationship between your mental and emotional nature. This principle is always in action and by understanding it, you will possess the key to creating the mental/emotional harmony you seek. This principle can be stated simply as:

$$\text{Think} \longrightarrow \text{Feel} \longrightarrow \text{Do}$$

First you conceive something mentally, then you have an emotional response to that thought. Based on that reaction, you act. This sequence of activity is so simple, yet so many times the relationship is confused—with disastrous results.

In the spiritual context, the mental part of you is the director of your consciousness. It is the part that's meant to guide your emotions. The emotional, feeling part of you is the doer. An emotion doesn't just happen; there has to be a thought behind it. I have to first think, "I love this" or "I hate this" for me to react to that thought emotionally. From this emotional response will come action.

Thoughts—the Kingdom Within

In the New Testament, when confronted by the Pharisees as to when the Kingdom of God would arrive, Jesus gave them an answer they were not expecting: "The Kingdom of God cometh not with observation . . . for, behold, the Kingdom of God is within you" (Luke 17:20). This statement has come to be interpreted in different ways. For some, it means acknowledging the God presence or divine spark within. For others, it means to look within rather than to the outside for change. These are all wonderful interpretations, but in understanding thoughts, this statement is a particularly important revelation.

In metaphysics, our mental body *is* the kingdom within. It's the king-DOME, the dome being the head, which houses our thoughts. Our mental division is the highest part of our conscious nature. It bridges our higher Divine Self and our lower human self. The mental body is the deciding factor in our evolution as to whether we will rise up into higher, Divine Self or stay in the lower self.

How we think controls the rest of us. So, the first place to make changes in our lives is in our thinking. If we know *how* to think, we probably know how to live. Mind is the builder. We imagine, design and create everything in our life from mind first. Thoughts create the world we live in and every aspect of our nature. Even the universe was a divine idea before it was a physical reality. So by redesigning our thoughts, we can redesign any part of our life. Without mind, we're like amoebas. This is why, above all, we must keep our thinking sharp and refuse to become slack in this area. Thoughts are far more than just little currents of electrical activity in the brain. They are living entities with energy behind them.

Thoughts are as real as our physical bodies. They are *more* real, in fact, because there is less constriction with thoughts. They create as we permit them to enter our consciousness and become part of us. As we have seen, enlightened thoughts can take the form of radiant, crown jewels of light. They shimmer with pearl luster colors and beautify the aura. Devolved thoughts can take hideous forms, choking and constricting the auric field.

The sad fact is that most of us are confused in our thinking. Even when we think we're clear, there can be confusion or delusion. The key to dealing with negative thoughts is to remember that they are artificial in origin. They were created at some moment in time, somewhere in our experience, but they are not part of our true nature. At some point, we entertained and accepted a false perception, creating a dark thought and allowing that thought to take root.

Thought is the first step in the Think—Feel—Do process. Mind always comes first. Some people try to reverse this process by putting their emotions first. Yet, even when we "act without thinking" we still have to give ourselves mental permission to do so. So thought still comes first, even when we permit our emotions to run rampant. It's our ignorance of this principle that can mess things up and permit our emotions to rule our thoughts, instead of the way it was meant to be.

In metaphysical parlance, there are three levels to our thinking self. These are the higher (divine) mind, the conscious mind, and the subconscious mind. When we're dealing with change, we're using our conscious mind. The conscious mind is our intellectual mind. Its focus of power is, as we have explored, in the mental center. The conscious mind is the part of us that reasons things through. It has the power to accept or reject thoughts. The conscious mind is the part of us that exercises our free will by making conscious choices. You can be reading this book and rejecting or accepting the ideas presented. No one can take that right away from you without your consent. And by your acceptance or rejection, you're either altering or reinforcing your perceptions, and hence your experiences of life.

The word *conscious* is very important. It indicates the ability to be self-aware. We have to be self-aware to make a conscious choice. Animals make choices, but they do it instinctually. They have yet to develop the capacity for self-awareness. We also have the subconscious, but of course, we're not self-aware of our subconscious mind unless we bring something from our subconscious to our conscious mind. We have our instinctual levels as well, but these are also subordinate to our conscious thinking.

God gave us this ability to choose in order to learn the difference between right and wrong, to distinguish the enlightened from the unenlightened. We are learning how to embrace the enlightened thoughts that strengthen the mental body, and we are also learning how to reject the negative thoughts and energies of others, as well as our own. Of course, until we really learn this lesson, the lines may be blurred. Very often we accept negative ideas and reject good ideas, then pay the price down the line when our creations are not to our liking. Eventually, by trial and error, we start to learn the difference.

As the mental body becomes more enlightened, spiritual power can establish itself much more easily. The light expands, creating radiant colors and bands of light. The beauty of enlightened thinking is its effortlessness. There's total clarity, decisiveness, and true inspiration when the conscious mind is enlightened. This is the goal of our thinking. Look back on times when you were in a very clear mental state, and remember how well things went. It all seemed effortless, didn't it? That's the state of mind you're meant to be in on a regular basis.

Most of us bog down our conscious mind with a lot of stuff we really don't need, or ask it to do things it's incapable of doing. The conscious mind also becomes colored and conditioned to think along certain lines, and in habitual closed loops. Upbringing, environment, and our own mental tendencies create this conditioning. As the mental body gets weighed down with negative thoughts, it becomes harder for the Divine Light to get through. The mind become confused and clouded, and moves farther away from the effortlessness of enlightened thinking.

Spiritual Energies & Thoughts

Abraham Lincoln once said, "Most folks are as happy as they want themselves to be." In other words, *you create the parameters* of what you will and will not allow yourself to do, and you do this through your thinking. You must recognize that, in whatever state you find your thinking, you can always change that thinking if you so desire. You are in control of your thinking! If you have relinquished that control, you must reclaim it. Then get the attention off your particular negative preoccupation and concentrate on a positive quality or trait that you want to have. If you have a persistent bitter thought about someone, you obviously don't want to start your meditation thinking of all the ways in which you dislike that person. You need to see yourself free of that bitterness and hatred. Or better yet, simply see yourself in a place of spiritual love where that bitterness doesn't exist.

You will be working a lot with the orange-red flame. Not only can this power ray cut loose specific negative thoughts, it can also cut through clouds of negative energies that may encircle you. You can work with the orange-red flame to release specific destructive thoughts or to conduct a general mental cleansing. The following meditative prayer is excellent for general cleansing. Use it anytime you feel mentally clouded or confused. If you've had a tough day at work or at home and you don't know which end is up, this is a great meditative prayer to use. Too, if you're trying to clear your mind before making an important decision, use this meditation. I suggest that you memorize it; let it become your anthem for cleansing the mental body.

Meditative Prayer for Mental Purification

"Down-ray the orange-red flame of purification into my mental body, releasing me from all mental confusions, illusions, delusions, all superimposed, distorted, and upside-down images. Let it out-ray in all directions, freeing me of all mental bombardments and impingements. I ask that all these black and gray atoms be dissolved in the mineral kingdom, in the light."

Feel and sense that flame going into the center of your mental body and out-raying throughout your whole mental division, bathing it in this flaming light and breaking up all negative energies. If you can visualize or actually see the process happening, all the better. Feel and sense those black and gray atoms being thrown off you as if you were in a sauna and the sweat is just rolling off you. Then see those atoms going directly into the mineral kingdom, dissolved in the light and forever out of your consciousness.

From the mental center, let the light shower your throat, Hermetic, and emotional centers to clear out any interconnecting debris. Let the light fill and activate these other centers, while also dissolving any negative energy in the mineral kingdom.

You may be surprised at how much negativity you've been holding in and how good it feels to let it all go. You don't have to qualify or justify anything. If it's a negative energy, you want it out of your life. As the orange-red flame is releasing negative thoughts, images or emotions may pop up unexpectedly. This is all part of the releasing process and simply means the light is doing its job. Look at these images as if they were a movie that you're just watching. Acknowledge them for what they are but give them no power. If you feel inspired, you can name any specific thought you want released as it comes up. Simply add at the end of the meditative prayer, "Free me of. . . ." and name the thought you want to be released from.

This purifying work can take on the quality of a confessional, discharging whatever torrent of negative thoughts you have been holding in. This is the time to surrender it all to the Divine Light, to the very altar of God. You may receive revelations you didn't expect. And yes, the old part of you may fight to hold on to those dark thoughts, but just keep letting go.

Before going on to the recharging process, let's look at some of these negative thoughts more closely.

Confusions

This word comes from the Latin, meaning "to mix together." Confused thinking comes about when two or more thoughts vie for attention and supremacy. You may be telling yourself you want something and at the same time telling yourself the thing you want isn't good for you. These conflicting thoughts create confusion in your thinking, and the result is inaction. Confusion shows up in the aura mainly as a creamy energy similar to the tan colors of lethargic thinking.

Illusions

Illusions are ideas and perceptions that you have accepted as real, but are not real. At some point or another, we all have illusions about something. Most of the time, we're unaware we're in an illusionary state. When you wear rose-colored glasses about someone, you're in an illusionary state. You can have illusions about your parents, friends, love interests, and yourself. There can be a feeling of disappointment and disillusionment when your bubble bursts. Nevertheless, part of the beauty of spiritual work is stepping out of these illusions and into greater realities.

Delusions

Delusion is similar to illusion, but there is more intent in delusions, more purposeful action. You delude yourself because you don't want to face something, and choose to escape from it. You might be under the delusion that things are fine at your job, when they are not. Or you might delude yourself into thinking you have great talents or abilities, when in fact you don't.

Superimposed Images

If you take two images, place one on top of the other and look at them, you'll see a jumbled mess. This is an example of superimposed images. I may hold a wonderful image of something. Then you come along and tell me that what I love is terrible. If I accept your image, I now have a conflict with the image I've held. Superimposed images tend to come from the outside rather than being self-imposed.

Distorted Pictures

Here you're twisting things out of their natural shape, creating scenarios that may have little or no bearing on reality. Paranoid people most often have distorted pictures of things, painting normal situations as doomsday scenarios.

Upside-Down Pictures

This is seeing something as the total opposite of what it really is, as in "Greed is good" or "Wrong is right." Upside-down thinkers have taken their distorted pictures to the extreme. This kind of thinking can be very dangerous. You see a friend where there is an enemy. Note how satanic imagery often involves inverting images to mean their opposite, as in upside-down pentagrams and crosses. This is no accident but rather a deliberate intent to invert natural laws for unnatural purposes.

Mental Bombardments

These are thoughts coming at you from the outside world. It could be people thinking negatively of you, knowingly or unknowingly. The problem with bombardments is you don't usually know they're coming. You may believe you're "under the weather" when actually you're under attack. This is why spiritual protection is so important (see Chapter 11).

Impingements

Whereas bombardments can come at you from anywhere and everywhere, impingements are much more specific. They come at you like stilettos, sharp and pointed, penetrating your aura. Certain people are very sharp in their thinking, and you can feel it. Impingements are not as common as bombardments but are still something to watch out for.

Once you've finished your purification, bring in the blue-white fire. This energy will recharge the depleted areas zapped by the negative thoughts. It will also serve as new spiritual soil, making room for a fresh crop of new thoughts and ideas.

Meditative Prayer for Recharging the Mental Body

"Down-ray the blue-white fire of eternal life to charge and recharge all depleted areas in my mental, brain/mind thinking with new life force, breathing in new spiritual thinking."

Give yourself equal time with the blue-white fire. You may feel a shifting and upliftment as it's doing its work. Again, feel and sense this energy radiating out from the mental center in all directions, charging and recharging all levels of the mental division and out-raying through the brain cells, drawing in new life force.

See that electrifying life force sparking new currents of divine life into all aspects of your mental being. Again, let it touch into the other centers as well.

Once you've replenished yourself with the blue-white fire, you can begin your building-up process. The key rays to work with are silver, lemon yellow, gold, and white light. Silver brings in greater powers of perception and a faster-thinking mind. The lemon yellow brings in powers of concentration, especially if there's been disorientation or laxness. Gold carries new wisdom, inner strength, and whatever dynamic qualities are needed. White light is especially good for lifting all the vibratory frequencies to bring in greater powers of illumination and vision.

After your meditation, watch your tendency of thought. Are your thoughts more positive, or are you still in the same negative state? Follow up your light work with positive action to establish new, constructive thinking, giving the light you have attracted the chance to express in every area of your life.

Emotions—the Spiritual Motor

Emotions are the engines that propel ideas into action. Once an emotion is wed to an idea, that idea has tremendous power and will move into realization. To put anything into action, we need the combined effort of mind and emotions. I may have a dream to be an artist or a doctor, but unless I attach a strong emotion to that dream, it has no chance of becoming real. Emotions may be likened to gunpowder, and thoughts to bullets. Without the firepower of gunpowder, the bullet will just sit in the chamber, no matter how strenuously we point and pull the trigger. Mind designs the plan of what is to be created, but once that design is in place, it is the emotions that get the energies going to realize that design.

It's not always easy to balance emotions with thoughts. We tend to lean one way or the other. Those who stay too much in the mental are more intellectual, and will conceive more than they create. "Doers," who stay too much in the emotional, can often paint themselves into corners because they don't think before they leap. Balance the two in a positive way, and we're steady, focused, and dynamic.

We need this balance because *emotions do not think*. This is perhaps the single most important thing to remember about emotions. Emotions *feel*. Emotions need thoughts to guide them. Have you ever tried to reason with a person who's in a rage? You can't, because that person is not operating from a thinking level at that moment. You have to approach the person gently, from a loving place. Let him or her calm down so the thinking levels are back in action, then you can communicate.

Our emotions are meant to flow in clear streams of love, compassion, inner strength, and all the higher attributes of life. In this mode, the emotional division of our aura radiates tremendous light. When we're in our higher emotions, we're very expressive, and others are attracted to our positive emotional force field. Yet, as we know, many times we fill ourselves with hates, jealousies, fears, and a host of unhealthy emotions. When we are in these dark states, our aura is darkened and weighed down, and the energies move out in a swirling chaotic manner.

We have to really work at rooting out negative emotions. We can't just say, "I'm not angry," for example, when trying to deal with anger. We have to free ourselves of that anger, because that anger will be smoldering inside, waiting for a chance to express itself. As with thoughts, the Divine Light can reach into the root of negative emotions and release them.

Often when we think we're operating from our mind levels, we're actually moving from our emotions. In this condition, we're bound to make faulty decisions and act wrongly. Most people live nearer their emotional self than their mental self and allow their emotions to rule their thoughts. When we make decisions solely by our emotions, it's like throwing ourselves to the wind. It may blow us where we need to go or it may not.

For example, say I'm the manager of a company, and I decide to fire one of my subordinates. I give several good reasons why I must do so, and claim to regret the decision. However, on closer examination, it becomes clear that job performance is not the real issue. The truth is, I'm actually jealous. Although new to the job, the person I wish to fire shows great potential, and I'm afraid that once my superiors catch wind of how good this employee really is, he may be promoted above me. So by getting rid of him, I'm no longer threatened. Since I refuse to see myself as a jealous person, I have to come up with a plausible reason for firing him, one that I can believe in myself. So I scrutinize his performance, looking for—and magnifying—little faults. Though the driving force behind my actions is jealousy, I've convinced myself it's a logical choice. In the think-feel-do principle, the sequence of this situation would look like this:

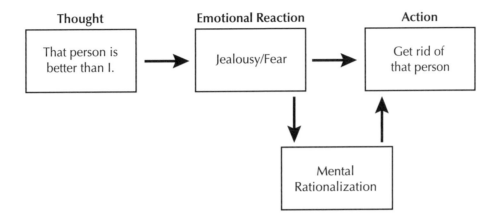

Figure 6–1: **Mental/Emotional Pattern**

In this situation, there is the added step of mental rationalization before action, but the results are the same. My rationalization has led me to believe that I'm coming from thought, when my actions really stem from emotional reactions to the original negative thought—which I have put out of my conscious awareness altogether.

Once we have an emotional response to a negative thought, we can do one of three things. First, we can act on that negative emotion, which will only compound the condition and create more destructive energy. Second, we can restrain ourselves, which shows control and discipline. This is better, but the negative energy will still be inside us, waiting to come out in other ways. Or third, we transmute our thoughts and feelings. No matter what the emotional reaction, we can always intervene with our thoughts and turn that reaction around. We can always "count to ten" and "turn the other cheek" to avoid acting rashly. Unfortunately, the majority of people automatically go with the first option and act on their negative emotions with little or no thought.

Negative emotions are deceptive. It's easy to feel justified in our negative feelings. If someone does us wrong, we feel justified in becoming angry or hateful. And herein lies the trap: As spiritual students on the path, we must train ourselves not to react with our lower emotions when wrongs have been done to us. We are *never* justified in retaliating, matching wrong for wrong, blow for blow, eye for eye. "Two wrongs do not make a right." Whether we are "right" or not, what are we doing when we react to that negative energy? We're tying in to the very situation that created that energy—which can only generate more negative energy. The result is that we're dragged down into the mud with the person who "started it." As humans, of course, we're going to have a reaction. It's unavoidable. The idea is to learn to react positively and constructively. Then we will have become the masters rather than victims of our own emotions.

Spiritual Energy & Emotions

When you're unbalanced in your emotional center, you'll feel it most in your solar plexus. It could feel like a stomachache, or nausea. Expressions like "sick to my stomach," "tearing my guts out" and "ripping me up" refer to feeling the emotional centers moving counterclockwise.

As with thoughts, the first energy to call on is the orange-red flame. This spiritual energy can reach deep into the emotions and cut through all emotional entanglements. If you find you're an overly emotional person to begin with, this energy can help to release the negative emotions that may have accumulated. The following meditation is for general purification of your entire emotional nature.

Meditative Prayer for Emotional Cleansing

"Down-ray the orange-red flame to my emotional body, cutting me loose from all destructive emotions, disturbances, confusions, false sympathies, and bombardments. I ask that all these black and gray atoms be taken into the mineral kingdom and dissolved in the light."

Once again, feel that spiritual energy reaching into the core of your emotional nature and out-raying through your entire emotional division, cutting loose all negative emotions. Working in this center can feel like taming wild horses. If you are asking for a specific emotion to be released, name that emotion and see it being dissolved in the light. If any other emotion pops up that you want to release, name that emotion and ask the light to release it from you. As with work on the mental body, let this light touch into your other centers as well, purifying all interconnecting destructive links.

Before going on to the blue-white fire, let's look more closely at some destructive emotional energies.

Disturbances

A disturbance is a counterclockwise movement within the emotional center that is usually caused by an upsetting situation. There's a problem at home that doesn't go away and you carry the disturbance wherever you go. Someone may have made a cruel comment that disturbed you. It's sometimes hard to trace where the disturbance came from, or what kind of emotion it is exactly. Yet you know it's there and that it's interfering with your normal activity.

Emotional Confusion

Emotional confusion comes about when two or more emotions are vying for attention. Love-hate relationships are an example of emotional confusion. Like mental confusion, emotional confusion tends to cause indecision and paralysis because you don't know where to go with your feelings.

False Sympathies

It's so easy to tie into the emotional energies of people around you. This can wreak havoc on your emotional body as well as your entire being. You can work hard to keep your aura clean and high, then mess it up by opening to outside influences. Although the entire auric field may be vulnerable to outside influence, the emotional division can be especially so through false sympathies. For example, I can be feeling peaceful, but if an agitated person comes near me, I will "catch" that agitation if I'm open to it. This can happen especially when I'm close to someone, like a spouse, parents, or children. If I have a sympathetic tie with you, I will relate to you emotionally. If you feel sad, I will feel sad. If you feel happy, so will I. This transference can happen quickly because in this case, there's little thinking involved.

Emotional Bombardments

Like false sympathy, bombardments involve taking in outside emotional energy that has nothing to do with you. Whereas false sympathy deals more with people you care about, bombardments may come from any source. There are so many emotional currents in the world you can unintentionally connect with. Bombardments can also be intentional—negative emotional energies directed specifically at you. If someone dislikes or hates you for any reason, that person will be transmitting an emotional current to you. You can easily pick up this energy if you're not paying attention, and absorb and aggravate the whole condition. By cutting loose these emotional bombardments, you steer clear of muddy waters.

Once you have finished your emotional cleansing, you are ready for the blue-white fire. Chances are, your emotional body will drink in this energy with gusto. Really feel it recharging all your emotions and replenishing all depleted areas, bringing them into a more vibrant place—especially if you are feeling emotionally exhausted.

Meditative Prayer for Emotional Replenishment

"Down-ray the blue-white fire of eternal life to charge and recharge my emotional body, filling it with new life force so that my feelings and actions are in a positive, creative place."

Again, give yourself all the time you need to replenish yourself with the blue-white fire. Feel it out-raying throughout your entire solar plexus area and drawing in new, spiritual power. Also let it flow into the other spiritual centers.

In addition to the blue-white fire, you will want to draw in pure white light as well. When the emotions are in their positive flow, there is a calm, centering gentleness to the emotions. After a heavy bout with negative emotion, calm and gentle will be the last thing you will feel. The pure white light can help to bring the emotions into the poise necessary to sustain positive, creative emotions. Use the following meditative prayer to help transmute any hidden traces of dark light not cleansed with the orange-red flame.

Meditative Prayer for Emotional Upliftment with the Pure White Light

"Down-ray the pure white light into my emotional body to steady all the feeling levels of my consciousness, bringing them into perfect poise and alignment."

Sometimes an emotional reaction can catch you off guard. You get sudden bad news and you're thrown completely for a loop, which throws off your emotional body as well. If you can bring in the spiritual light right then and there, you can save yourself a lot of grief later on. You'll handle the situation much better, especially if you have to make an important decision and need a cool head. In this situation, you want the purple ray to still your emotions. The following meditations are for emergency situations. If you can get to a quiet place for your meditation, great. But if you can't, simply close your eyes and just visualize that soothing purple ray right where you are.

Meditative Prayer to Still the Emotions

"Down-ray the deep purple ray to bring forth peace and serenity, quieting my emotional body."

If the negative emotion has had enough time to gather momentum, ask to receive the emerald green ray as well, to balance things out.

Meditative Prayer to Balance the Emotions

"Down-ray the emerald green ray to bring forth Thy balance into my entire emotional body, and move this emotional center clockwise."

Chapter 7

Transformational
Meditations

There will be many times when a general mental/emotional cleansing will not be enough to turn a negative condition around. You may find yourself in a specific destructive state of mind that resists your conscious efforts. In these cases, you'll need to *target* your meditations to focus the light on the particular aspect of your mental/emotional nature that needs transmuting. The beauty of targeted meditations is that they show how well the light can be applied to the most intricate and demanding of situations.

In these challenging conditions, try to identify the thought that originally started the negative momentum. Most of these conditions are a result of seeing things with physical eyes rather than spiritual eyes. By identifying the original misconception, you're that much ahead of the game. Both mental and emotional states are included in these meditations because they're so interconnected. However, if you notice the condition is more emotional, then focus more light there, and vice versa. In all cases, ask the light to touch into the four main centers and throughout your entire consciousness, permeating your entire auric field.

For most mental/emotional conditions, you'll start with the orange-red flame, and follow up with the blue-white fire. I've included slight variations on these meditations to show how petitions to the light will vary according to the specific need.

Please keep in mind that if any mental/emotional condition is severe or chronic, you should seek professional help. Don't try to remedy the situation all on your own. Personal light work will help a great deal, but when problems are intense, you will need the expertise of a doctor, counselor, or skilled healer. Seeking help is an essential part of the spiritual growth process when the situation calls for it.

Resentment

Resentment is strongly rooted in anger that is held in. Usually, resentment is directed at someone who is close to you, whether it's a parent, spouse, child, or a friend. The feeling of being wronged often takes the form of hurt that turns into anger, and then resentment.

Resentment is one of those tricky, stubborn and self-justifying emotions. You can say, "This person did this to me, and therefore I'm right in feeling this way." Now you've fallen into the emotional trap. All you accomplish when you give way to resentment is to spawn a host of negative reactions such as hurt, bitterness, anger and revenge, which will only tear at you and debilitate your aura. It takes energy to resent someone, energy that could be used for constructive, life-enhancing purposes.

In the aura, resentment usually shows up as vitiated red and gray energies in and around the emotional and Hermetic centers. These energies have a distorted, menacing quality. They're held in the Hermetic Center, because you've let them into your heart. The dirty red shows anger; it will sometimes darken to a black if the resentment is very intense and veers toward hatred. The gray appears because depression usually accompanies that anger or hatred. Of course, the centers would be spinning counterclockwise, and if the resentment were to persist, it would show up in other parts of the energy field as well.

To break the spell that resentment puts on you, first evaluate the situation. What really happened? Did that person really do this to you? Many times, resentment can build around imagined slights or misunderstandings. I may resent someone who got a promotion that I feel I deserved, when, in actuality, he or she may be better qualified than I. You must also make sure you have the full picture—that someone hasn't told you lies, or that you haven't misinterpreted the events. You can work with spiritual illumination to reveal the truth, so that you're coming from a place of clarity.

However, let's say someone has definitely offended you, and you resent that person. The first energy you would bring down is the orange-red flame to purify all the negative energy that came at you or was generated by you.

Meditative Prayer for Purifying Resentful Energies

"Down-ray the orange-red flame of purification to cut me loose from resentment toward (*name the person*) and any negative energies coming at me from (*name the person*). I hold to the knowing that this energy is being released from me and is being dissolved in the light. I am now free of all resentment and animosity."

After you've called on the light, become very still and receptive to the purification. See all the hurts, angers, hatreds and all the things that led up to this moment being cut loose from you. If you want to verbalize, let your heart spill out your feelings, allowing this negative energy to be purified by the orange-red flame and dissolved in the mineral kingdom. Whatever images, words, impressions or memories come up, let them all go into this cathartic light. Try to make the release as vivid as you can. Feel divine energy flowing freely, touching all the dark places created by this resentment. Hold to the knowing that this energy is going through all the centers and all aspects of your being, releasing every stickpin of resentment.

Give yourself a few minutes after you've finished to let any residual energy be cleared out, and then follow up with the blue-white fire and the following meditation.

Meditative Prayer for Spiritual Replenishment

"Down-ray the blue-white fire of eternal life to reestablish new life force at every level of my being."

Again, become still and feel the rush of this electrifying, life-giving energy. Now you are coming into a complete restoration of your aura from the ravages of energy-sapping resentment. Feel that new freshness entering your consciousness, bringing zest and enthusiasm, motivation and desire. Feel the restoring power of the blue-white fire going to every place touched by the orange-red flame and bringing those areas up to the energy level where they should be. You are beyond that dark thinking and feeling now. That energy is no longer a part of you. Let the healing quality of this divine life force restore your spiritual equilibrium and permeate every aspect of your being. Feel it charging you right up, giving you a new positive outlook on life.

Once this work is done, you can follow up with any additional energy you feel you need. Spiritually strengthened, you are now ready to begin your forgiveness work (see Chapter 9). Depending on how open you are and how deep the resentment, it may take several meditations for the light to take hold. If the resentment is longstanding, you also have to work strongly on the mind levels, because thought-forms and patterns have had a chance to set in. It will take more work on your part to cut them loose, but the light work remains the same.

Once the situation has been placed in the light, you must decide what to do. You may decide to confront that person from a place of love, and you may be surprised by that person's reaction. If you're somehow unable to meet with the resented one, and/or that person is not responding to the light, then you have to let the situation go, and ask that it be gently laid in God's hands. If the person who offended you isn't around, or alive, then send the light to that soul wherever it may be, and continue to practice forgiveness.

Hate

Hate is the lowest and most destructive of all emotions. No negative emotion is good, but hate operates on the very lowest vibratory frequency. It brings so much misery to all involved. In the aura, it presents itself in inky blacks. A person in a hate energy field is capable of just about anything, including murder. Like resentment, you hate something or someone who has done something to you, imagined or actual. However, unlike resentment that can be understated and secretive, hate tends to express openly. People are generally eager to tell you they hate you—unless they have a specific reason to hold back. If they don't tell you, they'll tell other people. The one advantage to such outspoken behavior is that you know where you stand with such a person. The bad thing is, hatred tends to want company. If I tell you that I hate this or that, I'm encouraging you to respond the same way. And since hate is such a strong energy, the passion of my hatred can influence you, even if you don't feel that way.

Hatred is especially strong on a mass scale. Most of the world's atrocities can be traced back to hatred. Look at aggressive rulers and evil dictators, and you'll find hate as their motivating force for conquest. The terrorist who is willing to kill others as well as himself for his idea of God thinks he is sacrificing to please that God. Yet what actually makes him pull the trigger is not love of God, but hatred for the misperceived person or idea that stands in his way. The hateful person can also be methodical. An angry person might do something impulsively and then it's over, but the hateful person can stew for a long time, giving ample opportunity for premeditated acts.

Hate operates void of divine essence. That's why it's so menacing. It's an active absorbing energy that, like a black hole, wants to draw things into it. You can't mess around with hatred. The same is true if hatred is directed at you. It's an aggressive energy that you must counteract with the highest attributes of the Divine Light. In the aura, hate can take on different forms, but the predominating energy is always black. Look at Figure 3–4 to see what hatred can look like. It is totally out of harmony with the divine nature of life. And as we know, hatred can harbor cruel and sadistic thoughts.

If hate is in your aura, you must make it a top priority to work on; with such an energy in your aura, it will be very hard, if not impossible, for you to progress spiritually. Hatred can be very difficult to let go of. As with resentment, chances are you are justifying your hatred. The wrongs committed are usually extreme. I'm certainly not excusing the behavior of those who have intentionally hurt you, but it's *your* choice how to react. Hatred is something you can control. You are choosing to hate.

There are several steps involved in clearing yourself of hatred. Once again, you start by calling upon the orange-red flame. You need this energy to come down very dynamically and begin to cut loose the black energy in the aura. I've seen this flame appear almost like a sword at times to sever the destructive energies. You can visualize it doing the same in your meditation.

Meditative Prayer for Purifying Hatred

"Down-ray the orange-red flame to strongly cut me loose from all hatred directed at me from (*name person*), and release me from all hatred and animosity anywhere in my consciousness that I have created and directed at (name person). I ask that You take these black and gray energies into the mineral kingdom to be dissolved in the light."

You must be very definite in your call to the orange-red flame, commanding these negative energies to be cut loose from your life. Then become still and feel this power working in you. With intense emotions such as hate, you may have to repeat the exercise several times to get the job done. With each meditation those dark energies will gradually lighten until they finally disappear. You must be very careful to not re-energize the hate by dwelling on it; otherwise you will have to repeat the work until you stabilize your consciousness.

After the orange-red flame, follow up with the blue-white fire, and feel the blue-white fire lifting your consciousness.

Meditative Prayer for Spiritual Replenishment

"Down-ray the blue-white fire of eternal life to charge and recharge all areas within me, bringing forth new life energy and lifting me into the consciousness of Thy Light."

After the blue-white fire, do the forgiveness work presented in Chapter 9. You may also work with the love ray just for yourself, to help bring in compassion and understanding.

If you have acted on your hate, it's especially important to finish your work using the pure white light. It will help to release any stickpins where hatred may still be lodged and to defuse any negative momentum you may have generated. It's also an uplifting energy to help take you out of the hate consciousness you've been living in.

Meditative Prayer for Upliftment with the Pure White Light

"Down-ray the pure white light to go into all levels of my being, lifting me into the vibration of Thy holiness."

Depending on your sensitivity to the light, you may feel relief during this process as you shift out of the dark state you were in. You will also begin to realize just how destructive that hatred was.

Anger

Anger is a common emotion that everyone has felt at one time or another. Generally, anger is more ephemeral than hatred. Some people get angry quickly and forget their anger just as quickly. If unchecked, anger can build and turn into rage. People with this type of anger are like a bomb waiting to go off. They can blow up at the least provocation. There's also an uncontrolled quality to anger. People don't plan to get angry, it just seems to happen sometimes against their will, and after the outburst they feel bad. This shows poor control of the emotional nature.

Anger is an explosive energy in the aura. Figure 3–5 clearly shows the firecracker-like energies of the vitiated reds and dark greens generated by sustained outbursts of anger. As mentioned before, one strong outburst of anger takes two weeks to work out of the aura! An angry person is hard to be around. He or she is usually insensitive, irritable, and likely to say terrible things, lashing out at people for no good reason. Many unpleasant personality traits can come through with anger.

To clear yourself of anger, begin with the orange-red flame to start clearing those streaks of vitiated red. See this energy bathing your entire aura as well as your energy centers.

Meditative Prayer for Purifying Anger

"Down-ray the orange-red flame of purification into my entire being, releasing me of all anger connected with (name person or situation) and dissolving all negative energy in the light."

Follow up with the blue-white fire.

Meditative Prayer for Spiritual Replenishment

"Down-ray the blue-white fire of eternal life to charge and recharge my entire being, bringing me new life force and creative energy."

In addition, you will need to work with the love ray to help bring you into the consciousness of divine oneness and to release the irritations associated with anger.

Meditative Prayer for Divine Love & Compassion

"Down-ray the deep rose-pink of spiritual love, touching my entire being and transforming anger into love so that I may have compassion. Let it flow into all levels of my being, bringing me into Thy body of Divine Love."

I also recommend bringing down the violet ray, which is a subtler version of the purple ray. This ray is excellent for bringing in a gentle peace. In anger, there is a harshness and agitation that the violet ray can help smooth out.

Meditative Prayer for Gentle Peace

"Down-ray the violet ray of Thy peace into my entire being, releasing all irritations and bringing me into a serenity and divine poise."

There is also something called righteous anger. You will not express this kind of anger as often. You may express righteous anger over an injustice done to someone who cannot speak for herself, or for unkindness being directed at you. Say someone is gossiping about you, lying and hurting your reputation. You have a right to tell that person, in no uncertain terms, to cease and desist. In this case, the emotion is not an uncontrolled outburst but a definite controlled expression. No one has the right to push into your aura, and you have every right to defend your good name. Righteous anger is not the same kind of anger that we have been speaking about. Righteous anger appears in the aura as bright red, not dirty red. It is a positive energy. You'll know the difference between the two, because with righteous anger you won't feel upset or displaced afterwards.

Jealousy

To be jealous is a sure sign of low self-worth. If you're jealous, you believe that someone has something you don't—but should—have. This can create all sorts of deceit and underhandedness as you go about trying to get the things you want.

The spiritual understanding missing is that what you desire on the outside is something you already possess *within*. If you find yourself feeling jealous of someone's talents or abilities, you must recognize that the very same talent can unfold in you—if you desire it enough. Just because a talent is active in someone else doesn't mean it can't be active in you. It's simply that the other has already worked at it, while you have yet to do so. In life, there will always be those who are further along the path than you are, just as there are others who are not quite as far along. This is all part of the natural evolutionary link that ties us all together and is why you can never compare yourself to others. If you do, "you may become vain or bitter," as the *Desiderata* warns. You will always be looking over your shoulder at what the other guy is doing.

In the aura, jealousy presents itself as a dirty, avocado green energy. It's a very ugly color to see. When people speak jealous words, I can sometimes see snakelike energies coming from their throat center. It throws the aura off kilter. There are often splotches of brown and vitiated red, because with jealousy, meanness and anger are never far behind. If the jealousy is more like envy, then the shade will be a lighter olive green.

Being jealous is one of the surest ways to destroy friendships. I remember two sisters who got along very well together—until they became interested in the same man. Both were in their early twenties and only a year or two apart. The man was interested in the older sister, who was prettier, and the younger one became very jealous. She did everything she could to win the man's affection, but it just didn't work. When she talked about her sister, I could see the snakelike energy coming out of her emotional center. It was an ugly sight. Of course, she had no idea what she was creating. Eventually, the man married the older sister. The younger sister, still seething with jealousy, couldn't take it and ended up moving away without resolving her feelings toward her sister. These sisters lost their friendship, and their once-beautiful sisterhood, to the "green-eyed monster," jealousy.

Jealousy can be insidious. Begin with the orange-red flame and ask it to cut you loose from all feelings of jealousy, wherever they may be lodged in your consciousness.

Meditative Prayer for Purifying Jealousy

"Down-ray the orange-red flame to release me from all jealousy and envy wherever it is lodged in my consciousness. Take all these black and gray atoms to the mineral kingdom, to be dissolved in the light."

Feel it showering your entire being. If you feel it more in the emotions, let the light stay there a little longer. If you've been talking about it a lot, you might feel it strongly in the throat center. You might be surprised at how much negative energy your jealousy can build. But don't dwell on that. Just feel the releasing. Afterwards, come in with the blue-white fire to recharge the areas depleted, asking to retain the power where you need it to fortify your energy field.

Meditative Prayer for Spiritual Replenishment

"Down-ray the blue-white fire of eternal life to bring in new life force to all levels of my being, and sustain its power wherever I need it."

Then use the love ray to bring in more compassion for you and the person you've been jealous of. Also ask for gentleness to come in with this love, because chances are you were harsh in your handling of the situation. You may also follow up with the forgiveness work (Chapter 9).

Meditative Prayer for Emotional Upliftment with Divine Love

"Down-ray the deep rose-pink of Divine Love to bring compassion into my entire being and to bring me into a consciousness of Divine Love."

To crown your efforts, you'll want to finish up with the emerald green to bring you into a harmonious state and to balance out your whole aura. Ask that this ray bring in serenity with the harmony. If you feel you also need to bring down the peace ray to really establish that tranquility, then do so.

Meditative Prayer for Balance

"Down-ray the emerald green ray to harmonize and balance all levels of my being."

After you have finished your light work, you must make an effort to remove your attention from the object of your jealousy until that negative energy is completely out of your consciousness. If there's been open friction, you may want to get it out into the open. Pay a genuine compliment about that person's talent. Confess to your feelings and ask forgiveness. The person may surprise you and turn out to be your friend. Remember, the divine spark shines in everyone. Admiring the God spark in others is a holy trait. Mother Teresa saw Christ in everyone she met. How can you be envious of Christ?

Later, after the jealousy has been totally cleared out, you can work with divine guidance to help create the things you want. If that quality/object/situation you'd coveted so much in someone is still a strong desire, then you must begin the building process for yourself. If it turns out you didn't want it as much as you thought, then you will know it wasn't that important to begin with.

Depression

Depression is a complex problem. It is usually due to taking in too much of the conditions around you. Even if you're watching yourself, it's hard not to absorb the outside world to some degree. Strong disappointments, sudden loss, and unresolved traumas can easily bring on depression. Physiological conditions can also bring on depression.

A spiritual principle often overlooked in depression is that events or conditions in your life are never permanent: "This too shall pass." When in a depressed state, you're not seeing the full spiritual picture. The negativity that seems to be engulfing you is a created condition that is temporary. In your true spiritual essence, these states do not exist, and therefore are not the originating reality. In God's kingdom, all is in its perfect flow, and since you are part of that perfection, part of you is in that perfect flow right now.

Unfortunately, depression is one of those conditions you can become strangely comfortable with, which can lead to many destructive habits. Alcoholics usually have depression as a motivating force that drives them to drink. Some people seem to love looking at the world fatalistically or cynically. Yet, having a fatalistic or pessimistic view will only serve to cloud the spiritual reality of life and make you an easy target for depression. The negativities you harbor stay with you only as long as you choose to keep them.

Granted, sometimes you may feel that you don't have the spiritual power to rise out of your present condition. This is where the spiritual work really comes to your assistance. The Divine Light will give you that "booster shot" to help you reconnect with your Source, so you can see things in their true perspective. In addition, you now know that by connecting with your Higher

Self, you're tapping into the higher spiritual awareness that is above the discords of Earth life. By stepping into that greater consciousness, you're letting go of your problems and putting them into God's hands. He will steer you over all the bumps and roadblocks along your spiritual path, and release the heaviness from your heart.

In the aura, depression most often shows itself as a gray cloud above the head. If the depression is severe, it can appear as a gray energy circling the entire person. Depression shows a lot in the Hermetic and emotional centers because of its connection to disturbing events and the emotional response to those events.

You must first cut loose these clouds with the orange-red flame. Like most of the work you will be doing in this section, it may take several tries before the gray clouds begin to dissipate, especially if the depression is long-standing.

Meditative Prayer for Purifying Depression

"Down-ray the orange-red flame to cut loose any gray clouds of depression and any negative energy, wherever it is lodged in my consciousness, dissolving it in the mineral kingdom in the light."

After the purification has done its job, follow up with the blue-white fire—one of the most effective energies to use for depression. If you have time to work with only one energy in connection with depression, use the blue-white fire. Its uplifting powers are truly dramatic.

Meditative Prayer for Spiritual Upliftment

"Down-ray the blue-white fire of eternal life to charge and recharge my consciousness, lifting me out of any depressive energies and into Thy renewing, electrifying and everlasting life force."

If there has been a lot of stress connected with your depression, you may want to work with the purple ray as well. It will help you break away from whatever it is that depresses you, almost as if you were going on an island cruise and dropping away all your cares.

Meditative Prayer for Peace

"Down-ray the purple ray of divine peace, releasing me from the burdens and pressures within my being and bringing forth Thy peace."

Once you feel the light breaking up the depressive energy, you will start to see things quite differently. If you can, take a little time off to give your whole psyche a rest. Your body and nerves will recharge, and that will help the whole process.

Depression can take time to be fully resolved; it's hard to say how long this process may take. The light will certainly begin the process of release and upliftment right away. If the depression is not severe, the light can clear it up within a relatively short time. But as with any condition that persists, if the depression is severe or chronic, seek professional help as well, whether it be a doctor, psychiatrist, or healer.

At some point when you feel stronger, start to work on resolving the condition that put you in the depression to begin with. It might involve letting go of something that's bothering you or gathering the courage to face something you've been avoiding. If there is more than one thing going on at the same time, take each challenge one at a time. Use your energy work with everything that comes up. Above all, try to maintain your spiritual, optimistic outlook, even if the condition seems to be lasting longer than you'd like.

Guilt

Guilt is directing anger or hostility toward yourself. Regret and remorse are often cousins to guilt. The funny part about guilt is that it usually becomes a form of self-punishment. By feeling guilt, you feel you're atoning for some wrong you have done.

In the aura, the basic color of guilt is gray. It can appear as a small gray cloud above the head or around the heart center and emotional center as well. Usually, remorse is there too, which will show up in tinges of darker, charcoal gray. The gray will be mixed with the color of whatever wrong was done. If you deceived someone, dark green will be mixed in with the gray; if you were mean or cruel, cocoa brown will tell the story. So the energy of guilt is rarely seen alone. This is what often helps to distinguish it from the gray clouds of fear or depression.

Guilt can be expressed in strange ways. I once knew a woman who owned a restaurant where I worked when I was very young. She had the strange habit of leaving the cash register open, which of course enticed customers and employees to take money from her, which they did. She would also make large accounting errors in employees' favor. It was as if she were deliberately inviting people to steal from her. One time, she made a thousand-dollar accounting error in my favor. I brought the matter to her attention and instead of being surprised or grateful, she was indignant! I could have just kept the money, but that's a form of stealing and I wasn't going to get caught up in that. I thought, "This is it. I'm going to find out what's going on here." I could see certain energies moving in her aura and knew something was happening.

It took a little work, but finally she told me her story. When my employer was a child, her mother had become hooked on morphine during a hospital stay. After using up all their money to satisfy her addiction, she would have her daughter steal. If they were visiting at a friend's house, the mother would be downstairs chatting while the little girl would sneak upstairs, go into people's bedrooms and take what she could. Other times her mother would have her crawl through windows at night or when no one was home and take money. The guilt of what she did weighed heavily on her, and she carried it into adulthood. When she found herself in a better financial situation, her way of reciprocating was to allow people to steal from her. It made her feel better and was her way of paying back the money she took.

Of course, if you make a mistake or hurt someone, there's bound to be regret and guilt. What you want to do as soon as you can is replace guilt with compassion—both for the person wronged and for yourself. You can't control what you did in the past, but you have complete freedom to work on things now. Forgive yourself for what you've done and certainly make amends. Recognize that the soul part of you is still growing and not fully perfected yet, so you will inevitably make mistakes. Sometimes, you will make *big* mistakes. That's part of your life experience. What you want to do is learn and grow from those mistakes, so you won't repeat them.

Begin with the orange-red flame. Ask it to cut loose not only the gray energies of guilt but also the negative energies that created the condition bringing about the guilt. If the wrong you did was severe, divide this process. Work on guilt separately as one purification, and then work on the negative situation.

Meditative Prayer for Releasing Guilt

"Down-ray the orange-red flame of purification to cut loose all thoughts and feelings of guilt, wherever they are lodged in my consciousness, and the accompanying destructive energies that created this guilt in the first place."

Follow up with the blue-white fire.

Meditative Prayer for Spiritual Replenishment

"Down-ray the blue-white fire to replenish all depleted areas of my consciousness with new life force."

Once you've revitalized yourself, you'll want to bring in a strong flow of the deep rose-pink as a healing and uplifting love, so that you feel the Divine Love. Remember: No matter what you've done, God forgives you, because He always sees you in the highest possible light—as the divine creation that you are. Regardless of our mistakes, God's love is unshakable. By working with this ray, you are opening up to that love flow. People often feel they don't deserve God's Love because of some of the things they've done, or perhaps not done. Yet, Divine Love is our inheritance, so it's already a part of us. Many people try to separate from that love and deny it to themselves. This only serves to draw them further away from their spiritual objectives.

Meditative Prayer for Divine Love Upliftment

"Down-ray the deep rose-pink ray as a healing love to bring me into the oneness of Thy love, releasing any self-hate or anger and uplifting me as one body in Thy body of Divine Love."

Finish up your light work with the emerald green ray to help harmonize your consciousness, especially if the guilt has been longstanding.

Meditative Prayer for Balance

"Down-ray the emerald green ray to balance and harmonize
all the levels of my consciousness—mind, body and soul—
with spirit."

Once you've cleared your energy field, begin your forgiveness work. Pray for yourself and the other person or persons involved.

After the light work, it's time to get cracking on turning around whatever situation you created. Look at it as objectively as you can and see what you can do to really help. If you cheated someone, pay him or her back. If you were cruel to someone, apologize and show kindness. If you deceived someone, come clean. Make every effort to do something concrete about it. And if you can't help the person you harmed, find someone else or someone in a similar situation and help that person.

Grief

It's impossible to go through this life without suffering a loss that brings grief. Everyone will lose someone or something dear to them at some point in their life and feel sorrow when that person or thing isn't there anymore. After all, this life is a visit. You and I are not meant to stay here forever. Yet, it's easy to forget this fundamental reality when we're caught up in the activities of the world. Although loss of loved ones occasions the strongest form of grief, people grieve over many things, including lost youth or ability, a bygone time when life was especially idyllic, and so on.

Grief is one of the most searing experiences you will ever have to face. Anyone who has lost a child or a spouse will attest to that. And because it is so difficult, so overwhelming, it also becomes one of the greatest spiritual tests. I've lost several dear ones in my life and understand grief very well. In love I tell you—sorrow is selfish. When you grieve, you're grieving more for yourself than for the other person. Should you be sad that the person you love is free from pain or old age? Do you mourn when a caterpillar turns into a butterfly? Your loved one has graduated from this existence and is free to go on to a greater existence. This Earth life is not the only life there is. When you pass on from Earth life, life does not end. You go on to the spiritual life from which you came. This is why one of the greatest services you can do for a loved one who has died is to let him or her go. Death cannot part you from your loved one—you will meet up again in the spiritual realms.

Prolonged grief will hold you back because it keeps you in the past. And if you're in the past, you cannot be moving forward. Understandably, if you've lost someone very dear to you, someone who's been an important part of your life, you're going to feel great sadness. It's only natural, and it's a good idea to give yourself time to mourn. There is a spiritual tradition that allows 44 days to mourn, and I highly recommend taking this time. But after the mourning period, it's wise to make every effort to move on.

Grief is another emotion that shows up as gray in the aura. I've seen it as a gray bubble in the heart center and sometimes above the head as well. If the person is angry with the person who died, there will be vitiated red in the aura. Self-pity or depression would bring in a darker cloud of charcoal gray and even black. The grieving soul might have unresolved issues concerning the deceased, bringing up a lifetime of feelings and thoughts, all of which will show up in the aura.

Begin with a thorough cleansing and replenishing, to lift you out of the heavy vibrations that deep grief brings.

Meditative Prayer for Releasing Grief

"Down-ray the orange-red flame of purification to cut loose all feelings of grief and loss everywhere in my consciousness, and dissolve all black and gray atoms in the mineral kingdom in the light."

Grief is another mental/emotional state that may be countered by a strong recharging flow of the blue-white fire.

Meditative Prayer for Spiritual Replenishment

"Down-ray the blue-white fire to replenish all depleted areas of my consciousness with new life force."

You will also need a strong dose of the emerald green ray to bring you back into harmony. With loss, your psyche will be thrown out of balance. Your world may feel upside down. You'll need the emerald green to bring things back into perspective.

Meditative Prayer for Balance

"Down-ray the emerald green ray to balance and harmonize all the levels of my consciousness as one body in Thy body of Divine Light and Love."

Of course, you will want Spiritual Love. This will help to uplift your soul and get you out of the loneliness you may feel. It also will help to strengthen your compassion so you can see things more from the level of Divine Love. Divine Love also brings in spiritual joy.

Meditative Prayer for Divine Love Upliftment

"Down-ray the deep rose-pink ray as a healing love to bring me into the oneness of Thy Love, embracing me as one body in Thy body of Divine Love."

Perhaps the most helpful energy of all is the deep purple ray of spiritual peace. If you have time to work with only one ray, use the deep peace. When you lose someone, there is almost always shock involved, and this ray can reach deep within to soothe and calm your soul. There may also be impulses to act rashly; this ray can put you in a place of serenity where you will see things more clearly.

Meditative Prayer for Peace

"Down-ray the purple ray of divine peace to all centers, especially my heart center, to give rest to my soul and to touch into all aspects of my being, releasing all grief and raising my consciousness into a state of harmony and peace."

After you have completed your light work, you're ready to start using the light in your life. Fill your days with fresh new thoughts and experiences. Surround yourself with positive, supportive people. Reassert your connection with God. Try to feel joy for the person passing on. Take care that you're not isolating yourself too much. There are as many ways of grieving as there are people. Some bereaved people develop a desire to die themselves, in the erroneous belief that it may bring them closer to the loved one who has passed on. Being around people and having good friends always helps. If you have unresolved issues with the person who passed on, be patient about that, too. Just because they are no longer in the body doesn't mean you can't still work things out within yourself.

Fear

Of all the negative emotions, fear is one of the strongest impediments to reaching your spiritual goals. Fear can cut to the very core of your being and paralyze you. Whereas hate can spur you on to negative action, fear encourages no action at all. How can you progress and go after the life you want if you're afraid to take the initiative?

Fear reaches deep into the instinctual levels of your consciousness. Yet, your fear doesn't necessarily have to be a big fear. You can have small fears that accumulate and even go unnoticed at first. But after a while, they add up. You can fear something very real or have neurotic fears wherein an innocent situation sparks terror. If it persists, fear can breed related emotions such as worry and depression. Worst of all, fear can breed more fear.

To fear something, you have to see yourself as separate from your Divine Source. Fear, by its very nature, creates a sense of separateness. In fearing something, you're accepting the belief that something or someone has power over you, and that you're powerless to do anything about it. If you return to your spiritual point of view, you can easily see the fallacy in this type of thinking. For if you are an essential part of the Spiritual Source that created the universe, how can there be any power greater than that? There can't be.

This sense of separateness is again a *physical* conception. In the spiritual realm, you are part of the One. You are "under the shadow of the Almighty." There is no separateness in the divine world. There is only one, unifying, all-powerful Source. This doesn't mean that you don't take normal precautions; it does mean that you're not coming from a place of fear and trembling. To the degree that you're in your divine oneness do you feel confident and courageous. You'll face adversity with dynamic power and courage. Look at the life of Saint Francis, who tamed the wolf and became his friend. Francis was a gentle man, yet he was able to save an entire village from a vicious predator without any bloodshed. If he had been afraid of what the wolf might do to him, what would have happened then?

You have to face your fears in order to conquer them. Most people will do just about anything to avoid a condition or situation they fear. Never allow fear to lodge in your being. It impairs your judgment, clouds your reason, and constrains your very being.

You're going to need a lot of spiritual power to get out of the fear state. Begin by asking yourself: Is what I fear a real or imagined situation? The key here is to try to identify the original experience or thought that created the fear. Once it's clear, you'll know where to start.

Fear shows very clearly in the aura as a gray energy, mostly in the emotional center. It can move in an odd, swirling motion from all the emotional turbulence involved. When the fear is very great, I have seen a whole band of it swirling around the aura itself. A very fearful person will also be lacking in some of the uplifting and dynamic energies, such as gold, orange, and red.

In working with the energies, bring down the orange-red flame and blue-white fire to do a clearing and cleansing and to build up your aura. You want the orange-red flame to touch into every thought, experience, and sensation that's producing the fear. The process may unloose some very specific pictures that evoke the emotion. If so, ask that they be cleanly cut away from your consciousness.

Meditative Prayer for Releasing Fear

"Down-ray the orange-red flame to cut loose all vibrations of fear wherever those negative energies have taken control of my life, and dissolve these black and gray atoms in the mineral kingdom, in the light."

After you're finished, bring in the blue-white fire.

Meditative Prayer for New Life Force

"Down-ray the blue-white fire to charge and recharge my consciousness with this electrifying life force at all levels of my consciousness."

Fearful experiences tend to pull you out of spiritual alignment quickly, after which it's hard to let any new energies take hold. Ask that the emerald green ray touch into your centers and entire being, especially your emotional body, bringing you into mind, body, and soul balance.

Meditative Prayer for Balance

"Down-ray the emerald green ray of balanced power to any areas of my consciousness that were thrown out of alignment by fear, and bring me into a divine centering and harmony at all levels of my consciousness."

Now you have to build up the aura with the gold light. Gold will help you to develop faith, courage, and strength. Bring in this ray very deliberately to establish the dynamic light. It was your lack of faith that put you in fear to begin with, but when you are in unity with God, you will feel nothing resembling fear. You will be handling situations with a swift keen hand and a sure step. The gold light will help you to reclaim that self-confidence.

Meditative Prayer for Inner Strength

"Down-ray the golden ray of wisdom light to touch into all aspects of my being, bringing me the inner strength, courage, confidence, divine faith and inner knowing to pull me through negative states of consciousness, so that I am in dynamic oneness with Thee."

Once you are in your spiritual power, you must use that energy. You'll have to face your fears one by one—ideally, as they come up in the heat of the moment. Constantly acknowledge the God power. Spiritual affirmations are of great assistance in restoring confidence and courage (see Chapter 13). Use the gold as often as necessary to reestablish that gold and the divine faith, and eventually you will conquer your fears.

Worry

Worry and fear show up very similarly in the aura. The gray is the dominating energy, but with worry the gray is lighter and not so oppressive. If the worry is chronic, it might also show itself in the color division as gray specks.

Some people are in the habit of worrying. They feel that somehow it accomplishes things, protects or prepares them for the unexpected, but it doesn't. When you worry you can exhaust yourself so much that eventually you must relax, and in your relaxed state come your answers.

When you worry, you're expressing a lack of spiritual trust, a lack of faith. If you are one with God, then you know for certain that God is working things out for you. If you really have confidence in God, there can be no worry. If you're unsure about what to do in your life, you need to consult your Higher Self to receive divine guidance (see Chapter 10). Be patient for that guidance to come. You can only do so much on your own. You are the channel through whom God works—which is all that's expected of you! Man often expects too much of himself and becomes stressed when his answers aren't forthcoming. If you worry too much, you will block the flow of light. If you really want resolution, stay quiet, and receive. Then act.

Follow the same steps that dispel fear, outlined above, to clear your aura of worry. Unless the worry is habitual, you don't have to use the emerald green ray.

Meditative Prayer for Purifying Worry

"Down-ray the orange-red flame to cut loose all patterns of worry and all anxieties and irritations connected with worry, and dissolve these black and gray atoms in the mineral kingdom, in the light."

After you're finished, bring in the blue-white fire.

Meditative Prayer for New Life Force

"Down-ray the blue-white fire to charge and recharge my consciousness with electrifying life force at all levels of my being."

Then you'll want to work with the gold to increase your faith and spiritual trust in God.

Meditative Prayer for Inner Strength

"Down-ray the golden ray of wisdom light to touch into all aspects of my being, bringing me the inner strength and confidence, faith and guidance to direct my life so that I am in dynamic oneness with Thee."

Then you really have to retrain yourself so that whenever conditions arise that call for you to act and make decisions, those old patterns of worry don't creep in. Once you start to really establish your dynamic nature, a lot of your fears will simply disappear.

Pride

It has been said that one of the first great sins man committed was inspired by pride. Throughout history, pride has been the cause of so much strife, yet many people regard pride as a positive quality. They ask, "Why not feel proud of an accomplishment well done? If I work very hard for something, I should feel proud of what I did." From a purely physical, human point of view, this would seem to make sense, but a deeper look at the spiritual root reveals the fundamental error in this thinking. Pride is a feeling of self-accomplishment. The keyword here is *self* and it is in "self" that you can be deceived. When you acknowledge and congratulate yourself as the creator of your achievements, you put the emphasis on *you*. This immediately moves you away from God consciousness and gives you a sense of being independent and disconnected from your Divine Source. You believe that the success is coming from your own efforts. If you continue along those lines, you will inevitably build the illusion of your superiority over others, which can quickly lead to arrogance.

The spiritual truth missing in pride is humility—the understanding of your relationship with God. This relationship is not always easy to act on. Even Jesus' disciples felt a sense of personal accomplishment when they felt their spiritual powers over evil growing ever stronger. Jesus quickly rebuked them saying, "Rejoice not, that the spirits are subject unto you; but rather rejoice, because your names are written in heaven" (Luke 10:20). In other words, marvel that God has allowed you to be such an instrument of spiritual power, but do not claim this power as your own personal possession.

When you are in tune with the Divine, many things will happen for you, and if you're not careful, you may start to claim these accomplishments as your own, or even as your God-given rewards for being such a marvelous person. This is a big test to see if you clearly understand the relationship between you and your divine nature. When you begin to recognize your spiritual root as the life-sustaining power behind all your accomplishments, and give all credit and glory to your Divine Source, then you have begun to overcome pride and master humility.

Some people have a hard time accepting humility because they think of being humble as a form of debasement or as an affront to their dignity.

They confuse being spiritually humble with being humiliated. This confusion is understandable because of the way the word is most often used. Yet, humility is just the opposite of debasement. Spiritual humility is seeing yourself where you belong in the spiritual scheme of things—as an instrument and co-creative being of God. If anything, true humility creates a greater sense of worth, because you understand how precious you are in God's eyes.

The Greeks have a word for when pride gets the better of you. They call it *hybris* from which the Anglicized "hubris"(overbearing pride) is taken. Everyone has felt this hubris at some time or another.

Pride usually shows up in the aura as burnt orange and distorted avocado green energies radiating from the emotional body in a jerky motion. Begin your light work with the orange-red flame. You may feel a little resistance to this energy, especially if your human ego has built up a lot of pride in your talents and achievements, but stick with it.

Meditative Prayer to Purify Pride

"Down-ray the orange-red flame into all levels of my consciousness to cut loose all insidious energies connected with pride, all feelings of arrogance, or feelings that I'm better than someone else."

As you follow up with the blue-white fire, feel how this divine power is the very source of your life force.

Meditative Prayer for New Life Force

"Down-ray the blue-white fire of eternal life and recharge all levels of my consciousness, breathing in the very life of God and helping me to recognize Him as my true source of being."

Once this is done, balance is important, because if you are acting under the delusions of pride, you are out of rhythm with the spiritual pulse. The emerald green can help you get back into harmony with the God flow.

Meditative Prayer for Spiritual Balance

"Down-ray the emerald green ray of spiritual balance to touch into all levels of my being, balancing all conditions in divine order and harmony."

Along with the harmonious green ray, you will need to work with the white light to bring you back into a spiritual understanding of your relationship with God. You can also work with the gold light if you feel resistance and need more dynamic power to establish this consciousness in you.

Meditative Prayer for Spiritual Awareness

"Down-ray the pure white light to touch into all levels of my consciousness and to cut loose all unnaturalness and all pretenses so that I may come into a spiritual inner knowing of my true relationship with God."

I would finish this work with the deep rose-pink ray to bring in more spiritual humility through its gentle and compassionate flow. When you are very proud, you cut yourself off from others, putting yourself in a special category, so you'll need to bring yourself back into unity and oneness with God and others.

Meditative Prayer for Spiritual Humility

"Down-ray the deep rose-pink ray of spiritual love, bringing in more compassion and understanding for others, releasing all feelings of arrogance or superiority, and establishing spiritual humility at all levels of my being."

In applying the light work, you can start by giving God all the "credit," and thanking Him for allowing you to be a channel of all good that is in your life. If you are having great successes, give credit to God. Look for all the ways in which you were inspired to follow the course you are on. If you are facing failure or difficulties, watch that hurt pride isn't getting the better of you.

Affirmations are a great help. They can keep your mind focused on your spiritual priorities.

Pride is not easy to release. You may even have a hard time recognizing it as something that needs to be worked on. Believe me—we all need to work on it! You have to stay on top of your very subtle enemy, pride, and learn to embrace humility in its place. Ben Franklin put it best when he said, "I don't think I could ever master humility because if I did, I'd be so damn proud of myself."

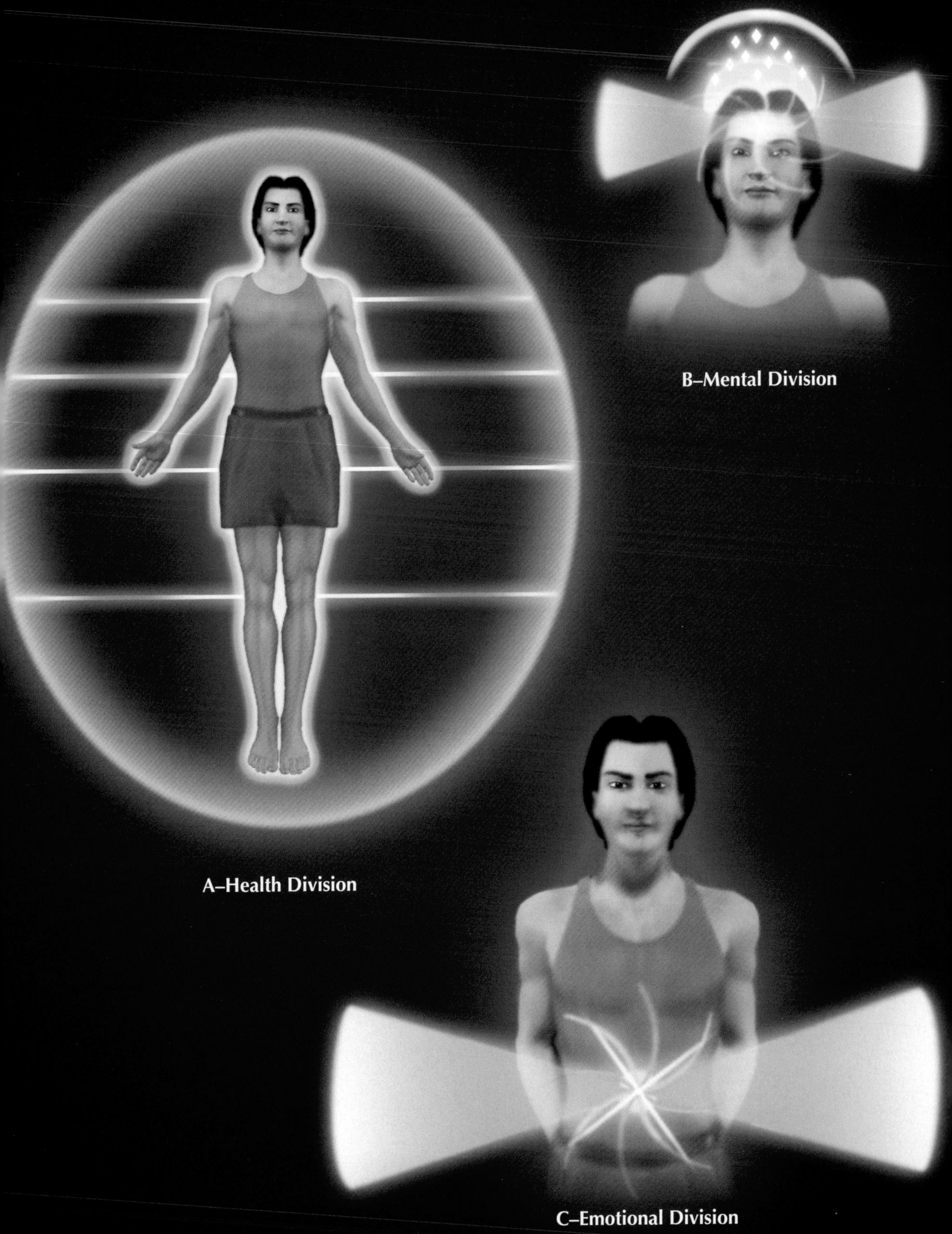

B–Mental Division

A–Health Division

C–Emotional Division

Figure 2–2: **Divisions of the Aura, A–C**

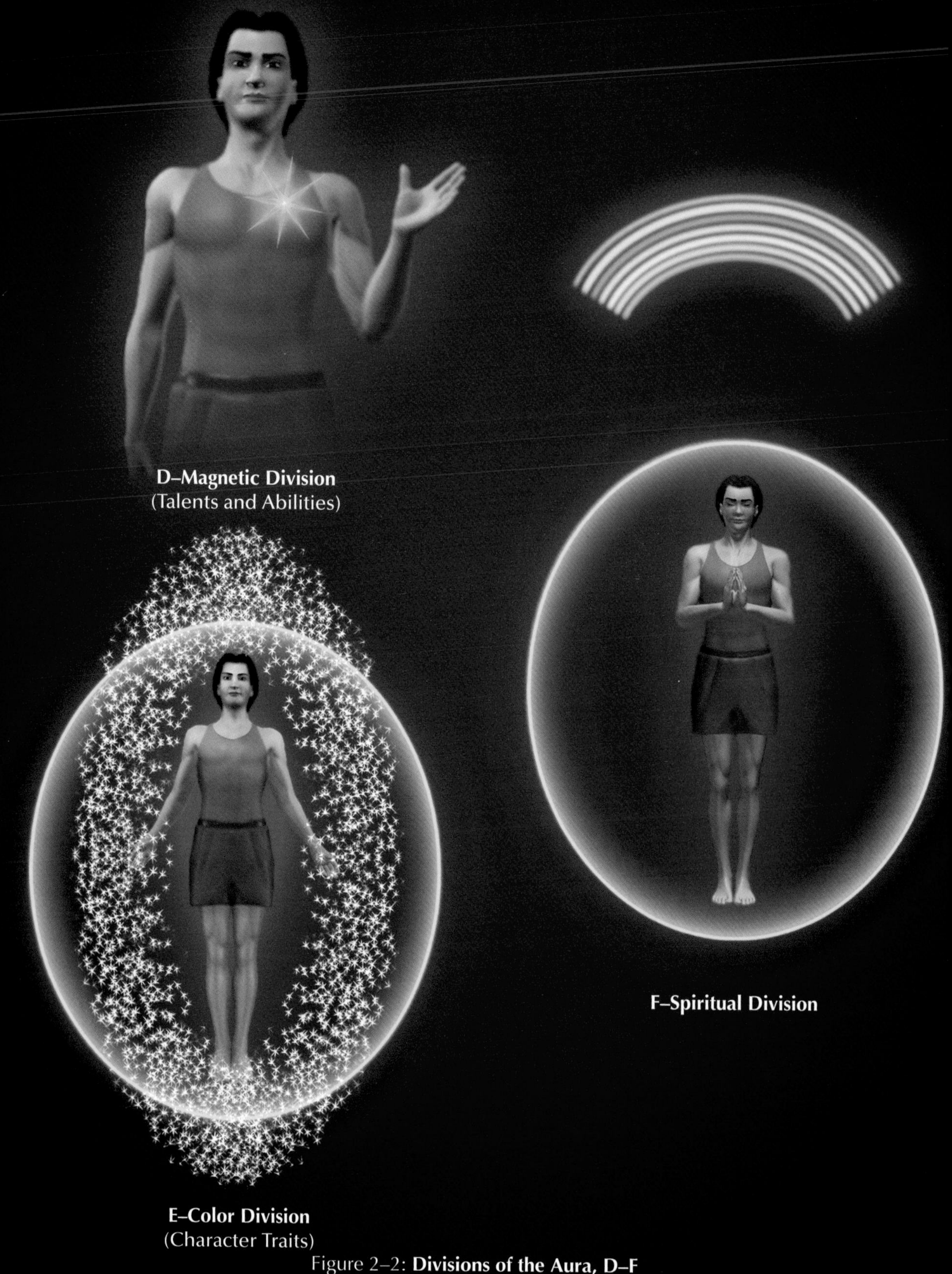

D–Magnetic Division
(Talents and Abilities)

F–Spiritual Division

E–Color Division
(Character Traits)

Figure 2–2: **Divisions of the Aura, D–F**

A–Stabilizers

B–Fanning Rays

C–Spiral Rays

Figure 2–4: **Energy Center Radiations**

Figure 2–5: **The Mixed Aura**

Figure 2–6: **The Devolved Aura**

Figure 2–7: **The Enlightened Aura**

Enlightened Colors

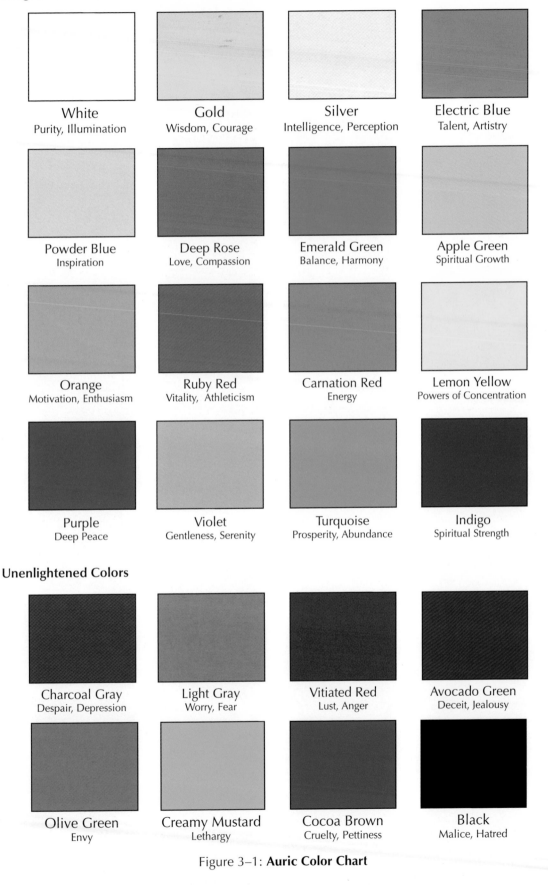

White
Purity, Illumination

Gold
Wisdom, Courage

Silver
Intelligence, Perception

Electric Blue
Talent, Artistry

Powder Blue
Inspiration

Deep Rose
Love, Compassion

Emerald Green
Balance, Harmony

Apple Green
Spiritual Growth

Orange
Motivation, Enthusiasm

Ruby Red
Vitality, Athleticism

Carnation Red
Energy

Lemon Yellow
Powers of Concentration

Purple
Deep Peace

Violet
Gentleness, Serenity

Turquoise
Prosperity, Abundance

Indigo
Spiritual Strength

Unenlightened Colors

Charcoal Gray
Despair, Depression

Light Gray
Worry, Fear

Vitiated Red
Lust, Anger

Avocado Green
Deceit, Jealousy

Olive Green
Envy

Creamy Mustard
Lethargy

Cocoa Brown
Cruelty, Pettiness

Black
Malice, Hatred

Figure 3–1: **Auric Color Chart**

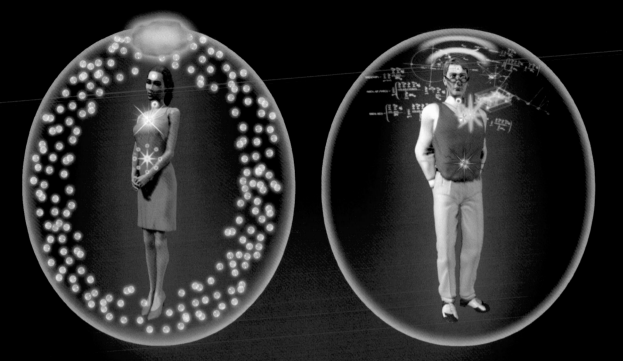

Figure 3–2: **Romantic Love**

Figure 3–3: **Intelligence**

Figure 3–4: **Hatred**

Figure 3–5: **Anger**

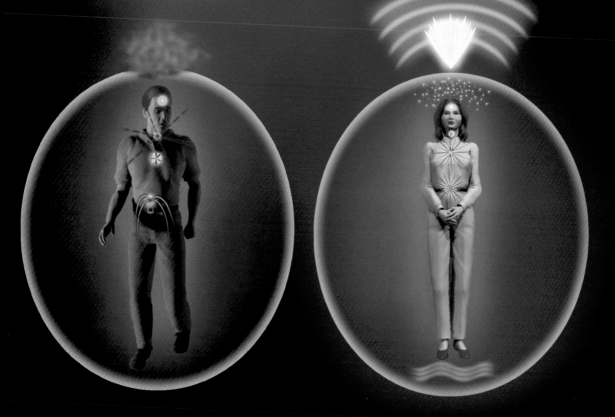

Figure 3–6: **Wealth Consciousness**

Figure 3–7: **Poverty Consciousness**

Figure 3–8: **Fear**

Figure 3–9: **The Spiritual Aspirant**

Figure 4–1: **The Higher Self Point of Spiritual Knowing**

Figure 4–4: **Light Process During Meditation**

Figure 5–1: **Light Just After Meditation**

Original Condition   After 8 Months of Light Work

Figure 5–2: **Releasing Depression with Spiritual Energy**

Improving Personal Affairs

In the grand scheme of our evolution, Earth is a schoolhouse for spiritual learning. We are students here to learn the lessons this schoolhouse provides. Behind our day-to-day affairs and dealings with our fellow men lies the true purpose of these interactions—our spiritual growth. Earth then is the testing ground of our spiritual mettle; it's the divine laboratory where we develop and unfold our soul. With such a mission, every action takes on divine significance, however great or small it may be.

Our daily affairs also provide testing ground for the Divine Light, for it's here that we put the tools of spiritual light to work. As we have seen, Divine Light is the key to success in all earthly endeavors. To create any condition in our lives, we must have the energy for it already present in our aura. And if it isn't there, we must generate the spiritual power so that it becomes a part of us.

I have worked with some very famous and successful people in my life, and it was clear from looking at their auras that their success was no accident. Their talents were already a part of them—already in their aura. So, it was no freak of nature that Mozart was a master musician or that da Vinci was able to paint the *Mona Lisa*. In the same way, it wasn't the apple that fell on Newton's head that gave him the concept of gravity. The accomplishments of great men and women down through the ages were born of spiritual power, and the passion to use that power for the greater good.

In the aura, the nucleus of all our relationships and world affairs is the Hermetic Center. (When I say world affairs, I am referring to our *personal* world affairs.) This center is responsible for directing spiritual energies that power our outside activities. All of our worldly conditions are reflected in some way in this center. This means that our relationships, our job, our finances, and our personal and spiritual life all converge at this point. In this energetic flow, we're the center of our own world—not *the* world, but our *own* world.

To handle all the activities of life, the Hermetic Center has twelve built-in power rays, representing the twelve avenues of our world affairs. We must keep these flows moving smoothly if we want to produce in our lives what we have in our hearts and minds. Because the Hermetic Center has so much to do, it can easily become burdened to the point that the world seems too much for us; we feel helpless and insignificant in the midst of all this activity. In this state, the Hermetic Center can become obscured by clouds of dark light, making it hard to create much in our lives. It can feel like we're putting out fires most of the time. It's also much harder to feel compassion for others because the heart is "heavy" with too much negative energy.

As with the other centers, we must work extra hard to keep the Hermetic Center moving, clean and clear, even when there is turmoil around us. We will not always have control over what's happening in our lives, but we *will* have total control over how we react to and shape those conditions. People often make the big mistake of judging their lives in terms of what's happening to them, rather than by how they're handling the inevitable challenges. If we're facing a difficult situation with courage, fortitude, and humility, we're strengthening and brightening the colors of our character by our actions. And it's by those actions that we build up light.

So the first step in clearing this center is to stay in our own divine harmony and rhythm, and not take on the world's problems. It's very important that we take charge of this part of our aura. Notice that the Hermetic Center, in addition to being the nucleus of our world affairs, is also the seat of the soul. This is not accidental. For it's here that the soul registers and absorbs all of life's experiences and lessons to grow and mature.

Of course, we don't ignore the outside world. We should definitely pray and work for a better, happier world, but we must not claim any world condition as our own. If we're *of* the world, we're going to do what the world requires, and our primary allegiance will be to the world and not to God. Our first allegiance must be to God, not to man and his world. We live with man, but it is God Who created us, God Who sustains us, and God to Whom we shall one day return.

It's very easy to put our trust in our fellow man first, because we're so close to one another. If someone is my boss at work, it's very easy for me to see him or her as my source of income. If I offend that person in any way, I could lose my job, and therefore my income. I might very well wonder, "Where does God fit into this picture?"

From the spiritual point of view, my employer is the instrument through whom God's prosperity is made manifest to me. There's a big difference between being the *instrument* and the *source* of something. If I see God as my source and my boss as the instrument, my focus changes. I still respect my boss, but I know that if this channel were taken away for any reason, my spiritual supply would still be there. It would simply have to find another channel of expression.

Under close examination we see that our problems in life stem from mankind—not God. Sometimes we want to blame God for allowing things to happen or for not interceding, but still it's man who botches things up. So why should we rely on man for our answers when it is he who creates the problems to begin with? The fundamental law of spiritual life, the First Commandment, is: Serve God first. When we're serving God, we're also serving man as the expression of our love for God.

The key to a harmonious Hermetic Center is to make sure it is moving *clockwise*. You want all your centers to be moving clockwise, but this is especially true of the Hermetic Center. If you're not sure what clockwise is in relation to your Hermetic Center, review Step 3 of the Higher Self meditation (page 53). If this center is moving counterclockwise, something is "off" in your affairs, and, as a result, you are experiencing problems. There are countless disturbances that could throw your center counterclockwise; generally, however, it will be a crisis situation. Serious friction with your spouse, deep financial trouble, intentional wrongdoing—all could throw this center off. And if one aspect of your life is off, that counterclockwise momentum can extend to other aspects as well. For example, your career may be going great, but if you're having troubles at home and those troubles are not resolved, eventually they will affect your work life.

When this center is moving clockwise, the rays of light move out in a beautiful flow. Depending on the development of the individual, energetic radiations can extend well beyond the body. When the center is moving counterclockwise, the light doesn't radiate nearly so far. It's more restricted and generally looks jumbled. Of course, there will be darker hues of color as well.

If you're facing life's problems, your Hermetic Center will rotate clockwise, but you have to be *really working* on your problems! You can't just sit on the fence and hope that things will somehow work out. If you have a problem in your life, you must either resolve that problem or be earnestly working toward resolution to keep this center moving clockwise. This is God's way of keeping us involved and active—and turned toward the light. Otherwise, we might just sit on a mountaintop and do nothing about our lives, thinking our meditations and prayers can do it all. In my counseling work, if someone comes to me with a problem, but I see their Hermetic Center moving clockwise, I don't concern myself with it too much. I know that as long as the center stays clockwise, that person will be okay and things will work out, regardless of present appearances. But when I see counterclockwise movement, I know there is something urgent that the person must do, and that they better make it a top priority.

You can use the light to quicken this center and bring in more spiritual power. Begin with a general cleansing to help cut loose the tangled energies that can disrupt your spiritual flow and throw obstacles in your path. The light will also help to harmonize and organize your many activities.

Meditative Prayer for
Purifying the Hermetic Center

"Down-ray the orange-red flame of purification into my Hermetic Center, touching into persons, places, things, conditions and situations and conditions that constitute situations. Purify all my comings, goings, and doings, releasing me from all destructive energies and obstacles in my path. Dissolve all these black and gray atoms in the mineral kingdom, in the light."

This is a very effective meditative prayer that covers a wide range of activities. You can add anything specific to your prayer that you feel you need. Upon finishing with the purification, bring in the blue-white fire. Feel the life force touching into all areas of your world affairs, drawing in new, divine energy to give you a fresh outlook on life.

Meditative Prayer to Replenish the Hermetic Center

"Down-ray the blue-white fire of eternal life to charge and recharge all twelve avenues of my human Earth affairs, establishing new life force and creative energy in all aspects of my activities."

The emerald green ray is one of the most essential rays you can use in this center. Even though emerald green is already part of this point, you will be using this energy a great deal to keep all your activities in harmony.

Meditative Prayer to Balance the Hermetic Center

"Down-ray the emerald green ray to balance all twelve avenues of my human Earth affairs, establishing harmony and divine rhythm in all of my activities."

In addition to the emerald green ray, I also recommend using the white light to uplift and bring in the holy vibration to this center, as you can often feel disconnected as a result of so much earthly activity.

Meditative Prayer to Uplift the Hermetic Center

"Down-ray the pure white light to bring forth Thy divine radiance in every avenue of my world affairs, spiritually uplifting me into Thy divine consciousness and activity."

Sometimes situations come up quickly. Things may be humming along smoothly and suddenly something pops up that throws your life off-kilter. In these situations, I recommend starting with the deep purple energy to still your consciousness. Even if you haven't the time to call down any other ray, bringing in the peace ray will help soften the shock element so that you can think more clearly.

Meditative Prayer to Quiet the Hermetic Center

"Down-ray the deep purple ray of spiritual peace to touch deep into my heart levels, stilling any stress and shock and bringing me into the silence of peace and the peace of silence."

Building Prosperity

I would like to now focus on an avenue of the Hermetic Center that seems to be of constant concern to us—prosperity. We go through the greater part of our lives earning, saving, and spending money. Money facilitates so many of our daily activities that some see it as one of the basic operating principles of life. Although money does indeed occupy a central place, many of us understand so little of its spiritual operation. It's no wonder that we often have problems with finances in one form or another.

To understand how to work with spiritual energy to build both supply and a consciousness of supply, we'll need to look at the basic spiritual principles of abundance. Prosperity, by the way, is not limited only to finances. We can enjoy a wealth of ideas, rich friendships, and abundance in just about every avenue of expression, but here we'll focus on prosperity as it relates to our finances and money supply.

Where You Stand Is Your Prosperity

This is the first principle of supply. It means that all the prosperity you'll ever need is already with you. And since it's with you, you don't need to look outside yourself to generate prosperity. Prosperity is with you even if it's not showing itself in your outer world.

Following the spiritual point of view that all physical manifestations are the result of inner, spiritual causes, it follows that all physical expressions of wealth result from an inner spiritual root of prosperity. As with everything else in life, wealth and supply originate in the spiritual realms. By touching into your spiritual core, you're touching into the divine source of all supply. This places you in the midst of an unending fountain of supply. This supply can materialize in a variety of ways, but regardless of the channel of expression, be it a person or job, the true source of your prosperity is always the Divine within you. If you look to the outside world for your fortune, your success will be hit-or-miss, at best.

To activate this spiritual power of abundance, God gave you a special power ray. One of the twelve power rays of your human Earth affairs is the turquoise ray of supply. It's your own special connection to your reservoir of spiritual wealth. This power ray gives you the jump-start you need to actually move the prosperity principles into action. Without this ray, it would be hard to draw on spiritual power to create what you need. In other words, it's one thing to have the consciousness of supply and another to have enough power to actually manifest that wealth. You build your consciousness of supply in your mental center, but you manifest that supply through your Hermetic Center. If there's difficulty manifesting, it's most likely a problem in one center or the other.

This turquoise ray is with you always, whether you use it or not. You could be dying of starvation or be homeless, and this ray would still be with you. Again, it's a matter of using or not using the power that's already there. When I was a little girl in Minot, North Dakota, there was a woman who walked around town like a beggar, scraping for money. It turned out she had a mattress full of cash at home. On a less dramatic scale, this is what happens with most of us: though blessed with unlimited power and potential for wealth, we often choose to live as if we weren't.

How you handle prosperity is one of life's greatest challenges. Money is a form of energy. It represents your Earth power, and by mastering the art of Earth power, you are showing your capacity to handle greater divine powers. In the higher planes of existence, issues of abundance are not a concern. Whatever is needed is created directly and immediately by mind and desire. In order to develop this kind of consciousness, each of us must first work in the physical medium, until we can master the conditions that are now facing us.

What does it mean to master the lessons of prosperity? Does it mean accumulating a great sum of money, becoming a king or one of the wealthiest persons on Earth?

The goal of mastering prosperity is to reach the point where you know your supply is there for you whenever you need it. This knowing is not an idle affirmation that can waver at the first sign of adversity, but a steadfast inner knowing. Once you're "set" in that divine knowing, you can manifest what you need, when you need it. However, the demonstration of that divine knowing won't always assume the form of great wealth. Becoming the richest man or woman on Earth doesn't mean you have mastered the art of prosperity. A surprising number of extremely wealthy people live in a constant state of fear that their money isn't enough, or will be taken away from them somehow. This is not a demonstration of the divine consciousness of wealth.

When you are in your true wealth, it won't matter how much you have, because you will be in direct connection with the very source of abundance. If you desire to generate supply, you will.

Give to Receive

This second great principle is best expressed in the adage, "The more you give, the more you receive." Notice the word *more*. The more you give, the MORE you receive. Not the *same* you receive, commensurate with your giving, but the *more* you receive! The spiritual principles of prosperity dictate that if you give a dollar, *two* dollars, in some form, will come back to you. When you send the energy out initially, not only do you create the conditions for its return, you create the conditions for its return *multiplied*. This is one of the great laws of the universe and may be seen operating at every level of life. By lending a hand, in some way you will be offered *two* hands to help you when you need them. This principle of spiritual multiplication is part of the ascension principle in your spiritual evolution and light work as well. As you climb the ladder of life, not only does your light expand, it expands exponentially.

Most people have trained themselves to think in reverse. They try to collect as much as they can. They hoard money and then give it out with great reluctance. There may be fear connected with money. When money gets short, what do you tend to do? You hold your money back, right? The tendency is to withdraw out of fear of losing what little you have. But this has the opposite effect of what you want. By holding so tightly, you're actually "strangling" your consciousness of supply and ensuring less for yourself. Now, I'm not saying to spend money recklessly. If funds appear low, sure you might have to cut back on expenses, but you must still keep the principle of giving very much alive.

Start by being generous. Open your heart. If someone asks for help, give it. Don't judge that person's merit, or do it begrudgingly. Give with your heart. The gift without the giver is barren.

You are the Steward of God's Supply

This principle is most often overlooked. It simply states that you are the channel—and not the owner—of God's abundance and supply. Most people like to think in terms of things being *theirs*. They live in their own houses, drive their own cars, and have their own bank accounts, their own families, and so on. In truth, they are the stewards of all these things. There's nothing in this world that belongs to you. All that you appear to possess is a result of a spiritual root that was alive long before it showed up in your life. It's by your alignment with the spiritual laws of life that you may enjoy your things and circumstances.

This knowledge can relieve you of much stress in relation to money. First, it takes some of the responsibility off your shoulders. As long as you're following the laws of supply, you can leave the rest to God. Did not the Christ say, "Take no thought for the morrow"? (Matt. 6:34) Or, as has been more accurately translated, "Take no *anxious* thought for the morrow." Being a steward of money rather than its owner releases you of possessiveness. It makes you aware that, as a steward, some of your money is obviously meant to go to others; it was brought into your life for just that purpose. Many times that's how God can reach those people—through you.

Poverty Consciousness

Before getting into the meditative work, let's look at what stops us from being in this wonderful awareness of wealth to begin with. In two words—poverty consciousness.

Poverty consciousness is the mental conditioning wherein we accept a negative, physical perception of a seeming lack as real. Poverty consciousness is so pervasive and automatic that we don't realize how often we actually talk ourselves out of abundance. For example, if your bank account has a balance of two cents, it would be natural for you to say you have no money. This negative affirmation would then begin a whole domino-like chain reaction, because you've accepted this condition as real, when in truth, you are seeing things as they physically appear and not as they are spiritually. Regardless of your physical situation, spiritually your wealth is unlimited and unchanged. The only reason you're experiencing a sense of lack is that somewhere there has been a disruption in your spiritual connection that you now must correct. Once that connection is reestablished, the condition will work itself out.

When you are in poverty consciousness, you'll feel like there's never enough money. You'll be thinking in terms of how limited your funds are, that you don't have enough to do the things you want. And you will think all these conditions are permanent, or at least stubborn, and difficult to change. Maybe the bills are stacking up with no apparent money to pay them. Maybe your clothes are a bit dated, or your home needs repairs, or your car is on its last legs. These are strong images, and if they're around you all the time, it's easy for you to let them make a deep impression on you.

Poverty consciousness, by the way, is not limited to "poor" people. Wealthy people can entertain feelings of lack and limitation just as easily. These people may be worth millions but still worry about money. I knew a man who founded a multimillion-dollar company, yet still lived in the simple house he grew up in. He even kept the same rotary phones he had when he started the business! Why didn't he enjoy his wealth? Because he still saw himself as the struggling young man with little money, even though he had long passed that point. Proverbs 13:7 says it best: "There is one who makes himself rich yet has nothing; and one who makes himself poor, yet has great riches."

This mental conditioning of poverty can come from a variety of sources. It may be that you grew up in a family with little money. Perhaps every day was a financial struggle for you, and you came to accept that as a normal fact of your life. You may have associated with other poverty thinkers who influenced and reinforced your thinking. Or, it may simply be your own mental tendency to think in terms of "never enough." There are many outside influences that encourage the consciousness of lack and limitation.

When you accept poverty, you have poverty. It's as simple as that. Be alert and reject thoughts of poverty as soon as they come to your awareness. Poverty consciousness, if allowed to grow, will have a paralyzing effect on your life. It creates low self-esteem and a feeling of futility that will stop you from going for the things you want in life. In addition, it creates a host of other negative emotions, including anxiety, fear, worry, and desperation. The longer you stay in such a consciousness, the more you will think that the condition is permanent.

There is a famous story about two brothers, both born into poverty. They were separated while still young. One went on to become a successful businessman while the other continued to be plagued by financial troubles. Now why did one brother rise above his situation while the other didn't? The brother who succeeded *believed* he could rise above his conditions, while the brother who struggled *accepted* his poverty condition.

Poverty Being Holy

One of the false conceptions of how money works comes from a deeply entrenched notion of poverty being holy. Many spiritually-minded people have adopted the idea that having money somehow inhibits their spiritual growth and have thus chosen to do without money or earthly luxuries in order to be spiritual. Many spiritual philosophies and anecdotes appear to support this idea. There's the familiar Bible misquote: "Money is the root of all evil" (1 Tim. 6:10). The actual words are, *"Love* of money is the root of all evil." Jesus spoke of how it was easier for "a camel to go through the eye of a needle than for a rich man to enter into the kingdom of God" (Matt. 19:24). There are even some religious sects in India that believe having furniture is a sign of decadence and moral corruption!

Metaphysically speaking, there is nothing inherently evil or wrong with having money. Quite the opposite is true. Money is a form of energy like everything else, and being in the flow of prosperity is sharing in God's light and power. If God is infinite wealth, why wouldn't He want you, as His beloved child, to partake of that divine wealth? You're meant to partake of all God's blessings, and prosperity is one of those blessings.

Where the confusion sets in is when you worship money as an end in itself. *Worshipping* money is an evil that will eventually bring spiritual and/or financial bankruptcy. If you make a false god of money, you are sure to have trouble. It's not that a rich man cannot enter the kingdom of God, but rather that a man who is *attached* to his possessions will not be able to enter the divine kingdom until he learns to let go of material attachments. If you worship possessions of any kind, it's much harder for you to come in to your spiritual consciousness because your mind is constantly on material things. You need to reverse your priorities and worship the spiritual life. Then your prosperity will flow, but it will be in balance with other aspects of your life.

There's a wonderful story about a young Indian boy who left home to search for the guru who would teach him the mysteries of life. He looked in many places but couldn't find his spiritual teacher. One day, he had come to a palace to ask for some water. As he was leaving, he heard a voice inside the palace asking, "Where are you going, little boy?"

The boy looked inside and saw the owner of the palace coming out. He looked like a rajah and was dressed in the finest clothes and jewelry. "I stopped for some water and must leave to find my guru," was the boy's response.

"What makes you think you haven't found him?"

The boy looked at the man in his fine raiment. "You? No, you can't be him. You're too rich. What do you know of spiritual things?"

"Why don't you come in and stay for a while. If you don't think I have something to teach you, you can go on your way."

The boy agreed, and the master of the house started teaching the boy many things. He was impressed, but still could only see the man's wealth and couldn't imagine how a man with so many material things could be so spiritual.

One day, as the master was teaching, a servant ran into the room crying, "The palace is on fire!"

The master didn't move an inch and simply replied, "Don't bother me, I'm busy."

A few moments later, the servant came up again yelling, "But Master, the fire is growing and coming up the stairs now!"

Again the master said, "Can't you see that I'm busy? Please, leave me alone."

Finally, the servant came again, beseeching the master, "Master, the fire's coming down the hall! You must do something or the palace will be lost!"

The man still did not move, but the boy, hearing such news, picked up his books and started running for the door. Suddenly, the master said, "Aha! I was willing to lose my whole palace and perhaps my life, and you were worried about your three little books."

So you are the one who passes judgment about what is spiritual and what is not. Clearly, in this apocryphal story, the guru was not interested in threatening the boy's life or boasting of his own spiritual development. He was using this situation to provoke the chela to help him break the illusionary picture the boy had regarding wealth and spirituality. This story also demonstrates that not only can a misapprehension of prosperity block the flow of prosperity, it can actually hinder spiritual development as well.

God is not interested in making you suffer. After all, the Creator knew very well when He made the world that you needed material things. Even the great Buddha, when he was searching for enlightenment, was said to have tried at one point to deny himself every physical dependency and live on one grain of rice a day, only to learn that this was not the way to enlightenment. This experience helped him to choose instead what he termed "the middle way" to spiritual maturity.

For every Mother Teresa who chooses to give up worldly possessions, there is also a King Solomon who is both spiritual *and* wealthy. It all depends on the soul's particular lesson or mission.

Tapping into the Turquoise Ray

In working with spiritual energy to build prosperity, you want to first clear misconceptions from your mind because poverty consciousness starts on the mental level. The orange-red flame is wonderful at clearing away these invasive weeds. Again, include the four main centers in your spiritual cleansing.

Meditative Prayer for
Releasing Poverty Consciousness

"Down-ray the orange-red flame of purification to cut loose all sense of lack and limitation, especially in my mental body, cleansing me of poverty consciousness wherever it is lodged in my being."

Feel those unenlightened thoughts dropping away from you. You will be surprised at how much you've been holding onto that needs releasing. You might find that you resist this process. Chances are, you've built a strong image of whatever your condition is, and it's not so easy to just let it go. In this case, pace yourself. Follow this meditative sequence to the degree to which you feel comfortable. Later on, you can repeat the entire process as often as you feel the need.

After you finish using the orange-red flame, bring in the blue-white fire to help establish new positive flows of Divine Light.

Meditative Prayer for
Replenishing the Consciousness

"Down-ray the blue-white fire of eternal life to charge and recharge all levels of my being, bringing me new life force."

Once you have replenished yourself, you're ready to build up your aura with the turquoise ray. This is a marvelous energy, one you can never use enough when building your prosperity. You may work with all the centers, but there is special emphasis on the Hermetic Center when working with this energy. As you bring it down, you want to get into the feeling and knowing of this divine flow of supply. Envision yourself as a mighty monarch who can buy anything.

Meditative Prayer for Prosperity

"Down-ray the turquoise ray of abundance and supply into my Hermetic Center, quickening all twelve avenues of my world affairs, and establishing this Thy prosperity in my human Earth affairs."

Sense and feel the activation of this center. If you like, you can add a short visualization to fully establish this energy in your aura. If you have seven cents in your bank account, see seven hundred dollars in your bank account. See this ray touching into your money supply and quickening in this light. See all your sources of income receiving a quickening with this spiritual flow. Ask that the light "Multiply and increase *this Thy money.*" And hold to the knowing that this is actually happening for you.

To finish your work, add the silver ray to quicken the turquoise and help manifest prosperity faster.

Meditative Prayer for Quickening the Prosperity Flow

"Down-ray the silver ray of divine intelligence into my Hermetic Center, quickening this Thy prosperity."

Once this power is established in you, give thanks, then let it go from your consciousness. Trust that the energy is in motion. Feel that power attracting the things you need. If you find yourself falling back into worry patterns, repeat the light work. You can do this three times in one day to get the energy moving and really make the connection. Of course, you can complement this work with any other light work you feel you need to strengthen this spiritual abundance.

Once you feel the energy is there for you, focus on the goals you want to achieve, the things you want to create, knowing that financial resources will be available as you need them. Visualizations are a great help at this point to create the conditions you want (Chapter 13).

Career

Most people probably spend more time at their jobs than any other single pursuit. In many professions, the forty-hour week has turned into the fifty-, sixty-, and even seventy-hour week. That's a lot of time to be focusing on any single activity. Because your career forms such a big chunk of your life, you want to be sure the time you're spending at it is time well spent. Directing the light into your career can help alleviate stress, create harmony in the workplace, remove stumbling blocks, and move your profession in the right direction.

The dictionary defines career as "a chosen pursuit." It comes from an old French word for racecourse. In staking your claim in the work world, a career can certainly feel like running a race, or, as some call it, a "rat race." The first thing to recognize when doing spiritual energy work is that your career is not an identity; it's an activity. It's not you. You are a divine spiritual being in the process of unfolding your spiritual powers. To do this, part of your purpose is to express yourself in focused activities that strengthen your abilities. That's the spiritual purpose of a career. Your job is an important part of your life, but you are not your job. If you identify with what you do rather than who you are, you will always be at the mercy of that activity. And there will inevitably come a day of reckoning, because no pursuit can satisfy all your needs.

A common misunderstanding about a career is that it must be money-producing. A "chosen pursuit" can mean anything that you diligently focus your attention on. It's come to be associated with a chosen profession, but any serious pursuit is a career. Motherhood, which has been so devalued in recent years, is not a job that brings in money, but is one of the most challenging and important careers a person can undertake. It's unquestionably a career in the best sense of the word, even though it's not a salary-generating profession.

Your chosen pursuit is strongly connected with your purpose in life. If Earth is a spiritual schoolhouse for the soul, then a career is one of the most important "courses" you'll be taking while attending this earthly school. Like any other aspect of your human Earth affairs, your career is a spiritual activity designed to help your soul grow. You may be here to develop your creative side, in which case you'll be attracted to artistic careers. Or it may be that you need to develop your social skills, in which case you will choose a profession where you'll interact with a lot of people, such as in business or the social sciences.

A positive attitude is probably the most important prerequisite to pursuing a career. There must be joy in work because work without joy is drudgery. You need to create joy even if it's not your ideal work. Of course, you should strive with all your heart for what you want, but in the course of reaching that goal, you may have to do work that is less than ideal. So attitude is everything. When there is joy and love in what you do, it's not work at all.

Many people do not have a good attitude toward their work. In focusing the spiritual light on your career, you must have a positive attitude about the work you're doing. From the spiritual point of view, no honest work is low or base. All work is valid and worthy in God's eyes. There is a story about Saint Francis of Assisi being confronted about work ethics. Saint Francis was sweeping a walkway to a church. It was a simple task, but he did it as if it were of great importance. A person came up to him wondering why he didn't assign that menial job to one of the monks in his order. When the man didn't get the response he wanted from Saint Francis, he tried to provoke him by asking what he'd do if he found out he was going to die in an hour. Saint Francis calmly replied, "I'd finish sweeping."

The way to maintain joy in your work life is to enjoy the process without being attached to results. This is work for its own sake more than for the rewards you may reap. Which doesn't mean you don't pay attention and strive to reach the career goals you've set; it simply means that you don't identify those goals as your primary motivation. You are not always in control of how things turn out. If a job doesn't work out the way you'd envisioned, you might feel like a failure and believe that your time was wasted. But if you put your heart into the process of work and recognized that your spiritual growth was in the journey itself as much as in the destination, then you'd know that no time was wasted at all. What appeared to be failure would contribute to success in the next try, and the one after that. The Bhagavad-Gita puts it well: "To work alone thou hast the right, but never to the fruits thereof."

The avenue of your world affairs that relates to career is the ray of pure white light. This ray quickens you to help manifest things in your career such as position, advancement, finding a new job, etc. Again, without this ray you might have the thought or desire to do something, but there would be very little power to actually manifest those dreams. This ray works automatically for you. By your actions, you're drawing on this power ray to facilitate your pursuits. If you lost your job or are looking for a job, this Hermetic ray will help you to generate that new job.

When someone is at full throttle in her career, happy and productive, the Hermetic Center will be very bright. It will be moving in a strong clockwise motion and will show active emanations of gold, red, and orange energies radiating from the center at least a foot in all directions. The white ray within the Hermetic Center will be very strong and pronounced.

The basic power rays you'll need to work with in strengthening your job situation are the gold, white, and silver. These energies help to open up the spiritual flow in this center. Of course, if there are mental and emotional problems, those concerns should be dealt with, too. Let's look at some specific job situations and how to work with the light in these situations.

Choosing a Profession

It's interesting how some people know exactly what they want to do in life while others are not so sure. For the ones who know what they want, there are few questions concerning which direction to take. However, for a great many people, deciding what to do is not such a straightforward matter. Fortunately, taking your cues from the aura is a wonderful way to discover exactly where your strengths lie, and what they suggest in terms of a lifetime pursuit. Natural abilities show up very clearly in the aura. With this kind of guidance, you can know very definitely which career would be most rewarding for you. This is a great blessing! Just imagine: a child who has pronounced musical ability would be encouraged to pursue a career in music rather than something else; someone who is very focused, with a sharp, analytical mind, would be assured that they had what it takes to become a very good scientist. In this way, "barking up the wrong trees"—whether of imagined abilities, parental expectations, or of immediate pragmatic returns—could be easily avoided.

For tuning in to the kind of career you are meant to pursue, you need to work with divine guidance and right direction (Chapter 10). We must remember that when it comes to something as important as career, there is a definite spiritual plan for each of us. Recognizing our true calling is a matter of tuning into that purpose. The reason some people are so clear about what they want is that they are in touch with their spiritual purpose. So, if you are unclear about your goals, it's time to get to work on releasing mental blocks and confusion, and opening up to inspiration and illumination.

The first thing you want to do is a thorough cleansing to release mental confusion and stress that may be blocking the clear picture of what you're meant to do. Once that clearing is done, the two key rays to work with are the gold and silver energies. The gold will help bring in the illumination to get a clear picture of the direction you should take. You can work with this ray from the Higher Self Point, as outlined in Chapter 10, or by using the following meditative prayer. This prayer will help steady your thinking and connect you with the inspiration that's always there for you. First, ask the golden ray to touch into your Higher Self Point. Then see that energy going into your mental body, quickening it with the light so that you connect with the guidance given.

Meditative Prayer with the Gold Light to Find a Profession

"Down-ray the golden ray of wisdom light into my Higher Self Point of Spiritual Knowing, to receive guidance and direction in finding my chosen profession." (Hold for a moment to feel the connection being made.) "I ask that this light down-ray to my mental body to connect me with the guidance being given so that I may envision what my true profession is."

After your meditation, hold to the knowing that your right work is forthcoming. As with all types of guidance, the answers may or may not be given to you at that moment. Either way, you have begun generating the power to manifest the work you are meant to do. Continue with whatever job search you are on, but try to feel which way the light is directing you. Generally, you will sense the light moving more strongly in one career direction than another. This is God's way of inspiring you to your right occupation and livelihood.

In addition to the gold, I recommend adding the silver ray to quicken your mental body so that you are receptive to spiritual inspiration and illumination.

Meditative Prayer with the Silver Ray to Find My Chosen Profession

"Down-ray the silver ray of divine intelligence to quicken my mental body to perceive and better comprehend the divine inspiration of my true profession being given to me."

Generating a New Job

If you're already clear about what you want to do, and you are looking for a specific kind of job, you can work precisely with the light to help you create the job you envision.

The key to generating a new job is to first get that energy moving for you on the spiritual level. Remember, everything that manifests physically was first created on the spiritual plane. So by building the light for your new job in the spiritual dimension first, you are taking the first step in creating that job on the physical plane.

Both the gold and white rays are helpful in generating a profession. The golden ray of wisdom light has the ability to quicken your Hermetic Center and open your path. Sometimes, you can be right for something, but there is outside interference. The golden light gives you extra power to break through any dissenting energy and open up the right path for you. Gold can also give you stamina when you may feel like giving up the fight.

Get in your Higher Self Point and use the gold to especially touch into your Hermetic Center.

Meditative Prayer with the
Gold Light to Generate New Work

"Down-ray the golden ray of wisdom light to touch into my Hermetic Center and generate new avenues of work, cutting through any negative blocks and giving me the inner strength and divine power to pursue my path and open up the job that's right for me."

Next, work with the pure white light. This ray will help to open the actual flow of whatever job you're seeking, thereby helping you to connect with it. Sometimes, you can be a little out-of-tune with the job you seek. It may be what you want and are good at, but you're just not clicking with the marketplace you're trying to enter. The pure white light can help you synchronize with the work you are seeking. It can also help to release internal blocks. However, if you notice a lot of internal strife, work on clearing that energy separately from this work. Again, work primarily with the Hermetic Center, but you can ask the light to touch into all the centers if you wish.

Meditative Prayer with the
White Light to Find New Work

"Down-ray the pure white light into my Hermetic Center, activating it in a clockwise motion to quicken all my human Earth affairs, helping me to tune in and open up to the work that's right for me, and giving me the vision to recognize that work when I see it."

You may add the silver ray here as well, asking that your new job open up quickly.

Meditative Prayer to Generate a New Job Quickly

"Down-ray the silver ray of divine intelligence directly into my Hermetic Center and out-ray into my human Earth affairs to bring forth my new job quickly, according to Divine Law and Love for the good of all concerned."

Once your light work is done, you need to trust that the light will do the job you've asked it to do. Conclude with the following prayer:

"I hold to the knowing that the work I love is forthcoming. So be it."

Dead-end Jobs

When I was still in college, I had many plans for my future. Financial troubles at home forced me to postpone my dreams and take up temp work to make ends meet. I was despondent, thinking I'd never do the things I really wanted to do in life. I went to ask the advice of well-known spiritual teacher and philosopher, Manly Hall. One of his many inspiring aphorisms was, "The universe always has work for those who are qualified to perform it." I respected his work and could see by his aura that he was a spiritually advanced soul. I started to pour my heart out, telling him all that was going on with me. I kept telling him, "I have all these obstacles." He stopped me at one point and simply said, "What obstacles?" That stopped me dead in my tracks. I recognized then that he was right. I was allowing all these immediate concerns to obscure my long-term goals. If I saw them as obstacles, I'd never get past them and on the road to what I wanted. Well, I did go through some tough times, but sure enough—things did eventually open up for me.

If you are in a dead-end job, the first thing to do is acknowledge that you need to make a change. You have to make an effort. This will take courage, but there is no other way. You need to get back to what it is you want in life and not let the momentary necessities cloud your vision.

When you're doing work that you know is not your calling, it can feel frustrating. Yet, here is where you have to apply the principle of spiritual joy in the workplace. The fact is, it only feels frustrating when you feel it's getting in the way of your true vocation. There are many times in life when you have to do things that are not to your liking, but there's always a lesson to be learned in these experiences. They only become stifling when you do nothing about changing these conditions. No matter what the job, you still need a positive attitude and must respect the work at hand; but at the same time, you need to make time to pursue your dreams. Then these present job experiences will not seem so frustrating or permanent.

You want to work with the gold to help create the courage needed to break the cycle you're in and to begin generating the job you need. Again, if there are emotional or mental blocks, you'll need to work on those separately. Also, work with the love ray if you're being too hard on yourself.

Meditative Prayer for Courage in Finding Work

"Down-ray the golden ray of wisdom light into my Hermetic Center and out-ray into my human Earth affairs to dispel any negative work patterns and to give me the courage and dynamic power to pursue the work I love."

Once you get the light working for you, you can either follow the procedure for generating a new job or for finding your chosen field.

Unhappy at Work

I have counseled many people who have good jobs but still are unhappy at what they do. They are unhappy because of friction with other people, or because they simply are not enamored with their work. The problem of friction is easier to resolve, because the difficult relationships will either improve, or the person will find a similar job elsewhere. Being disenchanted with the work itself is the stickier problem. I have found that many people who are unhappy with their work are not really suited for their jobs, and chose that line of work for the wrong reasons.

Too many people choose a career solely for the money. As we know, there are doctors who practice medicine not because they love the healing arts, but because the pay is good, the prestige high. A tremendous amount of dedicated work and responsibility go into being a doctor. Anyone whose main motivation is money soon discovers that he or she has paid a steep price for doing something without love. People also pick jobs because they appear glamorous. Or they may choose to enter a profession because others have influenced their decision. A father may want his son or daughter to follow in his footsteps, despite the child's wishes to the contrary. Too often that son or daughter complies out of love, or for fear of disappointing the parents. What inevitably follows is rebellion, a lifetime of "quiet desperation," or, with grace, an awakening and shift to their true calling.

Review your inventory list and see if you picked up on anything about your work by direct observation. If not, you need to do some reflecting to gain some insight into what, if anything, about your job is bothering you. Don't over-analyze the situation; just try to get a feeling for both the work itself and the conditions at work.

Until you've identified what's bothering you, it's hard to know exactly which power rays to work with. If the situation turns out to be more a people problem, turn to the chapter on relationships to see how to work with the light in professional environments. If the condition results from dislike of the actual work, then you need to call upon the gold and white, as you would to get out of a dead-end job. Even if you're in a high-paying job, if it's not for you, that job's not going to help you much in your spiritual growth. You'll need courage and vision to branch out in new directions. If you're not yet doing what you love, know that it is waiting for you somewhere else.

Another reason people are unhappy at work is that more and more jobs are becoming all-consuming. It seems that any job worth its salt these days demands ten to twelve hours a day, or even more. Many people really love what they do but still become miserable at their work and eventually "burn out" because the stress is just too much. Such demands put enormous pressure on your personal life—and what are you really gaining? By working so intensely, it's very easy to fall out of the spiritual rhythm of life. And when you're out of rhythm, anything can happen.

Watch out for jobs that demand too much of you. If you're already in such a job, work with the emerald green ray of balance to keep harmony. But you can't go on like that forever. No one can put in sixty- to eighty-hour workweeks for very long without paying a price.

To help relieve stress, don't carry your job home with you. Give it your best effort at work, and then cut loose when you go home. Change the pace. Many people don't take good care of themselves and carry their work with them all the time. Then they wonder why they're having health problems somewhere down the line. Release your mind, especially in bed at night. Don't let your last thoughts before going to sleep be stressful ones about work.

Getting Fired

There's certainly a strong element of shock in getting fired. If you are fired—for whatever reason—you'll want to work with the peace ray to release that shock. You'll also need to do some mental/emotional work with the emerald green, because once the shock has worn off, there's bound to be some sort of reaction such as anger, resentment, or depression. It's also easy for you to start feeling sorry for yourself and fall into a state of self-pity. This is the time to work things out. Don't give yourself time to sulk. Why did you get fired? If it was politics, then you know it was not about you. If you were fired because of something you did or didn't do, then you must take responsibility. Don't beat yourself over the head or feel humiliated; instead, find out where the problem is and fix it—so it will never happen again!

Here are two meditations to help you overcome the shock of losing your job and to help maintain your spiritual equilibrium.

Meditative Prayer to Overcome Shock

"Down-ray the purple ray of spiritual peace to touch into all levels of my consciousness, releasing me from all shock, and establishing the silence of peace and the peace of silence throughout my entire being."

Follow up with the emerald green to help keep things in perspective.

Meditative Prayer for Spiritual Balance

"Down-ray the emerald green ray to all levels of my being to balance my entire consciousness so that my thinking is clear and my actions are moving in divine rhythm and order."

Strengthening Relationships

Spiritual energy has a beneficial effect on all types of human relationships. The light helps dispel discord, clarify misunderstanding, and keep relationships moving harmoniously. It can also help to draw the right people to one another. Working with the light won't necessarily resolve every dilemma, but what it will do, if we are diligent, is help to resolve our part in that dilemma. Most of all, the light gives us the power to see other people beyond their human-personality self and in their true, divine self.

Applying spiritual energy will have different effects on relationships, all of which will be productive, but not always easy to act upon. Once the light has revealed the true nature of a relationship, that revelation will either serve to bring the people closer together, change the dynamics, or sometimes guide them in different directions altogether. I've had students who were surrounded by all the wrong people; once the light was really moving, they dropped these so-called friends—who were really only holding them back. Other times, the light will challenge relationships. As we are developing our spiritual powers, others may not understand our inclinations and behavior. They may want the "old" us, with all our faults and frailties, because that's the person they know and understand. Relationships test our character to begin with, and the added power of the light makes this testing all the more challenging. We will inevitably discover faults and weaknesses in ourselves that are affecting others, and we'll have to be forgiving and patient with ourselves as we go about correcting them.

Human & Divine Love

The primary element in any relationship is love. Without love, no relationship can work beneficently. Love connects us to each other, to creation, and to God. When dealing with others, we're going to work with the deep rose-pink energy, which is the love ray. I don't think there's such a thing as getting too much of this loving energy.

Love comes in many forms. Regardless of the expression, if love is real it emanates from the same spiritual source. The highest expression of love is Divine Love. Along with Divine Mind, Divine Love is the most powerful primary force in the universe. It emanates directly from the heart of God. Divine Love is the bond that holds all creation together. It's the heartbeat of life itself. Without this love, there'd be no purpose to life, no desire to create or act on anything. There'd still be Divine Mind, but no reason to express it. An act of Divine Love created each of us. God's love is what carries us through the trials and tribulations of our pilgrimage through creation and back to God.

The expression of spiritual love through each of us can be described as pure and unconditional when we love without thought of return. We see this love when people put others before themselves or risk their lives for others. This high love leads to the ultimate universal love in which we love all of creation unconditionally. Divine Love embodies all the attributes of the spiritual life such as gentleness, kindness, understanding, and compassion. There's a tremendous exhilaration and upliftment that accompanies such celestial love. Best of all, Divine Love is eternal. It's always there for us; it will never disappoint or let us down.

Human love is also spiritual, but is graded down to the physical level. This love is more restrictive. Human love desires things of this world. I may love having a big house, my fast car, the money I make at my job, the way my spouse looks, or the things he or she does for me. These are all more or less physical things—with limitations. There's nothing wrong with loving such things, but we must remember they are temporary, and will one day be gone.

Human love tends to be conditional, which makes it selfish. A person who loves on a human level will love what he or she is getting from the other person. If the quality or thing that the loved one is getting is diminished or taken away, then the love fades.

The goal of all our relationships is to transform them into acts of *Divine Love.* As part of our soul development, we're in the process of first developing our human love experience and then transforming that human love into Divine Love. When we can give love before getting love, without thought of payback, we've made strong strides toward that spiritual love state. To do this, we must first build the God Love within us. Loving God and putting that love into action accomplishes this. What did Jesus say? "Love God with all your heart and mind, and your neighbor as yourself." By loving God, we're reciprocating the love that God has for us. We're loving the power that fashioned and sustains us. We're loving the truest and best part of ourselves. By loving God first, we're automatically serving our fellow beings.

Sometimes, it's the most demanding things asked of us in relationship that can be the very key to our spiritual transformation. There is the story of a famous author who fathered a mentally handicapped son. The condition left the boy totally dependent on his parents to take care of almost all his physical functions. The father was a proud person, and was humiliated and embarrassed by his son's condition. He hated the boy, calling him his "little monster."

When the boy was several years old, it became evident that the child had a gift for music despite his handicap. This awakened something in the father. He realized that his son was not a "little monster" at all, and that there was a soul inside trying to express itself. The father's attitude completely changed. He realized that the issue was not his son's handicap but his own pride. He came to love the boy and dedicated himself to helping him in every way he could. It turned out that the boy grew up to become a famous pianist, more famous than his father. Yet, the son continued to need physical help for even the most basic things, like shaving, but his father was always there for him. This man showed a great spiritual transformation, from severe disappointment and ignorance to selfless love. His trial was a great opportunity to learn the spiritual lessons of love. We must look for and recognize these opportunities when they come up.

We're here to learn the lessons of life—and to learn them from one another. Once we learn how to love one another regardless of our imperfections, then we're showing our capacity to love the Divine. As the Bible says, "for he that loveth not his brother whom he hath seen, how can he love God whom he hath not seen?" (1 John 4:20) We can't be very close to loving God if we're at war with our fellow man. All problems in relationships stem from a lack of love shown in one way or another. So many people say they love, but do they really?

Most of us know how important love is. We can understand the principles of Divine Love in the abstract, but sometimes it seems so hard to actually apply these principles to real-life situations. Wise souls have been professing spiritual love for centuries. So why is it so difficult to put into action? Why isn't the world a more loving place?

Our nemesis is our own human ego—the petty ego, the puffed-up little "i" that keeps getting in the way of our natural love flow. Our human nature likes to hold onto its jealousies, angers, and hatreds, even though these are the very bonds that hold us back and make us suffer. In our petty self, we can't see beyond the immediate narrow field of whatever is happening in our lives. We're afraid to venture out beyond the familiar. Even though it's our nature to love, we get in the way of our own expression of that love when we allow the imperfections of our human ego to take control of our lives.

Love is an essential element to our auras. One of the first things I look for in reading auras is how the love energy is moving. This can quickly reveal the status and direction of a person's spiritual development. The primary energy to look for is deep rose-pink. I most often see this energy as a band of pink light around the perimeter of the aura, which shows a loving nature. The deep rose-pink energy is particularly tailored to the needs of our interactions with other people.

Most of us have some deep rose-pink in our auras, indicating that we have some of that spiritual love already, and are expressing it in some way. We may not recognize it as spiritual, but it is. What generally happens, though, is that we taint this love with our own selfish wants. I may love someone genuinely, but at the same time I may be very selfish in my love. I love what that person is doing for me, or giving me; I love the way that person makes me feel about myself. So, I will attract deep rose-pink, but it is mixed with some cocoa brown, which expresses my selfishness. Or I may be possessive in my love, which mixes the pink with avocado green. I may be lustful in my love, which adds vitiated red to the pink.

Much more rare to see is the high divine, selfless love. With this celestial love, a light pale pink and violet will accompany the deep rose-pink seen above the head. This is the love that expresses when people think of someone else's interest above their own. This high pink energy usually comes and goes in most people. It's very hard to sustain such an energy unless you're living a life of selfless service.

The avenue of our world affairs that deals with human relationships is, appropriately, the pink ray. This ray is our avenue of spiritual love here on Earth. It connects us to the celestial love and opens our feeling nature. Without this ray, we would be cold, heartless beings. This ray is for love in every sparkling facet: love of people, art, music, animals, nature, etc. Like the other rays of our human Earth affairs, this ray cannot be destroyed or disappear no matter what we do, but it can become inactive if we are set on closing our hearts. The deepest place in our aura that love registers is in our Hermetic Center, because this is where desires are born—in the soul. Fortunately, this ray within the Hermetic is active in most people; you can see it expressed in everyday acts of love, large and small.

You can work with the love flow directly to increase your spiritual capacity for love. Begin working with the deep rose-pink at all levels of your being. See it going into the four main centers, especially your heart center, and into your soul levels. You can follow the meditative prayer in Chapter 5 on love, or use the following meditative prayer.

Meditative Prayer to Increase Your Divine Love Flow

"Down-ray the deep rose-pink of spiritual love into all levels of my consciousness, igniting my spiritual centers with this Divine Light and especially touching into my Hermetic Center and soul levels to release any old hurts and soul wounds, and to uplift me into the divine ecstasy of Thy infinite love and everlasting embrace."

Auric Interactions

The greatest outside effect upon our aura is its interaction with other auras. Without knowing it, we can open ourselves to many influences from people—with a very definite effect on auric flow. Contact with other people's energies is a natural occurrence because we are constantly interacting with others.

As we work with the light, our aim is to draw less from others and more from our own reservoir of light. This serves several purposes. First, it begins to build our divine connection and helps us to tap into a source that we know is always pure. When we tap into the Higher, we can't get anything less than the highest spiritual energy. Second, it helps us to be less dependent on others because we are connected to that Greater Source. Third, it helps to keep our auric interactions moving on a positive, high level and prevents us from exchanging negative energy.

Most auric energy interactions occur within the energy centers themselves. Since these centers are receiving and transmitting stations, it makes sense that they play such a role in the exchange of energy. The aura itself can and does intermingle, but there is no actual exchange of energy within the aura as there is in the centers. Here is an example of how auras interact.

Two People Fighting (Figure 9–1)

In this scenario, Person A has started an argument with Person B. Vitiated red energy shoots from the emotional center of Person A to Person B. If B accepts this negative energy, which has happened in this case, then it will immediately hit B in the emotional center. Person B has now become incensed, and reacts with anger to Person A, sending a vitiated red energy back to A's emotional center, thereby accelerating the argument. At this point, the fight turns into a screaming match as the energies escalate into an emotional Vesuvius. As angry thoughts and barbed words fly back and forth, energy moves from the emotional to the mental centers, destabilizing the thinking levels and further inflaming the destructive exchange. This is a fairly typical example of a full-blown fight.

Refusing an Angry Outburst (Figure 9–2)

In this example, Person A is still directing anger at Person B, but this time B is completely refusing the negative energy. As a result, that negative energy does not enter the energy field of Person B. Instead, it simply dissipates. Not only does this keep B's aura clean, it also stops the escalation that would result if B were to give in to A's negative influence. In this example, B has put on a mantle of spiritual protection (Chapter 11), so the energy does not even penetrate the auric shell. Yet, even without protection, if B were still adamant about refusing to react, A's negative energy would still not get much farther into her aura.

Family

Let's now look at how to apply the light in specific types of relationships. We'll begin with family. We all know the importance of family and its relation to our well-being. The family unit is the backbone of any society, and one of our

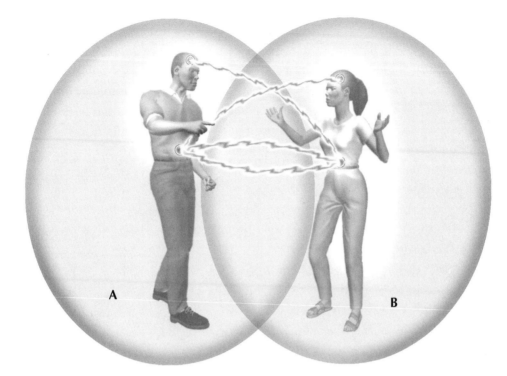

Figure 9–1: **Two People Fighting**

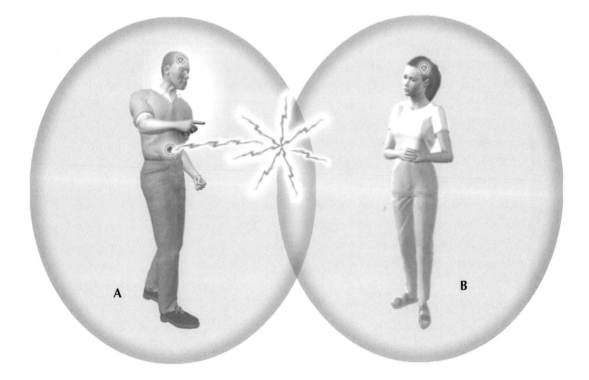

Figure 9–2: **Refusing an Angry Outburst**

main support systems in life. Our family experiences usually set the tone for our feelings and beliefs about ourselves, others, and life in general. Family is where we start building our relationships with people; it's where we learn how to give and take, and ultimately, to love. The importance of a strong family life cannot be overstated. When we have a good family experience, that basic stability and confidence carry throughout life. It's a powerful foundation we can build on. Conversely, growing up in a dysfunctional family takes its toll. It puts us at a disadvantage and, if we are unable to rise above that experience, can handicap us for life. Again, there's so much involved in family dynamics that we can only touch lightly on the subject, our main thrust being to show how effective the light can be in healing family friction, hostilities, resentment, and sorrow.

A great deal of my spiritual counseling has centered on helping to heal family traumas, past and present. I remember one case that was especially touching. There was a boy whose parents were killed in a car accident. He had no other living relatives and was put in an orphanage. A couple soon adopted him, and they tried to do everything for the child. The boy was heartbroken, and would often cry through the night for his biological parents. He would express his frustration and anger to his adopted mother, saying things like, "I don't like you. I don't want you. I want my mommy back." The woman did the best she could, but as time went on, things didn't get any better. The boy became more intolerant and difficult. The adoptive father was away a great deal on business trips, so it fell to the woman to care for the child. She didn't know how to handle him and wondered if she had done the right thing in adopting him. She loved him, but in her frustration at his lack of cooperation she made several mistakes, including slapping him a few times, which compounded the problem.

She came to me for counseling and began to work with the light to try to turn things around. First she turned to the love ray, to instill more patience and love in herself, so that her natural love could flow more freely. At the same time, frustration and anger that had caused her to mishandle so many situations needed to be released. She also brought in the silver ray to guide her in understanding and dealing with him better. Then she worked with the pink ray, sending it to the boy to help him heal from the loss of his parents and to show that she really loved him. She also used emerald green and gold for balance and strength to manage his difficult behavior. This went on for several months when finally, the boy started warming up to her. They began to go out and do things together, which had never happened before, and a very warm and loving relationship began to grow.

It is a fact that many of our most intense conflicts occur within our own family. This may seem a paradox: If the family unit is such a critical part of our development and character, then why does it so often turn out to be a major source of discord? Many dynamics come into play, but generally our biggest tests in human relationship will be with members of our own family. The family experience touches into the deepest recesses of our human soul—sometimes bringing out things that aren't so great. Karma plays a huge part in family dynamics (but the complexities of family karma are beyond the scope of this book). The main point to hold on to for now is that family discord is often essential to the learning and growing process. And fortunately, our human soul can overcome any obstacles we may face in family life. We can't always control the circumstances that are coming our way, but we *can* control the effects of those experiences so they don't haunt or limit us in the future.

Working with spiritual energy can have a very positive effect on even the most dysfunctional of families. Divine Light keeps us above our conditions, so their effects are not impressed as deeply. The best time to call on the light for help is when we're actually passing through these fires. If the family wars are past but their effects are still there, the light will cleanse the aura of those memories and blockages, no matter how longstanding.

Parents & Children

There's an old saying, "Give me the first seven years of a person's life and you can have the rest." Many believe that in the first seven years, a person's character and tendencies are established. How that person is brought up, the kinds of stimuli and experiences the person is exposed to, will shape his or her character from that time on. Such people argue that our character is determined mainly by our upbringing, with no inborn predisposition—nurture over nature. Metaphysical philosophy does not take that point of view. It teaches that even though our surroundings do greatly affect us, we have a life quite independent of our upbringing and environment. We are eternal beings, with a life prior to and after physical existence. Earth life is simply a stage in our spiritual evolution. Because of this, we are in control of our family influence.

From the spiritual point of view, the first seven years do indeed have a unique place in a soul's development. It takes seven years for all the auric energies to fully establish themselves within the physical body. There are many spiritual connections to be made, connections that must be made gradually. By the time a child is seven, the energy flow is set, and the person begins a rapid growth process. Within the first seven years, the auric flow is very pliable. If there has been a disturbance, it can easily be fixed. After seven, it can still be done but now it becomes more difficult.

This means that those first seven years are most critical. Love is important all the time, but it's especially important then. Such nurturing means sacrifice, time, and energy. It means learning how to lovingly attend to the physical, emotional, intellectual, and spiritual needs of the child.

It's important to recognize that it was no accident that we were born into our families. There's a reason we have this one particular family. It's all part of a spiritual growth pattern that we must work through. It doesn't matter whether we were born into wealth or poverty, good parents or bad parents, or even raised as an orphan with no parents at all. The most challenging experiences offer opportunities to grow spiritually.

We all handle family challenges differently. Some are very strong and pass through adversity with flying colors, while others are haunted by childhood traumas, which can stay with them for the rest of their lives. The thing to see is that we all have the ability to pass through and rise above any conditions in our lives, including the very worst of family scenarios. As trying as these situations can be, God always gives us the spiritual courage to pass through them. Abraham Lincoln grew up so poor he was not even taught how to read. He taught himself by moonlight. So whatever handicap or trying situation we're faced with, we can remedy it, or make things much better. If we had a difficult childhood and are still traumatized years later, we can release that energy. We now have the tools to heal those conditions. It actually becomes part of our destiny to work our way out of all limitations.

Siblings

Our brothers and sisters can be our best friends throughout life, or they can be irritating, a cause of friction, or even indifferent, drifting away to become strangers. The usual underlying cause of friction between siblings is rivalry or jealousy. One child may feel he or she got the short end of the stick. Perhaps a parent has a favorite child and the other child resents it. It's a mistake that parents often make, usually without even knowing it. Or it could be that one child has an outstanding talent and is getting more attention because of it, which may excite jealousy in a brother or sister. As we know, these rivalries can be carried over into adulthood.

The Light & Family

If you are having problems with a family member, you have to pull out all the stops to help turn things around. You want to be particularly careful not to simply blame the other person or persons for what's going on. Search your heart to see what your contribution is to the present dilemma, so that you are coming from a clear place. If you feel you are clear, then you must use the light to help keep yourself above the turmoil going on around you. This will not only help you, but will also help all family members involved, so they can begin to see things from a spiritual perspective. As in any type of relationship, sometimes the other person will respond to the light, sometimes not. The main focus should be on building your own light rays to endure what you are going through with courage and fortitude, so you can come out of the experience victorious.

You will most likely have to use a combination of energy techniques, including a mental/emotional clearing, forgiveness, and perhaps divine guidance. Your situation is not going unnoticed by your Higher Self. It understands the challenges you are facing and is doing everything it can to help. The spiritual life is far more understanding and attuned to the sufferings of humanity than we give it credit for; it does everything in its power to help alleviate that suffering.

In addition to whichever rays you feel you need to use for the particular situation you are in, I also recommend that you include these meditative prayers to help lighten the load of your family difficulties. Again, you need to be patient with these dilemmas. Their roots are deep, and it takes time and persistent effort for things to be worked out.

Meditative Prayer to Help Alleviate Family Discord

"Down-ray the pure white light into all levels of my being, releasing me of any animosities connected with (*name person*). I ask that the purity and power of this divine white light go to (*name person*) and me, touching deep within our souls and lifting our spirits and awareness of our oneness with God. I place this entire situation on the altar of God, releasing all lower vibrations and any heavy burdens or pressure."

Take your time with this prayer to really feel the white light touching deeply into your auric field. If you find you still have difficulty finding the strength to face the situation, add the following prayer. In this particular light work, you are bringing down two energies at the same time.

Meditative Prayer for Soul Upliftment

"Down-ray the gold and emerald green rays into all levels of my consciousness and especially my soul levels, to give me the courage and strength to resolve this family discord in Thy Divine Light and Love."

Keep the light and protection strongly around you after doing this work.

Friends

True friends are among our greatest blessings. The only reason for people to be friends is natural affinity and desire to be together. There's no formal commitment, just an assumed bond of loyalty, and the honest, benign exchanges of two people who are simply being themselves. In the aura, it's often seen as a beautiful exchange of lemon yellow energy at the mental level, because friends share common interests, and a pink exchange of energy at the Hermetic level, expressing the love and comradeship friends feel for each other. One of the greatest forms of friendship is the spiritual brotherhood that's formed by two people walking the path of light together.

The key to friendship is simple: "To have a friend, be a friend." If you feel lonely and wish you could have a real friend, don't bemoan your fate and feel sorry for yourself. Go out and express friendship! Eventually, people of the same affinities as you will be attracted to you. Now, there will always be fair-weather friends. These people are not really interested in you; they're interested in what they can get out of you. Sometimes, good friends will use each other for selfish reasons, too, and this is not good for the relationship. One of the best byproducts of working with the Divine Light is that you naturally attract people to you. As your aura brightens, people find themselves drawn to you, without really knowing why.

Don't push things. You can't make someone like you; it has to just happen. But you can use the deep rose-pink ray to create a more loving auric energy that helps to attract new friends. The following is a meditative prayer to help attract new people to you. The key energy to work with is the love ray, as it can act as a spiritual magnet.

Meditative Prayer to Attract New Friends

"Down-ray the deep rose-pink of spiritual love to all my centers, especially my emotional center, generating more love in my consciousness and strongly opening my path to attract new friends and to strengthen the bonds of friendship I already have. I ask this in Divine Light and Love for the good of all concerned."

Professional

Professional relationships can be very tricky. When someone is in a position to affect our lives by his or her actions, we tend to be very careful about how we act around them. We can be very friendly with an employer, but we still know that if we do anything to offend that person, we can be fired. Such a lopsided relationship can make us fearful or resentful of that person's authority. In the same way, employers may look at their employees with apprehension. Are they doing their jobs? Are they taking advantage of me? Do they respect me? Are they friend or foe? Needless to say, these fears and resentments can create a lot of tension.

Again, the spiritual point of view has a direct answer to this quandary. When involved in a professional relationship, remember this affirmation:

"God is the employer and God is the employee."

Too many people automatically cast their "superiors" in an adversarial role. If we're constantly getting bounced around because of friction with bosses, if they never seem to understand us, then it behooves us to look at our attitude toward them as well. There's almost always something we're doing to create these situations. It's soothing to remember that we have only one true boss, and that's God. If there's anyone we should be concerned about pleasing, it's God. Again, there's a spiritual lesson in playing the role of boss or employee, something crucial to be learned that will help us to grow. If we don't like our station in life, then we must work to change it. When dealing with a difficult boss or a disgruntled employee, we must first strive for insight and then try to work things out before bailing out.

The same demands of spiritual relationship apply to coworkers. There may be jealousies and competition among fellow workers for recognition and promotions, and this can create a lot of stress. We must look at our work associates in the same spiritual light as everyone else. They too are in their spiritual growth process. If they are doing something to tarnish our good name or reputation, we have the right and the duty to protect ourselves; but again, we must not do it from a place of anger or resentment. The Divine dwells fully within them, too. See them in their divine essence.

When it comes to professional relationships, the most important rays to work with are the deep rose-pink and emerald green to create greater love and harmony. Send these energies to the seeming antagonist and to yourself. If there's already been confrontation, do the forgiveness work and try for a fresh start. The silver ray is a good energy to work with when there is difficulty in communication. If the relationship has become adversarial, follow the meditative prayer on the next page for restoring harmony to relationships. The following is a good one to help keep harmony in the workplace.

Meditative Prayer for Harmony in the Workplace

"Down-ray the emerald green ray of spiritual balance and harmony to touch into my Hermetic Center and out-ray to my worldly affairs, quickening my workplace with this divine harmony. May all whom I come in contact with feel and respond to the divine impulse of this holy light. I ask this in Divine Light and Love for the good of all concerned."

Adversaries

Our "enemies" present our biggest tests. How we handle our adversarial relationships is one of the clearest indicators of our true character. There is a wonderful story about Mother Teresa, when she was first setting up her hospital for the destitute. She had encountered a great deal of resistance from a local Hindu priest. He did everything he could to stop her work, because she was not Indian and not a Hindu. Mother Teresa did not react to his diatribes. Even when the priest became deathly ill—and was ostracized by his own faithful—he continued to despize Mother Teresa. However, no one would help him during his time of trial and need—no one, that is, but Mother Teresa! When she heard that he was dying, she immediately took him in and treated him with the same love and affection that she showed to all the sick and dying. He could not believe that this woman could shower so much kindness upon someone who had hated her so. He eventually died, but not without asking her forgiveness. News of what she'd done traveled, because all knew how much trouble the priest had caused her. It was this particular incident that put Mother Teresa on the road to international fame.

If you are faced with intense animosity, the following exercise is very helpful in disconnecting the tangle of energies involved. It may or may not remove the person from your life entirely, but it will definitely help to release the destructive connections that most likely exist between you.

Begin your Higher Self meditation. When you are in your Higher Self, see yourself in a bubble of pink and white light. Feel it enveloping you and uplifting all levels of your being. See the other person sitting across from you in a bubble of pink and white light as well. Then, using the following prayer, ask the light to release you and the other person from the negativities that bind you.

Meditative Prayer to Release Adversarial Relationships

"I ask the Divine Light of God to go to (name person) and myself, releasing us mental to mental, emotional to emotional, physical to physical, astral to astral, and soul to soul. Free me and free (name person) in this Divine Light and Love. I ask it all in Thy Holy Name."

Repeat this exercise as often as you feel you need to. Notice on how many levels this meditation is working. The irony of an adversarial relationship is the strange attachment that exists between people who hate each other. Strongly negative feelings can attach you to the other person just as surely as love. Freud observed that the opposite of love is not hate, but indifference. You must detach from hate if you really want to be free of another person's influence.

In addition, you must keep your balance strong when dealing with such a person. They are trying to direct negative energy toward you, but it will only throw you off if you let it. You have to keep on sending them love, so that they're inspired to move toward that love, and away from the antagonism. If you too feel hostility toward them, you must work with the light to cut loose the emotional and mental turmoil this relationship may be causing you.

Romance & Marriage

Now we focus the light on one of the most volatile and dynamic of all human relations—the romantic interaction of men and women. There have been so many questions, debates, so-called rules, and conflicting opinions about the true nature of romantic involvement and sexual relations that many people are cynical and disillusioned about the whole process of dating. This has been reflected in unrealistic expectations, high divorce rates, broken families, and a host of mental and emotional miseries.

The male/female relationship is a sacred one. Physical evolution divided the sexes into male and female as a manifestation of its spiritual counterpart—the dynamic and magnetic nature of life. The dynamic/magnetic polarity is the very essence of all manifested life. It's the give and take, the ebb and flow of life. This duality of active life may be seen at all levels of creation. Even God manifests as the Dynamic Father principle and as the Magnetic Holy Mother principle. It is the cosmic union of these two forces of life that created each eternal soul.

The key feature of the dynamic nature is *mind*. God the Father is Divine Mind in action. He is the giving out, the initial step, inner strength, divine will and wisdom. The key quality of the magnetic nature is *heart*. God the Holy Mother is love. She is compassion, love, beauty, unity, nurturing, and desire. All created life interplays between these two poles, producing cosmic balance and the spiritual rhythms of life. Both aspects of God are of equal importance. When we appear to be putting God the Father principle before the Mother, it's only in the sense that there needs to be an action before there can be a reaction.

This brings us to the second principle of the male/female relationship: Within each of us exists this polarity of dynamic and magnetic activity. This means that our soul is neither male nor female, but contains *both* divine attributes of the magnetic/dynamic life. When we incarnate in physical form, we polarize either our dynamic or magnetic nature, depending on the sex we become. This doesn't mean the other isn't there. It means we choose to emphasize one over the other, but both must still be in balance. So, by being born male, we are meant to express the dynamic, father principle of our being and to bring it to the forefront. Yet we must balance that dynamic with our magnetic nature. If we are born female, we are meant to express our magnetic nature and balance it with our dynamic flow. The spiritual goal is to balance the two flows, so that we can express both spiritual qualities regardless of our gender.

There's a divine reason you are born the sex that you are. It was not a mistake or chance occurrence. The first step in creating greater harmony with the opposite sex is to be comfortable and in harmony with your own sex. If you are male, enjoy your maleness. If you are female, enjoy your femaleness. There's nothing wrong with expressing characteristics of your sex as long as you keep things in perspective.

Problems can arise when people of one gender try to dominate or manipulate those of the other gender. You must never use gender advantages over another person, but rather as a complement and counterpart. As part of your spiritual growth, you're meant to learn how to live in peace and joy with the opposite sex. It's one of the greatest blessings of physical life. A couple that loves, honors, and stands up for each other is an ongoing work of spiritual beauty! Romantic love helps to advance souls on the path to God.

These magnetic/dynamic flows express themselves very clearly in the aura. The right side of the aura brings in the dynamic flows of light and the left side attracts the magnetic flows (see Figure 9–3). This polarity is critical to a balanced aura. The right side tends to express gold, red, and other dynamic energies while the left side will have pink, violet, and other magnetic energies. This is not a hard-and-fast rule, but you will see it more often than not. Some energies can be both dynamic *and* magnetic, such as the green and blue rays. In addition, the Higher Self will down-breathe beautiful dynamic or magnetic rays to either the right or left side of the aura, depending on the particular need.

If the aura is unbalanced in its magnetic/dynamic flow, the energy will favor one side over the other. An overly magnetic soul will not have the dynamic radiation needed on the right side, and an overly dynamic person will generally not have the magnetic radiations needed on the left side. This condition exists only until balance is restored to the aura. Individuals must be magnetically/dynamically balanced, regardless of sex. If you are loving and kind but have no backbone, you must develop your dynamic side while continuing to be kind and loving. In the same way, if you are a go-getter at the expense of stepping on other people's toes, you must learn to be more giving and kind, but still be that go-getter.

Dating

The key element in dating is *compatibility*. People can date for all sorts of reasons, but for spiritual growth to occur, we want to find someone with whom we're extremely compatible. The aura is very good at showing the compatibility

**Right Side
Dynamic**

**Left Side
Magnetic**

Balanced Aura

Overly Dynamic

Overly Magnetic

Figure 9–3: **Polarity of the Aura**

of couples. When two people are compatible, there is a beautiful exchange of energy on the Hermetic and emotional levels. Usually there will be pink, showing the love flow. Orange reveals the enthusiasm and excitement that the couple have for each other. There will also be a violet energy exchange, showing that there is a peace and serenity with the other soul. They intuitively trust each other and are very comfortable with each other. When I see this kind of energy exchange, I know these people are meant for each other and would most likely make a fine couple. If the two are incompatible, there will usually be an exchange of gray energy. It will emanate from the Hermetic Center, showing that there is sadness and worry going on.

If you're having difficulty finding someone who's compatible, you can work with the light to help attract someone suitable. First you want to get an idea of what it is you're looking for. Are you looking for companionship or a marriage partner? Be crystal-clear about what you want. If you're simply looking for someone to date, recognize that this will most likely be a temporary situation. You may have a great time together, but chances are it won't last. On the other hand, if you're looking for a marriage partner, recognize that you're stepping into deeper waters and that you will have to make a much more lasting commitment.

Evaluate the qualities you have to offer another person. People often focus so much on what they want in another person that they don't look at what they themselves have to offer. You must be willing to give and sacrifice. Working with visualizations is very effective here. If you feel you have done all these things and still have come up with nothing, then you need to identify any negative thinking that may be getting in the way of attracting what you want. For example, you may say you want a marriage partner, but deep down, perhaps you're not ready to give up the pleasures and carefree quality of single life. Or you may want someone very sincerely but feel you're undeserving of a worthy companion. All these issues must be confronted and dealt with before you can attract the person you desire.

There are several ways to work with the light to attract the right person to you. Above all, you need clarity. If you're in confusion, you will often draw the wrong person to you because you're not clear about what you want. So, if you're having trouble attracting a truly compatible person, first do a spiritual cleansing with the orange-red flame to release any wrong pictures and patterns you may have developed.

Then, work with the pure white light and ask that it touch into your Higher Self Point to bring you a clear picture of the kind of person you need in your life.

Meditative Prayer to Identify
the Right Romantic/Marital Partner

"Down-ray the pure white light to quicken all levels of my consciousness. I ask that it especially touch into my Higher Self Point of Spiritual Knowing. And I ask my Higher Self to give me a clear picture of the person who is right for me."

Hold still to receive whatever is coming to you. Again, you may get the inspiration right then and there, or it may come to you later. What you are looking for in this meditation are the qualities, the overall essence, of the person who is best for you. This way, you have a much better idea of what to look for. Follow up this work with the silver ray to quicken the recognition in your mental body of the image being given to you. In this instance, the silver ray will also help to better stabilize that image.

Meditative Prayer to Quicken the Mental Body

"Down-ray the silver ray of divine intelligence into my mental body to quicken me in the recognition of the image of my rightful mate, given to me by my Higher Self."

I would also add the blue-white fire, because once you get that image, the blue-white fire can help intensify and sustain it until that person can become a reality for you.

Meditative Prayer to Sustain the Rightful Image

"Down-ray the blue-white fire of eternal life to touch into all levels of my consciousness and especially charge and recharge my mental body to hold and sustain the image of my rightful romantic partner."

With these three rays, you have greatly quickened your mental levels to get your mind focused in the right direction. This way, when the right person does come along, you will recognize him or her. Once you have worked on the mental levels, follow up with the wisdom light.

Meditative Prayer to Attract
a Romantic/Marital Partner

"Down-ray the golden ray of wisdom light to my Hermetic Center and out-ray in my human Earth affairs to attract the right person to me."

You may repeat this exercise as often as you feel you need to until the energy is established. Be patient when it comes to romance. You can't force the right person to appear in your life. In the same way, don't be lazy and expect the dream-person to just suddenly appear. You have to put yourself out there and make yourself available. As the saying goes, sometimes you have to kiss a few frogs before you find your prince (or princess!).

Meditative Prayer with
the Love Ray in the Emotions

"Down-ray the deep rose-pink ray of spiritual love to all levels of my being and into my emotional body. Let this light bathe all levels of my emotional nature, so I am coming from a place of love and kindness. And let this love ray open my heart and emotions, so I am accepting of the rightful person entering my life."

I would finish this work with the love ray. Obviously, love is the indispensable element in any relationship. It also helps balance the magnetic/dynamic flow. Ask the love ray to touch into all levels of your consciousness, but especially your emotional levels so that you are open and accepting of the person coming into your life.

Sex & Spiritual Energy

Sex is probably the key reason that so many people decide not to pursue the spiritual life. There's a common misconception that being spiritual means having no sex. Or if not total abstention, then at least a serious curtailment of sexual pleasure is believed to be called for. People see priests and nuns taking vows of celibacy and say, "If *that's* what it takes to be spiritual, it's not for me!" Many modern schools of metaphysics try to relax this point: spiritually speaking, they say, sex is not an issue as long as it's accompanied by love. Yet sex has a very definite effect on our lives and our auras. Of course, we all know that sex serves the critical function of perpetuating the species and that it's part of the attraction that brings people together. We also know that every human entering puberty experiences sexual feelings and that we all have these urges and sensations within us regardless of how we express them. So the question becomes not *whether* our sexuality should be a part of our spiritual life, but rather *how* our sexuality should be part of our spiritual life.

In the aura, sexual energy emanates from the Root Chakra. The Root Chakra operates a little differently from the other centers when it comes to how its energy moves. In the four main centers that we work with, energy is in a constant state of receiving and transmitting. As we have seen in Chapter 3, the Root Chakra does not function this way. The Root Chakra already has within it a special reservoir of power. The light within this center has been placed there as part of our spiritual design to serve a very specific function. This function is something we've been doing for eons in various forms. It's something that's an intimate part of our life and character. The energy of the Root Chakra gives us the power to *create*. It's not the actual creation, inspiration, or act, but the power, drive, and spiritual force necessary to put the creative energies into action and carry them to fruition.

There is an inexhaustible supply of Root-Chakra energy available to us. It's already been given to us as part of our spiritual heritage. Yet how we use this creative energy determines its effectiveness in our lives. This energy flows in one of three ways:

1. Generation
2. Degeneration
3. Regeneration

Generation uses the Root-Chakra energy for creating offspring. This root energy is necessary for the conception of children. Without it, conception could not take place because in addition to the physical union of egg and sperm, there is a spiritual connection that occurs as well. The power to procreate cannot be underestimated. The ability to reproduce is one of the most holy traits we possess, whether we choose to bear children or not. The procreative energy is not to be confused with the physical/instinctual desire for sex. That is a primal physical trait that would still be there regardless of this spiritual energy. Animals have the instinctual drive, but they don't have this spiritual Root-Chakra energy. God provides the spiritual energy for their conception in other ways. But in humans, this energy is necessary for physical conception.

Normal sexual activity without the goal of having children may also fall under the category of generation. This is because it still mirrors the procreative process even if the act doesn't result in the conception of a child. In this form, the procreative energy becomes purely sexual because the Root-Chakra energy is used primarily for pleasure and intimacy. The energy is not quite as bright as in the act of procreation, but it's still an elevating energy if the sexual activity is done out of genuine love and affection. This sexual interaction is part of the bonding and strengthening process that can bring two people closer together.

Degeneration is the wasting of Root-Chakra energy through the intentional or unintentional misuse of that creative force. We misuse the Root-Chakra energy through heavy excesses and distortions of sex. When we indulge in these practices, we may find them momentarily enjoyable, but they're serving no useful purpose. All perversions and deviate acts result in degeneration of Root-Chakra energy. We have to be very careful, because degeneration is a form of devolution. If we're determined and persistent in acting out degrading sex, we're going to distance ourselves more and more from our spiritual nature. In this situation, the root energy doesn't dissipate, but it becomes dirtied and defiled.

Regeneration means using the Root-Chakra energy for purely creative endeavors. We see this in people who refrain from sex before a big event, artists who abstain during creative periods. We need this power for all creative and productive endeavors: without it, we simply could not create, whether it's to design a building, sing a song or paint a picture. It's the power behind great artists, inventors, musicians, etc. It gives us the energy, stamina, and drive necessary to create something new and original.

We can also direct Root-Chakra energy for purely spiritual purposes. One of the greatest creative acts we can experience is our own metamorphosis from human consciousness to the realization of a fully matured divine being. This creative act will require a strong redirection of the Root-Chakra energy. And here's where the concept of celibacy comes in. For those who are aiming to reach the pinnacle of spiritual development, there is an eventual need for sexual abstention, so that the spiritual power can be completely directed to the spiritual goal. Such a sacrifice, however, is not necessary until a soul reaches the very advanced stages of spiritual development, and even then there are exceptions. To take a vow of celibacy before one has properly developed will only create problems. We end up repressing normal desires, which often results in perverted acts. So, the point is, we don't have to stop having sex to develop spiritually, but we do have to control our sexual activity.

**A–Normal
Generative Flow**

**B–High
Creative Flow**

**C–Spiritual
Mastery Flow**

**D–Degenerative
Flow**

Figure 9–4: **Root-Chakra Energy**

When the root energy is in the generative mode, the energy in the aura beams upward from the root center, concurrent with the spine (see Figure 9–4A). It usually extends to the level of the emotional center in a carnation-red color. If the person is trying to conceive children, the color will be a very bright red with white light around it. It's a vital, beautiful energy to see. If the person is simply in a romantic relationship, there will only be the red energy moving upward, but it won't be as bright. If the person is a little too intoxicated by sex, the energy will still move upwards, but the red will now be dirtied and dulled to the maroon red. On the other hand, if the person is in a strong degenerative mode, the root energy now moves in a downward motion, sometimes reaching below the feet—indicative of a devolving consciousness (Figure 9–4D). The energy is deep, vitiated red.

What's always very interesting and beautiful is to see the light moving in a regenerative flow. If the person is in a high creative mode, the root energy will be moving all the way up to the mental body, giving it tremendous energy and power (Figure 9–4B). This helps to regenerate and replenish the brain cells and can make you look and feel young. It's one of the reasons so many productive and creative people have youthful vitality and stamina. If you find yourself confused, or uninspired, one of the best ways to get on target is to start (or resume) being productive and creative. It renews and vivifies the whole landscape of your thinking. In the case of the spiritual master who has directed all his or her energy to spiritual purposes, the root energy will move up beyond the head and into the Higher Self Point (Figure 9–4C). In this case, there will also undoubtedly be a strong flow of kundalini energy moving up the spine as well.

Most of our problems with sex come from a misunderstanding and misuse of this energy. Instead of using the creative power of sex to its fullest potential, we limit its power, squandering its vitality to no particular end. We do this mainly out of ignorance. If you are unhappy in your sex life, first look to see if you are placing too much emphasis on sex. The truth is, when the sexual energy is balanced, it will not be such a preoccupation. Sex will feel like a natural part of life. Oversexed people are most always compensating for a lack in another area of their lives. These people end up still feeling dissatisfied, even after they've had their sexual conquests, because the energy's not balanced. People who have balanced the sexual energy with all other aspects of life enjoy sex, but it's not an issue with them. The truth is, as you climb the spiritual ladder, there will be less and less desire for sex because more of your root energy will be flowing into creative and spiritual avenues.

Working with the Divine Light in this center will help to clear and cleanse misused energies and get the whole flow moving the way it should.

Most important, it will help to elevate and spiritualize the Root Center so that we can use it for more creative purposes. The following prayer may be used before sex to put the Divine Light into the act of making love to raise its vibration. Ideally, it's best if both partners say this prayer together.

Meditative Prayer to Uplift the Sex Act

"Down-ray the pure white light into my Root Chakra and sexual organs to uplift and elevate this sexual act into an expression of Thy Light and Love."

Regardless of where you are, you want to begin the process of spiritualizing and rarefying the sexual vibration. By getting a handle on this part of your nature, you're harnessing one of the most potent forces in you. I recommend using the orange-red flame to help cleanse and clear any dark energies.

Meditative Prayer to Purify the Root Chakra

"Down-ray the orange-red flame of purification into my Root Chakra to purify all depleted and defiled sexual energies. Cleanse all black and gray atoms and impurities, taking them to the mineral kingdom where they are dissolved in the light."

Although you can't extinguish the power of the Root Chakra no matter how you may misuse it, you can deplete its potency. The blue-white fire can help to quicken the regenerating process, so it's still necessary to use this energy following the purification.

Meditative Prayer to Replenish the Root Chakra

"Down-ray the blue-white fire into my Root Chakra to charge and recharge all depleted and exhausted areas with new spiritual energy and vitality."

You can also use the emerald green to balance the flow in your Root Chakra, which will help to get the energy moving in the direction it needs to.

In closing, my advice is to use the sex act sparingly. When you do have sex, do it with good intentions. Care for and love the person you're being intimate with. There's a great deal more going on than just copulation. The physical act of love is the closest two auras can get. Not only do you affect your Root-Chakra flow by your sexual actions, you also draw energy from the other person's aura. So you want to be careful that your partner is coming from a place of love. Respect this sacred energy God has given you, and it will serve you better than you can imagine.

The Sacrament of Marriage

The sacrament of marriage in its true form brings couples to the highest level of male/female relationship that can be experienced on Earth. The union of a man and a woman before the eyes of God is designed to assist human souls in their spiritual evolution. It's part of the spiritual plan, the vehicle that the Divine chose to procreate the species. Maintaining a nurturing environment for new, incoming souls, husband and wife also serve God by serving each other. Through love, respect, fidelity, and sacrifice, the couple learns to serve God. One reflects the other: loyalty in marriage demonstrates loyalty to God.

Many intelligent people question the need for marriage, especially when there is no intention of having children. They ask why, if two people love each other, is it essential for them to marry? The answer is very simple: Marriage is not just about two people in love. It's about two people and God. We can't take God out of the equation. This is why we marry *in the eyes of God*. Marriage has to be under the aegis of ultimate authority—and absolute love! When we sign that marriage license, we're signing part of ourselves as well. We're making a commitment. We can't escape that it's like any legal document. When a student graduates from school, he or she gets a degree. When a medical student becomes a doctor, he or she is bestowed the honor of M.D., and obtains a license to practice. The same is true of marriage. We all have to make commitments; they exist on every level of life. So, the challenge of marriage is not in the design but in our ability to live up to that design.

When we marry, we're giving part of ourselves—part of our human selves. The Divine always remains Its own, but each of us does give of our human self. Many people are afraid of this sacrifice. They fear that it will stifle their creativity, that they will lose their identity in this union called marriage. Look at the stereotype of married life as "the old ball and chain." Those who have gone through a stifling or harsh marital experience will often say, "No more!" Their fears are understandable, but they are just that—fears. The truth is, we are all in the process of surrendering our human self to our divine self. That's the whole point of spiritual evolution. Day by day, we drop a little of our old self to pick up our true self. Any opportunity to drop some of the human opens us up to more of the Divine. If we do the marriage thing right, we're not restricting ourselves at all. Quite the contrary. We're opening our creative flow to new heights, and expanding our identity to new dimensions. On top of that, we're forming a support system that's unbeatable. And the auric exchange between strong marriage partners is a great enhancement to life.

Marriage born of true love brings a wonderful blessing from the Higher. Not only is there a physical and legal marriage—there is a spiritual marriage as well. Spiritual marriage can be seen in the aura as a thread of pink light connecting the spouses at the emerald hub within the Hermetic Center. This thread is the spiritual blessing of the Divine, and is created when there is true love and earnest commitment between a man and woman. Such spiritual connection is essential because it keeps the love flow going. It unites at the Hermetic Center because that is where this commitment is made in the human Earth affairs. However, it does not affect the soul levels. Even in marriage, each partner is still on his or her own evolutionary ladder. The marriage becomes part of the learning experience but each is still a spiritual individual. This spiritual bond is created only in the sacrament of marriage. The marriage can take place civilly, in a church, etc., but must take place legally. And it must be done out of love. If you date someone, live with someone you love dearly, even have children with that person out of wedlock, you may have a beautiful exchange of energy, but this special, sacramental bond will be lacking. It's a spiritual blessing that stays with the couple throughout married life until death or divorce.

There are just as many ways to work with the light in marriage as there are spiritual traits to develop—harmony, fidelity, loyalty, understanding, gentleness, patience, adaptability, commitment . . . the list goes on. If there's a problem in your marriage, you must do everything in your power to remedy it. Call on all your divine tools, everything in your possession, to turn things around.

Meditative Prayer for
Spiritual Harmony Between Couples

"Down-ray the emerald green ray of balance and the deep rose-pink ray of spiritual love into all levels of my consciousness, restoring and reestablishing mind-body-soul harmony between (name person) and me. May (name person) also receive this mind-body-soul harmony at all levels of consciousness and may this light strengthen our marital bond in the fires of Thy light and everlasting love for the good of all concerned."

The meditative prayer given on page 180 is designed to start the energy moving in the right direction and to strengthen the spiritual commitment you have made to each other. In this meditative prayer, you are down-raying the emerald green ray with the deep rose-pink ray at the same time to harmonize and stabilize the love flow between the two of you.

To Forgive is Divine

To round out our work on applying the light in relationships, we need to include forgiveness. Forgiveness is essential to healing any relationship and also an essential part of the light work. In our experiences, we're bound to step on each other's toes at one point or another. We're not perfected yet, so we're inevitably going to make mistakes. As a result, there'll be countless times when we'll need to ask forgiveness, or be forgiving, so we'd better become good at forgiveness or we'll not get very far in our spiritual growth.

As we know, it's not always easy for people to ask for forgiveness or to forgive. Our human ego gets involved and wants to hold on to its anger, grudges, and so on. On the one hand, we may not recognize or want to recognize that we have done anything wrong to warrant asking someone's forgiveness. On the other hand, it may be doubly hard for us to forgive others for wrongs done, especially if they are serious. There are people who have gone to their graves without forgiving the people who injured them. Perhaps what makes the act of forgiveness so difficult is the notion that if we forgive someone, we're letting him or her off the hook. In truth, when we forgive someone we're letting *ourselves* off the hook. There's a tremendous freedom in forgiveness. When we forgive, we're breaking the negative connection that has been forged between the other person and ourselves. For example, when someone has wronged you, he or she has sent out negative energy toward you. This negative energy will make a connection with you somewhere unless you're wise enough to totally refuse that energy, which is not likely. So, chances are you've picked up some of that destructive flow and are suffering the consequences. By forgiving, you're severing that destructive connection. This frees you from the painful bond that existed between the other person and you.

There's the famous story of a woman who was forced to endure the Nazi concentration camps of World War II. She survived the experience but had been misused by one jailer in particular. Well, years passed, and the woman became very religious, which helped release many of the horrible memories she carried. Yet, the experiences with this jailer still haunted her.

As fate would have it, she was at some public function when she spotted the guard who had abused her. Her initial reaction was to walk over and kill him right then and there. Fortunately, her religious convictions took hold of her. She realized that this was her opportunity to apply all the spiritual principles she had learned over the years. With all the strength she had, she walked over to the astonished man (who recognized her) and told him that she forgave him for all the things he had done to her. She said it sincerely and with conviction. To her amazement, after truly forgiving him, the first thing she felt was relief. For the first time since her whole ordeal, she felt a deep sense of peace. She had truly let it go from her life.

Do her actions free this man from his offenses? Of course not. He still has a great deal of work to do to redeem his soul for all his misdeeds. But she is now free of him, and, in the process, has helped him along his road to redemption. There is enormous power in the act of forgiveness, for the more we exercise it, the more we can access that power.

No matter what the situation, all forgiveness begins with God. When we commit an offense, the first thing we need to do is ask God's forgiveness, for it is God we have first offended. The beautiful thing is, since God is love, God will always forgive. He's actually forgiven us before we've even asked for forgiveness, but we must still ask. God can pull us out of any dark hole we find ourselves in. Even if we've committed an atrocity, God forgives us, and we can still come clean of that mess. By asking God's forgiveness, we're reconnecting with God's Light and power to begin our redemption.

One of the greatest stories of God's forgiveness is the life of Saul, who became Saint Paul. Saul, as we know, was a persecutor of the early Christians. Locked into his own religious traditions, he felt that the Christian faith was a threat to his system of belief. He was persistent and cruel in his systematic attacks on the early Christians, killing many. Yet this very man, after his spiritual awakening on the road to Damascus, became Paul, one of Christianity's greatest exponents. And as Paul, God imbued him with great spiritual power and authority. What better example of God's forgiving power than this?

In addition to God's forgiveness, we often overlook forgiving ourselves. We, of course, want to do all that we can to help those we've offended, but we want to do it from a place of compassion and love—not guilt. If we condemn our past actions, we're only reinforcing the negative traits that precipitated those acts in the first place. Guilt or remorse at the beginning is inevitable and understandable. However, once we have the picture of what we've done wrong, we don't want to "feed it" by dwelling on it. We want to get on with our lives and do what we must to rectify the situation. No one is immune to moments of weakness, not even spiritual masters. There's a saying that even the angels have to be reprimanded every once in a great while!

In the forgiveness prayer we will be offering shortly, we include both forgiving and asking forgiveness. This reciprocal activity is important because from the human point of view, it's hard to be sensitive to the full range and interplay of energies that created a wrongful action. It might be very obvious that someone did wrong to you, and that you need to forgive that person. Yet, there may also have been something *you* did that contributed to this person's acting the way he or she did. By returning the forgiving act, you're ensuring your spiritual release.

The Forgiveness Principles

In working with forgiveness, keep these three simple principles firmly in mind. They will take you a long way toward success in your forgiveness work.

> 1. *Forgive quickly.*
> 2. *Forgive and forget.*
> 3. *Forgive "70 x 7."*

1. *Forgive quickly*—Try to forgive or ask forgiveness as soon after the incident as possible. If anger or resentment has time to seep in, it's not good. When negative energies have had a chance to work into the aura, they're harder to eliminate.

2. *Forgive and forget*—Someone may have done a hundred good things, but what do you remember? It's that one rotten thing that was done to you. That's human nature. You must forgive and forget. If you say you forgive, but constantly dredge up mistakes from the past, you haven't really forgiven. You must forgive from your heart and *truly mean it* to let it go.

3. *Forgive "70 x 7"*—Many times mistakes will be repeated. If you're in the process of learning an important life-lesson, but it still hasn't quite "sunk in," you're going to repeatedly make the same mistake, sometimes hurting the same person, until that lesson is completely understood. This is why Jesus said you must forgive not once, not seven times, but "seventy times seven" times. There can be no limit to forgiveness. You must continue to be supportive of your forgiveness. You can't say, "I'll forgive you this time, but if you do it again, I'll never forgive you." That's the same as *not* forgiving.

The Forgiveness Prayer

Once again, the key energy to work with is the deep rose-pink ray. Meditate with this energy before doing your actual forgiveness work to bring more love and compassion to yourself. You should feel an actual lifting with this energy, as though a dense cloud were being taken away from you. If the wrong is very serious, include meditating with the pure white light as well to redeem the defiled energies.

Get into your Higher Self Point and begin the forgiveness prayer. In this case, you're not working with a particular light ray, although you can use the love ray if you want. You're working primarily with your Higher Self.

Forgiveness Prayer

"I ask forgiveness for anything I may have done that injured you in word, thought, act, and deed, knowingly and unknowingly.

"And I forgive you for anything that you may have done to me that injured me in word, thought, act, and deed, knowingly and unknowingly.

"I ask that all these negative energies be dissolved in the holy fires of eternal love, freeing us completely in God's Divine Light and everlasting peace."

Notice the words "knowingly and unknowingly." Many times you can hurt people or are hurt by others unknowingly. Since you're not always fully conscious of your motives and actions, you need to include the unconsciousness factor. Fortunately, one of the magnificent things about working with spiritual energy is that it gently brings more of your unconscious thoughts, words, and actions to conscious light, so that you can do something about them.

In addition to your forgiveness prayers and light work, you'll need to confront the person face-to-face. If the person is adamant and refuses to forgive you, you're still free. You did your part to open your heart and show your true remorse and willingness to mend things. Just continue to do your best to heal the relationship. You can repeat this prayer as often as you feel the need. If you wish to forgive or ask forgiveness of someone who has passed on, you can still use this prayer. Remember, the soul of that person is still very much alive, and your prayer and light reach them wherever they are.

Chapter 10

Divine Guidance

Sometimes we get stuck in life's activities. Like a lesson in school we just can't seem to master, there are times when we simply don't know how to handle a situation we're confronted with. We try to solve our problems by ourselves, but the right answer just doesn't come. Here's where we are meant to take advantage of the most important tool in our spiritual arsenal—divine guidance.

Divine guidance manifests in myriad ways, some subtle, some obvious. Calling on the divine power to help steer us in our pursuits, we can be absolutely certain of a perfectly loving response. Because our human soul is growing and learning, it's bound to get lost and confused at times. It doesn't have the ability to anticipate and negotiate all the twists and turns along its path of light. If we relied only on our own wits to climb the spiritual ladder, we'd get stuck very quickly. So, an essential part of our spiritual growth entails learning how to work with spiritual energy to guide and direct our lives. By calling on the light for help, we're strengthening our spiritual connection, with the automatic effect of uplifting our lives. The key is to actively call on the light for help, and then to use the inspiration given.

Our Higher Self Point plays a crucial role in connecting with spiritual guidance. In addition to acting as intermediary for the spiritual light, the Higher Self will help us step into the spiritual awareness that enables us to comprehend the divine answers given. The Higher Self sees the whole spiritual picture of our Earth life, and part of its job is to steer us, so we stay on the evolutionary path. As the essence of our answer flows from God through the Divine Light, it makes a strong connection with our Higher Self, which then quickens this inspiration into a form we can understand. The Higher Self then sends the inspired light to our human aura to speak to our soul. Thus, it is this spiritual union of light and consciousness that brings our answers.

Becoming Receptive to Inspiration

To receive guidance, you need to be clear about what you need help with. When you're in the throes of an important decision, you can lose sight of the real issue. So take a moment to reflect on what you want the light to do for you, and formulate that thought into a sentence or question. You may have an important decision or dilemma on your inventory list for which you are seeking spiritual assistance. An urgent situation may have just come up, and you need help in making a decision quickly. Whatever is going on in your life, if you've done all you can to resolve things and you can't, it's time to call on the light for help.

Once you've clearly defined the problem or dilemma, let it go from your conscious mind. If trying to solve your problem has been taxing your mind and emotions, you're not leaving room for the light to inspire you. You want to switch your conscious brain/mind thinking to a receiving mode rather than a sending mode. In this receiving mode, your conscious mind listens to the spirit part of you.

Begin your work by relaxing. In this relaxing there is a trust, a knowing, that you are putting things into God's hands. With this trust comes a belief in the unlimited capacity and readiness of the Higher Power to help you. Jesus advised us to "ask, believing." There is great power in belief. In believing, you know there is an answer even if you can't see that answer yet. You're not challenging God. You're opening to God. You're saying, "God, I know You know the answer. I open myself up to receiving that answer." There has to be open-mindedness and an open-heartedness on your part for this whole process to work. If you're assuming a doubting or challenging attitude, essentially telling God to "prove it," all you're doing is blocking the very flow you're trying to open.

Letting go of your problems can be much more difficult than it seems. Chances are, your most tenacious problem is still "hanging in there" simply because you yourself have been holding on to it, and not letting your higher nature work with you. The problem most often confronted in asking for help is that you get in the way of yourself. Your answer could be staring you right in the face, with you refusing to see it. The issue is not the spirit connecting with you, but you connecting with the spirit.

Some people resist the idea of being helped altogether. They want to do it on their own. Of course, there will be times when you must pass through a trial on your own, no matter how you may pray and call on the light. However, in most cases, you are meant to make your decision in conjunction with your higher nature. That's the whole point. You're supposed to be building a bridge between your higher and lower nature. How can you do that unless you learn to make contact with the Higher through repeated practice?

Most people who come to me with problems show confusion in their auras. Confusion shows up in a lot of gray and creamy mustard energies, especially around the head area. Their aura is generally out of balance, which can be detected by its lack of emerald green. Often, people in a confused state will be restless, which can make the energy field jagged and disoriented as well. With such an aura, it's not surprising that the person is having difficulties and not able to make logical decisions. There can be lethargy in the mental body if the problem has been active for a while. If you feel confused, begin your meditation by working with the orange-red flame and the blue-white fire in the mental and emotional areas; they will help to cut loose all confusion and indecision and create a clear receiving station for the divine ideas to make their impression.

After someone has received a dose of inspirational light, I'll often see a white glow around the head area, showing the guidance at work. This is a temporary situation while the light is doing its job. There will also be active emanations of violet and light pinks, showing that the Higher is trying to quiet the soul so it can be receptive to the inspiration given.

Connecting with Your Source of Inspiration

The two main energies to call upon for guidance are gold and white light. The silver comes into play if you're having trouble comprehending information given to you. Your answer can come through either the gold or white ray, depending on the situation you're facing. Gold is wonderful for inspiring decisive action. If you're ambivalent or allow others to confuse and influence your decisions, the gold can bring in a dynamic power to straighten things out. It's great for clear-cut decisions, calling for yes/no answers. The gold is the energy I personally call upon the most when making important decisions. The gold gives the power to put inspiration into action.

In calling for guidance, you will work your meditation a little differently. Still follow the meditative steps as before, but when you begin down-raying, you will be asking that the light down-ray to the Higher Self only. The reason for this is that you want to hold your attention in your Higher Self Point as you are making your connection with the light and asking your spiritual question. On its own, the light will touch into your aura as needed, but again, you want to stay in as high a level of consciousness as you can while asking for help. By keeping your attention on the Higher Self Point, you're making a more direct contact with your source of inspiration and staying out of any human-level confusion. The actual idea or inspiration will come through with the light. The Higher Self will quicken this divine idea, so you can recognize and understand its meaning. Begin by calling on the gold light with the following meditative prayer.

Meditative Prayer for Divine Guidance with the Gold Light

"Down-ray the golden ray of wisdom light to my Higher Self Point of Spiritual Knowing, bringing forth the pearl of Thy wisdom and guidance to reveal that which I need to know, and that which I need to know now, concerning (*name situation*)."

Feel the light beaming down into your Higher Self Point, activating it. Once you feel the connection has been made, then ask your question. After you ask, be still and see if any thoughts come through for you. Keep your mind as passive as you can. The guidance might come as an image or idea. It might be a quiet voice speaking to you, but it will be something very definite. Generally, you'll know you've hit on something because you'll feel exhilaration. Regardless of what does or does not come through, conclude with the following expression of gratitude.

"I thank Thee that this is so, and I hold to
the knowing that my answer is forthcoming."

This prayer will help to establish your connection with the answer to your question, so that at precisely the right time it can reveal itself to you.

You can work with the white light in conjunction with the gold, or separately, as needed. The white light is a purifying ray as well as an uplifting energy. It is especially good for situations in which the answer is not so clear-cut. You may not even be sure what a real decision might consist of. You know that something is wrong and that you're being called upon to act, but the exact nature of the issue eludes you. The white light, in addition to being a great illuminating energy, is also an effective revelatory energy to show things about your situation that you may not have known or considered.

Meditative Prayer for
Divine Guidance with the White Light

"Down-ray the pure white light into my Higher Self Point, bringing forth Thy perfect illumination, revelation, and divine answer concerning (*name situation*)."

Feel the light igniting your Higher Self Point, activating it. You may then ask your question. Be still and see if any inspiration comes through for you. Inspiration may or may not come at that moment. It doesn't matter. Either way, you have put the energy into motion; your answer will come.

Accept and Use the Guidance Given

If your answer does not come through during your meditation, it may yet come to you at any time, according to your receptivity and the timing of the need. The answer could manifest during contemplation or even in the midst of an animated conversation. Someone might say something that sparks an idea. You may not even recognize it as inspiration, but it is. Again, you will know you have the right answer because there will be an ease about the whole thing. With spirit, there's no hesitation. You recognize its wisdom. If there's doubt and you're not sure, then there's a strong possibility you haven't got the answer, or you're still blocking it.

Many people have asked me, "How do I know that the thoughts I may be getting are truly divine inspirations, rather than just my own thinking?" If you have done all the preparatory work correctly and really made your connection, then chances are you're on the right track. The Higher knows what you're doing and is going to make every effort to make that connection work. There will undoubtedly be some trial and error in the beginning. The voice of the Higher Self and the light has a quality all its own. The first step in receiving guidance from the light through your Higher Self is to establish clarity. If there is indecision, mixed motives, faulty information, or rigid preconceptions, take an honest look at what's there: you may be unintentionally interfering with what you're doing. If you're stepping into this process with vested interests, the guidance won't get through, or will be misinterpreted.

Divine guidance isn't a servant. It's not going to help you win the sixth race at Santa Anita. Its sole purpose is to guide you in your spiritual evolution. Sure, it helps with everyday life situations, but it will answer your questions strictly in terms of guidance that is directly relevant to your growth process. Many people who receive guidance still don't "get it" because they are approaching the question devoid of any spiritual foundation. Little wonder they're not getting the answers they want! Guidance is not about demanding things of God; it's about putting your life into God's hands and letting Him steer for you. Your job is obedience to this light and power. If you're stepping into this process with the best of intentions, most ambivalence will clear up.

Your spiritual guidance will most likely reach you through some type of prompting. There will be something that will urge you a certain way. Now that you're on the lookout for spiritual guidance, you'll be more attuned to its prompting. You may be fortunate and make a strong connection right away in the form of an epiphany or spiritual revelation. Eventually, you could build the connection with your Higher Self to the point where you are in full conscious awareness, continuously receiving guidance. Of course, you have to have been acclimated to the light for a long time to operate from this level, but it can happen if you are dedicated. Many spiritual initiates, avatars, and saints work from this high spiritual level.

Most people connect with spiritual inspiration through what is commonly called intuition. Intuition and divine guidance walk hand in hand. So many people tell me they had a feeling they shouldn't have done this or that, but then went right ahead and did it anyway. They didn't trust their own intuition. They permitted another part of themselves to speak for them. You must *listen* to what is said to you—and act on it. Divine guidance doesn't mollycoddle: the answer you get may not be the one you're expecting. And it may not be to your liking. Yet, it will be what's best for you and what you need at the moment.

Don't sweat what comes through. If it feels like you're on target, try it. God would never inspire you to do something hurtful or dangerous. If you get such thoughts, you can be very sure they're not from God. So when you get inspiration that feels right, try it out and see what happens. By seeing your ideas in action, you'll know right away if your receptivity to divine inspiration is on target. If it doesn't work out, you'll learn how to better recognize when Divine Light is talking to you. Be flexible. Even divine guidance is not set in stone. Life is fluid and things change. But if you're in the divine flow, you'll have no problems that can't be solved.

If you feel that something is being communicated to you but that the answer is still not clear, work with the silver ray to quicken your powers of discernment and comprehension. Again, let it work at your Higher Self Point.

Meditative Prayer for
Divine Guidance with the Silver Ray

"Down-ray the silver ray of divine intelligence to my Higher Self Point to quicken my awareness of this Divine Light and inspiration You have given me. I ask to be released from all blocks or resistance to my full reception and comprehension of Your guidance."

Right Direction

Sometimes dilemmas are not so much a matter of getting lost along the way as knowing where the way is to begin with. Perhaps you're trying to find your career path, deciding if marriage is right for you, or whether to have children. Maybe you simply want to change your life in some way but are unclear about where to start. In these cases, you can work with another spiritual tool very similar to guidance—right direction. The two can work together very nicely. You work with right direction when you are trying to find your way. Work with divine guidance to help steer you once you are on your chosen path. Right direction points you in the right direction and divine guidance helps to keep you on the right path and steer you over bumps or obstacles along the way.

Right direction is connected with your destiny here on Earth. Each of us is ideally suited to accomplish certain things in life. Intuitively you already know what that purpose is, but as so often happens, you can become distracted and confused to the point that you lose your way. Right direction may be used for decisions, big and small. By tuning into right direction, you're tuning into an energy already in motion.

In working with right direction, I've found it effective to ask the light to come down and touch directly into the Hermetic Center. In looking for your direction, you're trying to connect with an energy that's active on the Earth plane. By asking the light to work on the Hermetic level, you're making a conscious effort to connect with this energy. The gold and white light work equally well in this situation.

Meditative Prayer for
Right Direction with the Gold Light

"Down-ray the golden ray of wisdom light to my Hermetic Center, bringing me clear thinking and decisive action concerning (*name situation*), all in accordance with Thy divine will and right direction."

Once you feel the point being activated, ask your question and wait for an answer to come through. You can end your work there, or down-ray the white light as well.

Meditative Prayer for
Right Direction with the White Light

"Down-ray the pure white light into my Hermetic Center and all levels of my being, lifting my consciousness and illuminating me to see with Thy spirit eyes, that I may choose the right path for me."

When you're finished with your meditation, if no answer has come forth, end with the following:

"I thank Thee that this is so and I hold to the knowing that my answer is forthcoming. So be it."

Spiritual Illumination

Perhaps you have a problem but can't pinpoint what it is exactly. The nature of the problem may elude you altogether. Spiritual illumination can give you the vision to better understand the nature of the decision to be made.

Spiritual illumination is seeing with spirit eyes. Call on spiritual illumination when you want to gain a greater understanding or comprehension of something in general, not necessarily for specific guidance or direction— although it is excellent for this too. You may have done your personal inventory but still not have a clear understanding of why there are certain problems in your life. Spiritual illumination can explain why you're in a particular mental or emotional state. You may then make a decision about what to do. You need that clarity to effectively work with the light. The key energy to work with here is the pure white light.

Meditative Prayer for Spiritual Illumination

"Down-ray the pure white light into my Higher Self Point, lifting me up into Thy divine consciousness that I may see with Thy spirit eyes, illuminating and revealing what I need to work on in my life."

After you've made your connection, become still and receptive. There's no question to pose here because you've simply asked to see what you need to work on. So be quiet, and let God speak to you. You may get an answer right away or it may be revealed to you later.

The Light in All Aspects
of Your Life

You now have a strong working knowledge of the Divine Light process. You have the tools to call on your Higher Self to access your reservoir of spiritual energy and many examples of how to implement that energy in your active life. In this chapter, we will explore techniques you can use in conjunction with the Higher Self meditation that will amplify the light process to an even greater extent.

A World of Energy

All life is teeming with spiritual energy in one form or another. Even what we think of as empty space is really filled with some type of spiritual activity. Because we live in this sea of energy, we're constantly intermingling with other energy flows. Think of how many people each of us interacts with on a daily basis. Each one of these people has their own auric flow, which may be good or bad or in between. This means that anyone can have a potentially positive or negative effect on our own aura. So in developing our auras, we need to be aware not only of our own vibration, but of how we are interacting with other vibrations. We must learn how to maintain our spiritual equilibrium, maintain a healthy interaction with the world around us, and not pick up any negative vibrations along the way.

Protection

The first requirement for staying in your own auric flow is to keep spiritual protection strongly around you. People who are unaware of the interaction of auric energies always ask me, "Protection from what?" and I begin to explain all the ways you can open up to negative energy. Fortunately, the aura has protective energies built into it that buffer a great deal of the negative energy hurled at you. But even with that protection, unwanted energy can still touch in, and you'll need all the protection you can get.

Golden Sphere with Orange-Red Flame

This is an excellent protective exercise. It is very similar to the gold-bubble protection you use when going into meditation. The only difference is that you surround the circumference of your golden bubble with the orange-red flame to dissolve any negative energy that might be trying to push in. Again, this exercise only keeps out negative energy. All positive flows continue normally.

In the same manner as in Step 2 of your Higher Self meditation, stand up and hold your arms out, envisioning yourself surrounded by a golden bubble of light about arm's length from your body. Sense and feel this sphere of golden light as vividly as you can. Envision seven flows of this living light enfolding you in a protective sheath. Once the gold light is established, envision the orange-red flame surrounding the golden sphere and making the bubble look like a fireball of living light. Envision the protective light surrounding you while saying the following prayer.

Golden Protection with the Orange-Red Flame

"Encircle me now in a golden bubble of protective light. I ask that seven flows of this light surround me, keeping me in perfect protection. And I ask that You place the orange-red flame around the circumference of this protection, dissolving any negative energies that might try to penetrate this bubble."

Put on your protection every time you leave your house, and reinforce it as needed throughout the day. This protection is especially important if you're going into a crowd of people, whether at a party, business meeting, concert, movie, or any gathering. Protecting yourself and your loved ones will quickly become second nature to you and is one of the most important spiritual tools you possess. As you work with the protection, it will grow. After two weeks or so of consistent effort, you will have established your golden bubble. You don't need to stand to do the exercise. You can simply close your eyes to reinforce the light as the need arises.

Closing the Psychic Door

One of the first spiritual exercises I give my students in building their spiritual protection is what I call closing the psychic door. The psychic door is an interesting part of your spiritual anatomy. It's the gateway to your subconscious mind. Your subconscious mind is particularly susceptible to outside influences. It is like an incredibly sensitive recording device that picks up everything that's happening around you, without your conscious awareness. As a result and without your intending to, the subconscious mind can take in negative

Figure 11–1: **Closing the Psychic Door**

flows, from which you'll suffer the effects. To protect the subconscious part of you, the aura has built into it a subconscious filtration system. Its purpose is to shut out destructive energy, allowing only positive energy to enter. However, this door can swing open through emotional outbursts, if you've had too much to drink, or are thinking unkindly of someone. Then you're open to *every-thing*—the good, the bad, and the ugly. This door can become an Achilles heel if you're not careful. It's not at all uncommon to have the psychic door burst open, yet it is mercifully easy to close.

The psychic door is located just behind the right ear and looks like a blue flap when it is open. It's very important to make sure this door is kept closed at all times, permitting only good thoughts to enter. Having a stiff neck, or feeling that someone is a "pain in the neck," can be a sign that your door may be open. The actual spiritual mechanism by which this door is closed is too involved to describe in these pages, but by following this sim-plified procedure, you'll get the job done.

Place your right index and third fingers behind your right ear over the psychic door and envision a golden gingerbread man in the center of your head. See his right hand extending out and shutting the door from the inside. Then see that door being sealed with three impenetrable golden-white locks. As you are doing this, make the following decree.

Closing the Psychic Door

"I command my psychic door to be sealed and locked with three impenetrable golden-white locks, and I refuse to per-mit anything negative to enter therein."

I personally envision my door sealing like the locks on a bank vault. Once you have successfully performed this exercise, your door is closed. If you feel it's come ajar during the course of the day, just repeat the exercise.

The Energy We Leave Behind

Albert Schweitzer once said that whatever we do in life, we should "leave the footprints of love behind us." We've all felt the ripple effect of our actions. How many times have you entered a home for the first time and felt either comfortable or strangely repelled? This can be even before we meet the person living there. Why do we feel this? Because the house has been "charged up" with that person's vibrations. Churches and temples demonstrate this principle very noticeably with their chanting, glowing candles, incense, holy water, etc. Having accumulated the spiritual vibrations of these inspiring expressions, not to mention the years of prayers that have become thought-forms, people can't help but feel spiritually uplifted just by being there.

This works at both ends of the spectrum. Houses that are supposedly haunted can be charged up with negative energy, which is why we can feel creepy just by walking into such a place, even if we don't see or sense any apparition. There is a story about the Black Bridge in London. It's particularly famous for people committing suicide by jumping. This in itself isn't so unusual. What makes this bridge so unusual is that a very high percentage of these people jumped from the same exact spot. Of course, they were unaware they were doing this, but they usually gravitated to the same place. Why would they do this? Because that certain area had been charged up with the vibrational energy of suicide, and people in this frame of mind were intuitively drawn to that energy.

This auric effect works at all levels of interaction, including chairs you sit in, places you visit, the clothing you wear, and everything you interact with. I have a dear friend who bought an ancient chair from the Ming Dynasty that a king was supposed to have sat in. She was proud of this purchase and placed it prominently in her home. Yet for some reason, having it in her house made her feel very uncomfortable. She told herself she was just being irrational. As the days passed, her uneasiness only grew. She invited me to see if I could tune in to anything that would explain her unsettling feeling. The chair was jet-black and somewhat plain for a piece of furniture designed for such a regal purpose. The moment I got close to it, my stomach did several flip-flops, which told me something was very wrong. I clairvoyantly looked at the chair and saw black light around it. I knew right then and there that the chair had been connected with terrible things. The person or persons who had sat in this chair had been responsible for many cruel acts, and those vibrations were still embedded in the chair. My friend did some research and discovered that the king associated with the chair had been a tyrant responsible for many executions and barbaric acts. We purified the chair, but she decided to sell it anyway.

As you work with the light, you will get into the feeling and knowing of where and when you need to send the light. My first recommendation in working with energies around you is to send the light ahead of you to places you'll be going to and people you'll be meeting. In my morning meditations, I add the following prayer, asking the light to walk ahead of me to prepare every person and place I will be dealing with that day. If I know specifically who or what they are, I name them. This sends a signal to the Higher Self to begin the energy process.

Meditative Prayer to Send the Light Ahead of You

"I ask the Divine Light to walk ahead of me to prepare the way as I go to (*name place or places*). Let it touch into (*name people you'll be in contact with*) and purify them of any black and gray atoms, dissolving them in the mineral kingdom in the light and bringing in new life force and divine energy."

You can name any other energy you feel is appropriate as well, such as love or peace. This prayer will help to dissipate any negative energy you may encounter. You can also purify things as you go along. If you get a letter that may not be so good, you can ask the light to go into it before you read it. If you're going to make a difficult phone call that might be distressing, ask the light to touch into the person you'll be calling and into the call itself to help keep things moving on a positive level. Even when you go to a movie theater, you'll want to purify the seat you're in so as not to pick up the spiritual atoms of the person before you.

The purification for cleansing objects is also very simple. If you can hold the object in your hands, hold it in your left hand with your right hand on top. If not, ask the light to go to the object. Ask your Higher Self to cleanse whatever you feel needs it with a prayer like the following.

Meditative Prayer for Object Cleansing

"Down-ray the orange-red flame into my right hand and into (*name object*), purifying it of any black and gray atoms and dissolving them in the mineral kingdom. Then bring in the blue-white fire to establish new life energy within this (*name object*)."

It may take several minutes for the energy to start working. You can ask that the cleansing be done for you either in meditation or right as the need arises. By the way, material cleanliness has nothing to do with this process. An object can be immaculate and germ-free while also being spiritually dirty.

Purifying Your Home

A very important place to concentrate your purification work is in your own home. This is your place of sanctuary, and obviously a very important place to keep spiritually clean. If a hateful person walks into your house and directs hatred at you, after that person leaves, there will be a residual energy of that hatred in your home, which needs to be cleared up. Otherwise, you could pick up that negative energy without even knowing it. The purification needs to go to your door, mailbox, telephones, and especially to the bed you sleep in. Many people burn incense to cleanse their home. Greek Orthodox people have a tradition of asking a priest to come to their house to bless it. These are all wonderful practices and should be done periodically.

To cleanse your home with the light, burn orange and blue candles in what would be the center of your house. Place a large bowl of salted water between the candles. Let the candles burn for about ten minutes before and after the meditation. Do your Higher Self meditation and, with the following prayer, ask the light to touch into your home.

Meditative Prayer to Purify Your Home

"Down-ray the orange-red flame into the center of this house, including all rooms, grounds, and property. Take all black and gray atoms at least ten feet into the mineral kingdom and dissolve them in the light. Upon completion of this purification, down-ray the blue-white fire to charge and recharge all aspects of this home, retaining this energy and bringing this house into the highest vibration possible."

Sense the light touching everything inside your home and thoroughly cleansing it. The process by which the light goes through your home is a little different from how it reaches your aura. It still involves the Higher Self, but all you need to do is visualize the light doing what you're asking it to do. If you need to focus on one room in particular that feels off, place the candles in that room and do a cleansing for just that room. If you live in an apartment building, see the light radiating throughout your own unit and also dissolving any negative energies from adjoining units. I have found that burning sage and taking that sage to all rooms of the house effects a wonderful cleansing as well. If you do this, ask the light to go into the sage itself to amplify the cleaning process. I would repeat this exercise every day until you feel it's well established. After successfully doing this exercise, you will feel very different inside your home.

Follow up your housecleaning with a prayer of protection. The prayer itself is a power that builds up over time, helping to keep negative energies out, while also uplifting visitors who come in.

Protection for House

"Down-ray the golden ray of Thy divine protection to surround this home in seven flows of this light, strongly protecting everything herein and everyone who enters. In Thy Holy Name I ask this."

Chapter

12

Reflective Meditation

Reflective meditation is a wonderful and simple way to work with the light. If the Higher Self meditation feels a little complicated at first, if you're having trouble concentrating during your meditation, or if you're simply not in the mood to go through the steps of down-raying light, reflective meditation is another way of drawing energy to you. It's wonderful for stilling the consciousness when you are looking for spiritual inspiration and guidance, or simply to feel your oneness with God.

In reflective meditation you're focusing your attention on an image that's pleasing and uplifting. In your imaging, you strongly visualize the color of the energy you want. By doing this, you're attracting the energy and vibration you're envisioning. For example, if you envision yourself running through a field of bright yellow flowers, you're putting your attention on the beauty and vibrancy of that yellow color. If you really connect with that image and really feel and sense those yellow flowers, this actually triggers the effect of drawing in the lemon-yellow energy to you. The energy will not come with the same intensity as it would with your Higher Self meditation, but the connection will be made. This principle of attraction is nothing new.

You experience this reflective power when you daydream and let your mind wander to a beautiful tropical island you would like to visit, or in contemplating the face of someone you love. These daydreams have a quality of automatically uplifting you because, for that moment, your consciousness is actually connecting with the person or thing you're contemplating. Reflective meditation is simply applying this principle in a meditative environment.

More often than not, if you're having trouble in your light work, the problem exists on a mental level. Somewhere there is resistance, confusion, or fatigue. In these situations, you will not be as good a channel for the Divine Light because your attention is weak. Reflective meditation helps relax the conscious mind from its stresses. By concentrating on mental images that are pleasing and soothing, you will quiet the mind. Once the mind is stilled, the spiritual energy can flow more freely, energizing the mental levels and making them more receptive to the higher flows of light. Why do people go on trips? To relax, unwind, and renew themselves. Well, going on a *mental* trip can have a wonderful positive effect as well, and you don't have to leave home to do it.

You can use reflective meditation for any condition you would work on with your Higher Self meditation, but now you are using specific imagery instead of down-raying to attract the light you need. To begin your reflective meditation, find a quiet place to do your work as you would with the Higher Self meditation. Light a candle if you wish. You can play a little music if that helps to set the mood. Put your protective light around you and begin. In this case, the only preparation you need is to decide which energy you want to work with and what imagery you want to associate it with. Make the image something that really appeals to you and something you can envision vividly. Then close your eyes and mentally see yourself there. Take your time with this so you really step into the picture, feeling and sensing just what you're envisioning.

The simplest use of this imagery is to see yourself receiving a shower of the light you desire. For example, if you're calling on the purple ray of spiritual peace, simply see this color showering your entire body like water. Let it touch into every part of your being, soaking in through the pores of your skin, relaxing and uplifting you in this peace. You can follow the same exercise with each energy you feel you need.

You can use scenes to generate the energy you want. If you're depressed, visualize yourself in a waterfall, and feel orange-red water rushing down over you, releasing you from those dark atoms. Once that's established, envision scintillating sprays of shimmering blue-white water, caressing your entire being with beautiful, energetic life force, lifting you out of depression and soul sadness. Enter a pool of emerald green water and feel the balance and harmony of this brilliant green water surrounding you. Try to envision the colors as rich and as pure as you can. If it is difficult for you to visualize such scenes, let your feeling and sensing take over as you go through your reflective meditation.

If you wish to endow your mental body with more powers of concentration and studiousness, you can take a stroll through a meadow of bright yellow tulips, breathing in and filling yourself with their vibrant yellowness as you become one with its power. Continue to stay in this field until you actually feel energized. If you are lonely and feel unloved, sit on a hill and merge with a deep rose-pink cloud and just float, dropping away all the cares of the day. Feel yourself in this beautiful pink cloud, resting in the arms of love. Or run through a field of pink roses and feel the beautiful essence of that pink swirling around you and filling you, until you feel the spiritual love established.

There are infinite variations. Through practice, you will find the imagery that works best for you. Let your imagination really take over. Reflective meditation adds wonderful variety to your meditations.

Guided Imagery

In this form of reflective meditation, you are following along rather than creating the scene you're envisioning. This could be someone else's inspired imagery, or something you have prepared beforehand. With guided imagery, there is nothing to do but experience. The meditation should be experienced as though you were actually there, and you should encourage your feelings to come through. The best way to follow the scenes depicted here is to record the words on a tape recorder and follow along as you play it back.

Forest Setting

Picture yourself at a mountain campsite. It is the start of a rosy-fingered dawn, and the singing of birds is just awakening you. Inside your sleeping bag, you're snug, warm and cozy. You feel a hint of cool, crisp mountain air brushing your cheeks, inviting you to leave your tent and explore the beautiful forest around you.

You slip quietly out of your sleeping bag, put on your boots, pick up a towel, and step out of your tent. You then breathe in deeply the pine scent of the forest, feeling the life-giving breath filling your lungs and igniting every cell in your body. You stretch your body and lift your eyes, following the line of emerald green pines all the way up to the rosy skies of dawn. You see a path leading away from your campsite and into the forest; you want to find out where it goes. The rich red-brown earth is soft, but supports your steps with gentle strength as you proceed along the path. You step on pine needles and hear them snap beneath your feet. You feel the tingle of the cool morning air around your nose and cheeks. You hear a gentle breeze rustling through the leaves. You sense the powerful life force flowing freely all around you, from the rich earth to the tops of the majestic trees. The trees tower over you, enveloping you in their eternal strength and stillness. You are at one with the tranquility of the forest's deep verdant green.

You proceed along the path and discover a clearing, which opens to a gentle cascading waterfall that feeds into a clear shallow pool, the source of a mountain stream. The pool reflects and shows the sky above. Clear blue, with streaks of pink and dancing golden sunbeams sparkle on the water. The sun is warm and the shimmering pool invites you to bathe in its pure fresh waters. You remove your clothing and wade into the cool, invigorating water, feeling warm golden light as the sun streams down all over your body. You look down to the bottom of the pool and see brightly colored pebbles. They glisten and sparkle like precious gems and jewels, and all at once you feel wealthy, as if you had discovered secret treasures. You stand beneath the waterfall, and, as it washes away all impurities from your being, you feel clean, and renewed as never before.

You leave the pool and the very cells of your skin tingle, clean and alive in the cool air. You dry yourself with your towel, dress, and proceed away from the waterfall, mounting ever higher up the path. The breeze greets your nose with a fragrance so sweet, you feel compelled to learn what awaits you further along the path. You climb steadily, and suddenly the path opens onto a vast green meadow filled with dazzling wildflowers in full bloom: oranges, reds, violets, pinks, whites, purples, yellows—all swaying joyously in the breeze. You run through the meadow, the brilliant green grass and flowers brushing against your legs, and you feel the warm sun shining down on you. The meadow sweeps upward, and you arrive at the crest of a peak. Your eyes behold panoramic vistas of rich green valleys, majestic purple mountains, and a turquoise sky, resplendent with white and rose-pink clouds.

One of these rose-pink clouds drifts near you, and you are enfolded in its billowy, loving pink softness. You drift away with this cloud, up into the sky, peacefully, higher and higher. The sun's rays warm and bathe you in the very essence of this deep rose-pink light and love. This love and light flow in a rich pink through your mind, your entire nervous system, your entire physical body, and all around you on every side. This love enfolds you. You're feeling its healing power coursing through you, and opening you up to receive greater love, greater peace, and greater joy than you have ever known before.

The cloud now carries you gently back past the meadow, past the waterfall. The cloud then becomes a pink parachute. This pink parachute gently carries you back down to Earth. Gently, gently, it carries you as you slowly drift down to the campsite where your adventure began. You breathe deeply of the morning air once again, and you hold to the feeling, the sensing, and the knowing of what you have experienced in the very heart of your being, knowing that you are renewed. You are at peace, and you will keep that deep peace, tranquility, and serenity with you throughout the coming week.

Island Monastery

You are on a boat going to a tropical island where no one has ever been before. The water is a clear blue with shades of brilliant emerald green. You disembark and walk across a sparkling white sandy beach. The sand feels like velvet. As you walk, you see a beautiful flower garden and walk into it. The flowers are in beautiful hues and geometric shapes, vibrating their colors to you, enfolding you in their splendor. There are many beautiful birds and animals in the garden. They know you're there and are happy to see you. Beautiful fruit trees also send their vibrations to you. You are attracted to a particular tree that has a profusion of fruit you've never seen before. You pick one of the fruits and bring it to your lips. It's the most delicious morsel you've ever tasted! You are energized by its very flavor. You now move through the garden and realize that you are walking on a brilliant golden path that goes straight up a mountainside. You seem to be gliding effortlessly as you walk the golden path, climbing up the mountain.

Off in the distance, you see a monastery. You climb effortlessly toward it. As you approach, you hear bells chiming—beautiful tones!—and you sense an atmosphere of power and light. You approach the monastery and go through the outer gate. This is like no monastery you've ever seen. It's large, with several white buildings, and filled with radiant gardens and fountains. There are brilliant colors everywhere. A monk greets you, dressed in golden robes. No words are spoken, yet there is a sense of love between you and the monk, and you understand each other perfectly. You see the grounds, and buildings of many rooms. The monk lets you wander through the halls on your own. You walk into one of the rooms and see paintings and sacred manuscripts. In a courtyard are enticing, multicolored fountains. You take your clothes off and step lightly into one of the fountains. The water seems to be made of pure light, moving in indescribable, symmetrical formations. You are in awe of the beauty.

You step out of the fountain feeling refreshed, and put on a magnificent white robe that has been placed on a bench just for you. You then see a circular glass building. You wonder how you'll get in. You don't see a door. The monk appears next to you and places his hand on a panel of glass; the glass slides open and you enter. The monk vanishes again. You walk to the center of this huge circular room. There is a circle of violet living light and a golden chair within that circle. You sit in the chair and feel the energies of the room. Your thoughts and feelings keep rising higher and higher. You look around and admire a magnificent golden dome above you. And as you're looking, a beautiful flow of light from the dome encompasses your entire being, establishing that flow of spiritual light deep within you. The light flows in different colors and seems to be exactly what you need. Then the light stops flowing from the dome. The violet circle that you are sitting in starts rising up all around you, a flame of life-energizing light surrounding your entire being and reaching all the way up to the golden dome. You stay in that flow for a few moments but feel like you could stay there forever. The flame subsides, and you leave the glass building. The monk guides you out of the monastery and down the mountainside. You end up at the boat that brought you to this beautiful place. You say good-bye to the monk, get in the boat and sail away feeling completely refreshed and revitalized.

Plantation Setting

You see yourself wearing a beautiful pink robe, sandals, and belt. You are walking along a gorgeous pathway of pure white light. On both sides of you are nothing but flowers. On the right side are warm colors of pink, red, orange, and yellow; on the left are cooler shades of green, blue, and violet. As you come up the path, you are met by a beautiful white horse. You mount that horse and immediately feel its tremendous spirit, life, and strength. It seems to know exactly where it is going and begins galloping in a flowing rhythm. You feel the breeze blowing through your hair and you feel a thrilling sense of freedom. The horse takes you through a green meadow and, as you ride, it gets greener and greener.

The horse takes you to a pillared mansion that looks like it belongs on a Southern plantation. You get off the horse and go up the steps into the mansion. No one is around. You think to yourself that this is one of the most beautiful homes you have ever seen. You walk inside, and the interior is even more beautiful. You're immediately drawn to a spiral staircase. You ascend to the second floor, which has a long corridor. There are six rooms to the right and six rooms to the left. You go to the first door on the right and enter. The room is huge, lavishly furnished with Louis XIV furniture. The bedspread is a beautiful light blue with little yellow flowers embroidered around its edges. You go to a magnificent bay window, and by that window is an ornamental golden chair, which faces a wall. On that wall is a very large painting.

You sit and study the painting. Your eyes are at once drawn to its focal point—a beautiful emerald-green stream. It's very refreshing to look at. Alongside it are trees and little animals scurrying among the rocks. The sun seems to be directly overhead, in its full glory, rays streaming down. As you're looking at all the different things in the painting, suddenly the stream begins to move and become alive. You can feel the rays of the sun and you become one with that light. As you feel that flow enveloping and lifting you, you suddenly find that you have entered the picture, and are walking by the water. You pick a spot that calls to you and sit by a rock, looking at the stream.

As you're sitting there, a beautiful ray of white light beams down on you, touching into the very center of your being. You drink deeply of this light, feeling yourself becoming more and more elevated. Then every home you have ever lived in starts flashing through your mind. You feel this light touching into every one of those homes, releasing any unhappy experiences or memories and establishing the radiance of this light in each of them. You feel thankful for what the light is doing. Then you feel another flow of this light touching into every vibration and every person who has ever lived with you in those homes, enfolding them in this light and lifting their spirits.

Then the light fades. You feel like a new person. You get up and start walking by the stream, again sensing the sun sending you strength and love. All at once you're back in the bedroom, sitting in the golden chair. Through the window you can see the horse waiting for you. You bid farewell to the room, descend the spiral staircase, pass through the entrance, and get back on the horse. It takes you back to the path of white light where you first began your journey. Once again, you feel completely refreshed and revitalized.

Chapter 13

Affirmations & Visualizations

Affirmations and visualizations are two very effective spiritual practices that we can employ to accentuate our spiritual energy work. I have found that not only do these work well by themselves, but used in conjunction with the light, their effect is enormously amplified.

Affirmations

The beginning of the twentieth century saw the blossoming of a spiritual movement called New Thought or, as William James called it, "The Religion of Healthy-Mindedness." The philosophy behind this movement is that our thinking has a direct impact on the quality of our lives, and that by changing our thinking, we can change any aspect of our life. Although we understand this philosophy much better today, at the time it was first introduced, such thinking was revolutionary. The famous aphorism "Mind over matter" grew out of this movement. New Thought attempted to show the spiritual dimensions of our thinking, and how by using our mind in the proper way, we align ourselves with the divine scheme of life. Pioneers such as Norman Vincent Peale, Ernest Holmes, Charles Fillmore, and Thomas Troward were the forerunners of this movement, and several very successful religious organizations grew around it. Even today, New Thought is very much alive and continues to prosper and grow.

One of the most effective tools New Thought employs to facilitate mental change is the use of affirmations. The word affirmation comes from the Latin word meaning "to strengthen." The theory is that a strong declarative statement can have the effect of reversing a negative belief or attitude. For example, if you're constantly telling yourself, "I'm worthless," and really believe it, you probably have created some corresponding negative condition in your life. By refusing that negative thought and replacing it with a sincere, positive affirmation such as, "I am a precious child of God," you may then create a positive change in your life. Affirmations follow the spiritual point of view that life works from the inside out. If you're already trying to focus on your positive qualities, affirmations can help to keep your consciousness set on your desired goals.

Designing Your Affirmations

Once you get in the flow of how affirmations work, you can have a lot of fun with them. If you're trying to overcome a negative mental/emotional habit or trait with the light, you can use affirmations to help strengthen your mental body. Or if you're working on a relationship problem, affirmations can help keep the energy of attention focused in a positive way as you work things out. Here are a few guidelines for designing your affirmations.

1. Word Your Affirmations as if They Were Already a Reality.

Your affirmations must express the consciousness and full reality of the condition you're aspiring to. You don't want to project an image of something that will happen in the future. For example, creating the affirmation "I am losing weight" isn't nearly as effective as saying, "I am at my perfect weight." By seeing yourself already at the goal, you're keeping yourself in the present, and that has the effect of drawing the condition to you.

Use statements like "I am," as they keep you focused in the present. If you use tentative phrases such as "I will" or "I hope," there's not much conviction there, and your affirmations will have far less positive effect.

2. Avoid the Word "Not."

Using the words "not" or "never" are negations, not affirmations. Your consciousness responds best to affirmations. Your affirmation must be a *positive* declaration. You want to affirm what you want—not what you don't want. Instead of saying "I am not sick," for example, you would say, "I am in perfect health," or "I *accept* only perfect health," which are both affirmative statements.

3. *Feel* What You Say.

You have to really mean what you say; otherwise, what's the point? This is supposed to be coming from your heart. In designing affirmations, find the truth and meaning for you before using them.

The Light & Affirmations

If you were sitting at a table in a noisy, busy diner and in a quiet, meek voice asked the waitress for a cup of coffee, what do you suppose would happen? How fast would you get that cup of coffee? Would the waitress even hear you amidst all the noise and activity? You'd have to speak clearly and strongly in such an atmosphere to be heard. Affirmations work in a very similar way. If you repeat affirmations but put no power behind them, they will have little meaning. You'll become like a parrot, merely repeating words with little understanding of what you're saying. As a result, they will not carry the force of conviction needed to impact on your consciousness.

If you want an affirmation to have impact, it must have power and conviction behind it. Your mental body is busy with many things, and you have to impress it strongly for it to respond to you. We're not talking decibels here; I mean *spiritual power* and sincerity. I have found that by putting the Divine Light into an affirmation, you give it far more power and authority. And perhaps most important of all, by using the light with your affirmation, you're infusing the words with some of the divine essence of what you're affirming.

You can call on the light to work with affirmations as a meditation in itself, or use them before or after your normal light work. Either way, begin your Higher Self meditation as you normally would. If necessary, do a mental cleansing with the light first to get your mind as clear as possible. When you are in your Higher Self Point, bring down the pure white light to touch into your mental body, quickening it in the light. You can also ask the light to touch into your throat center as well.

Meditative Prayer for Affirmations

"Down-ray the pure white light into my Higher Self Point and into my mental center to flow into my affirmations, giving power and conviction to bring forth Thy divine results. Let this light also touch into my throat center, quickening it in this Thy Light, so that the affirmations spoken move out with spiritual tone into the vibrated ethers."

When you feel the light is established, start saying your affirmations. Repeat each one three times, feeling the light touching into every word you say. Declare your affirmation unequivocally. You don't have to force it or scream it out, but make it definite. Leave no room for your conscious or subconscious mind to misinterpret what you're saying. As you say the words, see the light moving out with the verbalized thought from your mental center. Hold to the knowing that that thought is now moving into the spiritual ethers, putting into motion and manifesting the affirmation in your life.

Examples of Affirmations

There are many fine examples of affirmations available today. It doesn't matter if you use your own or others', as long as they work for you. I use affirmations a great deal in my classes, because I find it's one of the quickest ways to unify a group of people and get them moving in a creative, positive way. Below are thirty affirmations I have used with great effect.

1. I am perfect Health, Harmony, and Happiness.
2. I am perfect Power, Ability, and Success.
3. I am perfect Poise, Peace, and Plenty.
4. The kingdom of God, the glory of God, are here and now. I am forever a part of its being.
5. The perfect law of God is now operating in my affairs.
6. I am free of strain, stress, and fear in my life.
7. I am in the presence of radiant joy, of Divine Love, and of perfect power.
8. I know that I am drawing my good to me.
9. There is a silent power of attraction within me that is irresistible.
10. I am without worry about what happened yesterday. I know that today everything is made new.

11. I let go of all sense of limitation and I take the hand of God. My Father and I walk into the garden of Divine Love and everlasting light.

12. I give my full attention to the positive, creative, dynamic powers of God, RIGHT HERE, RIGHT NOW. I erase all illusions and beliefs that obstruction exists, and relax and establish divine order in me now.

13. The Divine Spirit of the Conquering Christ transcends all discord.

14. The Holy Presence of the Living God has full possession of this body temple, and is in complete charge.

15. My mind, body, and soul respond only to perfection, beauty, wisdom, purity, and loving thoughts.

16. I give thanks that I am the ever-renewing, ever-unfolding expression of infinite life, love, health, and energy.

17. Divine Love and wisdom go before me, making my way easy and successful, for I am now guided, healed, prospered, and blessed.

18. My Father and I are One.

19. The light of love shines forth in me as new energy, new peace of mind, new power and dominion, new poise, new beauty, new prosperity, new harmony, and new good in every phase of my life.

20. Divine Love foresees everything, and richly provides for me now.

21. The Spirit of God that dwells within me blesses my mind, heals my body, and prospers my way.

22. The divine child of God knows only total freedom and the unlimited life of the Eternal Being.

23. God is the creative principle of life, and I am one with all the creative intelligence and wisdom of the Father.

24. My life is guided by divine intelligence.

25. My creative flow is magnificent and perfectly expressed.

26. I am prosperous beyond my wildest dreams.

27. I am open to give love and to receive love.

28. My energy is boundless and I am filled with vitality.

29. I have excellent motivation to fill each day fully with harmonious thoughts, words, and deeds.

30. I release my past mistakes and the results of those mistakes.

Visualizations

Visualizations work much like affirmations in that they strengthen the power of the mental body. Here the creative aspect comes strongly into play, because you are inventing scenarios you wish to manifest.

The ability to visualize is one of the most important spiritual traits you possess. You cannot create anything tangible if you have not first visualized it in your mind's eye. When you strongly imagine something, you make an impression on the spiritual fabric of life. That impression has the immediate effect of moving toward materialization. If this image is consistently and constantly reinforced, it cannot help but eventually become a reality. Visualizations are actually God's attribute of divine sight acting in and through your mind. This power of creative visualization exists at all levels of activity, from the simplest creative acts to the greatest inventions or works of art. The universe itself was created from an envisioned, divine idea. So when you are consciously picturing in your mind a desire or a wish that you want fulfilled, you are using the most powerful tools of creative invention that exist.

I've seen some wonderful things happen working with visualizations. There was a woman in one of my classes who was not particularly metaphysical, but she really caught on to the idea of visualizations. She was a real estate broker working for a prestigious agency. She somehow knew that by working with the light and visualizations, she could really build up her business. She began using the turquoise ray, and visualized that she was closing deals and that lots of money was flowing in. She was so single-minded and diligent in her work that within a few months she had doubled her sales, becoming her company's top producer.

Planning Your Visualization

Because the ability to visualize is so powerful, you have to be clear on what you want to create. The old saying, "Be careful what you wish for because you just might get it" is especially true when it comes to visualizations. If you're not thorough in planning your visualization, you might create something you didn't exactly want, or neglect to create something you do want. I worked with a woman who was visualizing a new job. She was very careful to construct exactly the kind of job she wanted, visualizing her salary, exact duties, and even the hours she wanted to put in. Then, after careful planning, she worked very hard to manifest the situation she designed. She eventually did get the job she wished for, and the salary she wanted. But she'd left out one critical element that came back to haunt her—harmony in the workplace. She was so concerned about the nature of the work and the money, that she neglected to envision a congenial work environment. As a result, she had nothing but friction at work from her boss and fellow workers. She eventually transferred to another division where things went much better, but she'd learned her lesson about designing a well-rounded visualization.

Before planning your visualization, recognize that you're never alone in this process. God is always your partner in every constructive visualization you create. After all, it's God's vision you're calling on, God's power you're using, and God's spiritual fabric onto which you're impressing this visualization, so God must be consciously recognized as the all-pervading presence and power in your plan. An ancient spiritual teaching states that God is the Doer, the Doing, and the Deed of every right form and action that has ever been sent into the world of manifestation. A well-executed visualization is, in essence, tapping into the very creative principle of God and the divine plan for you.

With this understanding in mind, begin to plan your visualization. The first step is to really determine a definite goal or desire to be fulfilled. You have to stop and think: What exactly is it that I wish? What do I want to bring forth? It should be constructive, honorable, and worthy of your time and effort. Are you looking for a new job, or trying to find a romantic companion? Are you looking to buy a new car or house? Your visualization can be as simple or elaborate as you choose.

I recommend taking a week to plan your visualization. Write down all your ideas of what you want to create. By writing it down, you can look at it more objectively and see if that's what you really want. You can more easily add or take things away. You want to make sure your list includes everything you want. If you get stuck, work with divine guidance, saying: "Tell me if there is anything I've left out." Sometimes, the Higher will flash in something you haven't seen or thought of. You may be picturing all the physical features of your visualization and forgetting the essentials, such as peace, love, and joy.

When you are writing down your ideas, do not actually visualize them. All you're doing is starting your plan. Once you have the ideas you want, then organize your thoughts and state your plan in words as concisely and clearly as possible. The following are some guidelines for planning your visualization.

1. BE SPECIFIC.

The more specific you are, the better. For example, if you're looking to buy a new car, don't just visualize a car. See the specific make, model, and color if you can. If you're unsure of the exact thing you want, be very specific about the quality you want. Sometimes, specific qualities are more important than anything else. For example, if you're looking for a companion, you don't want to go into physical features as much as the specific qualities you're looking for in the person. Perhaps you want that person to be kind, funny, exciting, etc. This will help you get into the feeling more clearly of what you want.

2. Be Realistic.

Anything's possible, but obviously the more outlandish your visualization, the harder it will be to realize. If your goals are reasonably doable, you're going to see results much faster, creating more excitement and drive. You have to use common sense. However, there's nothing wrong with visualizing long-range goals. Just recognize this as a plan that will take greater energy and time to manifest.

3. Watch Your Motive.

Examine your motives for bringing such a creation into expression. You must approach your work constructively. If you're thinking selfishly, you're not going to connect with the God vision and you'll create problems for yourself and others. Your visualization must be a win/win situation for all involved. This is why in the meditative prayer you must include the phrase "according to Divine Law and Love for the good of all concerned." By including that phrase, you are making sure you're putting things in God's hands.

4. See Yourself in the Act of Doing.

Whatever you design, see it as something finished, complete, and perfect. If you're visualizing a new car, see yourself driving that car. If you're visualizing a mate, see yourself with that person, having fun, laughing, walking hand in hand. Or if you're visualizing a new job, see yourself already at that job. As with affirmations, you want your desiring to be active, in the present tense.

5. Have Complete Faith.

Before you start a visualization, it has to be with complete faith in the inevitability of success. If it's really part of God's design, how could it NOT come to pass? If you harbor fears, then you'll be projecting them, which is just the opposite of what you want. You'll be creating two antagonistic images and the result will be confusion.

6. Don't Put a Time Limit on It.

This can be hard, especially when you're in desperate need. But once you do a visualization, you must let it go and grow in God's time. If you've done things right, the energy is in motion and will eventually materialize, but you can't dictate the exact route it must take, or even have a preference as to how and when it will come about. If, after a period of time, it still hasn't come to pass, you can reinforce the visualization, or reevaluate the situation.

7. Keep Your Visualization to Yourself.

Your visualization is your own business. It is very unwise to excitedly tell others your plans. I've seen more beautiful plans be knocked off course when people deflate and dilute the whole thing by talking about it. A visualization needs time to grow, and if you talk about it too much, you won't be giving time for the spiritual energy to accumulate, which will most likely neutralize the effectiveness of your entire visualization.

The Light & Visualizations

As with affirmations, putting the light into your visualization makes a much stronger impact and reduces the time it takes to materialize. It also helps to keep your visualization constructive and in the light of God's will. The light accentuates God's power, acting within your consciousness to propel the picture you are projecting into your outer world.

If you feel you need to, do a purification first to clear your mind. Use the Higher Self meditation to bring down the pure white light to activate your visualization. You especially want the white light to touch into your brain cells so that they're receptive to the whole process.

Meditative Prayer for Visualizations

"Down-ray the pure white light into my mental body, charging and recharging all levels of my consciousness, especially quickening my brain cells. I then ask this light to out-ray into my visualization to manifest according to Thy Divine Law and Love for the good of all concerned."

Once you feel your connection with the light, begin your visualization. Feel and sense that the white light is quickening and amplifying the power of whatever you're imaging. Again, see yourself actually doing whatever you wish to create. Act it out in your mind. Really *feel it* already happening for you.

When your visualization is complete, you don't have to do anything more. You've planted the spiritual seed. You don't need to go back and dig it up to see if it's growing. Keep yourself in the knowing that your visualization will come to pass according to divine will. If you do something to disturb that knowing, simply repeat the visualization. If, after a reasonable period of time it hasn't happened, then you can repeat the visualization, or reevaluate your plan.

Chapter 14

Parting Thoughts

It has been my privilege and pleasure to bring forth the knowledge contained in these pages. I hope I've instilled in you an enthusiasm to change your life, and shown that you have a glorious and divine potential. You are more precious in God's eyes than you can imagine. It is said that if one person were missing from creation, the universe would be incomplete. You are indispensable in the grand plan of life no matter how vast that plan is. In this great adventure, your aura and the spiritual light are true friends you can always rely on, and are the mainspring of your life's activities and endeavors.

Life cannot stay status quo. Activity and change are inevitable. The question is not whether life will change but *how* life will change. The answer to this question is entirely up to you. If you treat life laxly, you won't get much out of it, and your progress will be slow. You need to be bold and take chances. As growth opportunities arise, you must take advantage of them as best you can.

You are the aura you radiate. When you leave this Earth and move into the hereafter, you're going to leave with the aura you've earned. If your life hasn't been the best, you're not going to suddenly come into a beautiful, saintly aura. You're going to be exactly who you are, so you need to start improving your aura right here and now. Aim to leave this life with a better aura than the one you entered with by continuously building your light through your good thoughts, words, and actions. The light you accumulate will give you a spiritual wealth beyond measure, a wealth that can never be taken from you.

Be alert. The world is a very active place today, and you need to keep your mind keen and razor-sharp. Just as there are greater opportunities to grow than ever before, there are also more temptations and distractions that will only steer you away from your true destiny and delay your progress. Take advantage of your spiritual knowledge and awareness to live life according to the highest ideals you can imagine. Recognize that everything you do makes a difference to you and to everyone in the world, for better or for worse. It doesn't matter if your deeds go recognized or unrecognized by others. God sees your actions, and those actions are registered in your aura.

Make it a point to work on your aura every day, to connect with the light, and to infuse your every thought, act, word, and deed with this light. Remember that you carry the spiritual blueprint of yourself with you every minute of every day. Let that blueprint become an expression of Divine Love and wisdom, uplifting not only yourself, but all those who come in contact with you. It's a magnificent path of evolution that leads us upward to the heaven worlds, and eventually to God our Father, Holy Mother.

Quick Reference for Meditation

Three Keys to Working with Spiritual Energy

1. Decide what you want the light to do for you.
2. Draw the light into your aura.
3. Use the light to effect the change you desire.

Six Steps to Down-Ray Light

1. RELAX

Before beginning any meditation, get into a relaxed state of mind. Take your shoes off and uncross your legs. This helps the energy to flow more freely.

2. PROTECTION

Envision yourself in a bubble of golden light. Ask that it surround you in seven flows of this magnificent energy with the meditational prayer for protection.

"Encircle me now in a golden bubble of protective light. I ask for seven flows of this light to surround me, keeping me in perfect protection."

3. CHECK YOUR CENTERS

Make sure the four main centers are moving *clockwise* (as if you were the clock). Check your centers by placing your hands, right hand over left, over each center and feel if it's moving clockwise. If not, ask the white light to go to that center and move it clockwise.

4. CONNECT WITH YOUR HIGHER SELF

While sitting upright in a comfortable chair, legs uncrossed, right hand on left over the emotional center, envision a golden sun 24 inches above your physical head (Higher Self Point). Say the invocation:

> "Heavenly Father, Holy Mother God, I raise my consciousness into Thy consciousness where I become one with Thee. I ask to receive that which I need and that which I need to know now."

Feel yourself in a beautiful state of being as you place your attention in your Higher Self.

5. DOWN-RAY THE LIGHT

Ask that the light be down-rayed to you by making a verbal petition (meditative prayer). When you do this, envision the light going first to the Higher Self Point and then beaming down to your four main centers and aura. Three to five minutes for each ray is all you need.

6. GROUNDING

When you are finished, give your thanks and take a moment to feel the light equalized throughout your aura. Feel you are grounded and centered before ending your meditation.

Ten Spiritual Energies to Work With

THE ORANGE-RED FLAME

Purification, cleansing. Releases black and gray atoms and dissolves them in the mineral kingdom.

THE BLUE-WHITE FIRE

Replenishment, new life force. Always bring it in after working with the orange-red flame. A wonderful healing ray.

THE GOLDEN RAY OF WISDOM LIGHT

Wisdom, courage, inner strength, self-confidence, faith, divine will and protection. It brings in the dynamic power of God.

THE DEEP ROSE-PINK RAY

Spiritual love, compassion, trust, and understanding. It brings in the magnetic, nurturing power of God.

THE PURPLE RAY

Deep peace. Wonderful for healing grief.

THE EMERALD GREEN RAY

Balance and harmony. Especially important to have in the Hermetic Center.

THE SILVER RAY

Divine intelligence, perception. Especially important in the mental body and brain cells.

THE LEMON YELLOW RAY

Powers of concentration. Very effective when you are studying for a test or assimilating new material.

THE TURQUOISE RAY

Prosperity, supply, and abundance.

THE PURE WHITE LIGHT

Spiritual upliftment. It helps to equalize, align, center, and attune the consciousness to the divine impulse.

Four Main Spiritual Centers

(All centers should be moving *clockwise*.)

MENTAL CENTER (TRINITY CHALICE)

Located in the middle of the forehead, this center is the nucleus of our thinking levels. It's the point where we link up mind, body, and soul with spirit.

Throat Center (Eternal Ego)

Located in the middle of the throat, this center is where we express the power of our words. When we speak positively, our words move out in *spiritual tone*.

Hermetic Center (heart center)

Located in the middle of the chest, this center is the nucleus of all our worldly affairs, including persons, places, things, conditions, situations, and the conditions that constitute a situation.

Emotional Center (Spiritual Heart)

Located in the solar plexus behind the navel, this center is the nucleus of our emotional nature, positive or negative.

INDEX

H

I/J/K

L

N/O

P

R

About Barbara

Sometimes called "The Mozart of Metaphysics," Barbara Martin is an early pioneer in the field of metaphysics and is well-known for her work with the aura and spiritual energy. Born with highly developed clairvoyance, Barbara could see *complete* auras as well as other spiritual phenomena from the time she was a little girl. She became one of the first persons to get on the public lecture circuit and speak about the aura in depth, even before Kirlian photography brought the aura to public awareness.

Barbara has had extensive experience as a speaker before universities, scientific organizations, civic and community groups. She has written books and articles on metaphysics and the aura, appeared on national television, and counseled numerous celebrities. Most recently she has co-founded Spiritual Arts Institute, where she teaches workshops and classes on the aura and metaphysics.

Dimitri Moraitis—Collaborator

Dimitri Moraitis was originally trained in film/television production and has had a wide variety of experiences in entertainment and advertising as producer, writer, and director. He has received several awards and distinctions, including an Academy Award nomination for his film short, *Don't Let It Bother You*. Dimitri has been Barbara's writing partner for many years and is co-founder of Spiritual Arts Institute.

To Contact Barbara Y. Martin

If you would like to learn more
about Barbara's private aura consultations,
classes, seminars, books, and CDs,
please contact:

Spiritual Arts Institute
P.O. Box 4315
Sunland, CA 91041-4315

Tel: (818) 353-1716
Toll Free: (800) 650-AURA (2872)
Fax: (818) 353-2269

Or visit the Institute's Web site: www.SpiritualArts.org

Quick Order Form

Fax orders:	818-353-2269
	Send this form
Telephone orders:	818-353-1716
E-mail orders:	orders@spiritualarts.org
Postal orders:	Spiritual Arts Institute
	P.O. Box 4315
	Sunland, CA 91041-4315

Please send the following books, cassettes, CDs:

_____

_____

_____

I understand that I may return any product for a full refund
—for any reason, no questions asked.

SHIPPING ADDRESS

Name: _____

Address:_____

City: _____ State:_____ Zip: ____

Telephone: _____

E-mail Address:_____

Do you wish to be on our mailing list? (We do not sell lists.) ❑ Yes ❑ No

SALES TAX: Please add 8.25% for products shipped to California addresses.

SHIPPING CHARGE: $4 for the first book, tape, or disk and $2 for each additional product. International: $9 for first book, tape, or disk; $5 for each additional product (estimate).

PAYMENT: ❑ Check ❑ Credit Card: ❑ Visa ❑ Mastercard

CARD NUMBER: _____

NAME ON CARD: _____ Exp. date: _____

QUICK ORDER FORM

FAX ORDERS: 818-353-2269
                 Send this form
TELEPHONE ORDERS: 818-353-1716
E-MAIL ORDERS: orders@spiritualarts.org
POSTAL ORDERS: Spiritual Arts Institute
                 P.O. Box 4315
                 Sunland, CA 91041-4315

Please send the following books, cassettes, CDs:

_____

_____

_____

I understand that I may return any product for a full refund
—for any reason, no questions asked.

SHIPPING ADDRESS

Name: _____

Address:_____

City: _____ State:_____ Zip: ____

Telephone: _____

E-mail Address:_____

Do you wish to be on our mailing list? (We do not sell lists.) ❑ Yes ❑ No

SALES TAX: Please add 8.25% for products shipped to California addresses.

SHIPPING CHARGE: $4 for the first book, tape, or disk and $2 for each additional product. International: $9 for first book, tape, or disk; $5 for each additional product (estimate).

PAYMENT: ❑ Check   ❑ Credit Card: ❑ Visa   ❑ Mastercard

CARD NUMBER: _____

NAME ON CARD: _____ Exp. date: _____